D0213768

MOVIE MUSIC,
THE FILM READER

From silent film accompaniment and classical film scores to jazz, rock 'n' roll movies and pop soundtracks, *Movie Music, the Film Reader* argues for a broader understanding of the roles of music in film.

Bringing together key articles on subjects such as rockumentary, fandom and animation, *Movie Music, the Film Reader* comprises an important resource of writings about one of cinema's most powerful and pervasive elements. Articles are grouped into thematic sections, each with an introduction by the editor. These include:

- *The meanings of the film score* – looks at instrumental scores, their production and reception, and questions the onscreen power of nineteenth-century-derived classical scores
- *The place of the song* – turns to popular music, asking how the pop score expands the film narrative
- *The formal politics of music on film* – questions the subversive power of cinematic music
- *Crossing over into the narrative* – addresses the use of musicians within film narratives, from rockumentaries, such as the spoof *This is Spinal Tap*, to pop-stars-as-movie-stars, such as Madonna in *Desperately Seeking Susan*

Contributors Theodor Adorno, Tim Anderson, Philip Brophy, Kay Dickinson, Hans Eisler, Krin Gabbard, Ian Garwood, Claudia Gorbman, Lawrence Grossberg, Kathryn Kalinak, Keir Keightley, Lisa Lewis, Carl Plantinga, Jeff Smith, and Anastasia Valassopoulos.

Kay Dickinson is Lecturer in Film Studies at Middlesex University, London. She has also co-edited a forthcoming volume, *Teen Television*.

IN FOCUS

In Focus: Routledge Film Readers

Series Editors: Steven Cohan (Syracuse University) and Ina Rae Hark (University of South Carolina)

The In Focus series of readers is a comprehensive resource for students on film and cinema studies courses. The series explores the innovations of film studies while highlighting the vital connection of debates to other academic fields and to studies of other media. The readers bring together key articles on a major topic in film studies, from marketing to Hollywood comedy, identifying the central issues, exploring how and why scholars have approached it in specific ways, and tracing continuities of thought among scholars. Each reader opens with an introductory essay setting the debates in their academic context, explaining the topic's historical and theoretical importance, and surveying and critiquing its development in film studies.

Exhibition, The Film Reader
Edited by Ina Rae Hark

Experimental Cinema, The Film Reader
Edited by Wheeler Winston Dixon and Gwendolyn Audrey Foster

Hollywood Musicals, The Film Reader
Edited by Steven Cohan

Horror, The Film Reader
Edited by Mark Jancovich

Hollywood Comedians, The Film Reader
Edited by Frank Krutnik

Movie Music, The Film Reader
Edited by Kay Dickinson

Forthcoming Titles:

Marketing, The Film Reader
Edited by Justin Wyatt

Reception, The Film Reader
Edited by Barbara Klinger

Stars, The Film Reader
Edited by Marcia Landy and Lucy Fischer

MOVIE MUSIC,
THE FILM READER

Edited by Kay Dickinson

Routledge
Taylor & Francis Group

LONDON AND NEW YORK

First published 2003
by Routledge
2 Park Square, Milton Park, Abingdon, Oxon OX14 4RN

Simultaneously published in the USA and Canada
by Routledge
711 Third Avenue, New York, NY 10017

Routledge is an imprint of the Taylor & Francis Group

© 2003 Kay Dickinson for selection and editorial matter;
individual chapters, the copyright holders

Designed and typeset in Novarese and Scala Sans
by Keystroke, Jacaranda Lodge, Wolverhampton

All rights reserved. No part of this book may be reprinted or reproduced
or utilised in any form or by any electronic, mechanical, or other
means, now known or hereafter invented, including photocopying and
recording, or in any information storage or retrieval system, without
permission in writing from the publishers.

British Library Cataloguing in Publication Data
A catalogue record for this book is available from the British Library

Library of Congress Cataloging in Publication Data
Movie music, the film reader/edited by Kay Dickinson.
    p. cm. – (In focus–Routledge film readers)
    Includes bibliographical references and indexes.
    1. Motion picture music–History and criticism. I. Dickinson, Kay, 1972–
    II. Series.

ML2075 .M877 2002
781.5'42–dc21   2002032632

ISBN 0–415–28159–8 (hbk)
ISBN 0–415–28160–1 (pbk)

Contents

PART FOUR: CROSSING OVER INTO THE NARRATIVE   153

Acknowledgements

1. Kathryn Kalinak, "The Language of Music: A Brief Analysis of *Vertigo*" from *Settling the Score: Music and the Classical Hollywood Film* (Madison, University of Wisconsin Press, 1992), pp. 3–19. Reprinted by permission of University of Wisconsin Press.
2. Theodor Adorno and Hans Eisler, "Introduction" and "Prejudices and Bad Habits" from *Composing for the Films* (London, Athlone Press, 1994), pp. li–lii, 3–19. Reprinted by permission of Athlone Press.
3. Claudia Gorbman, "Why Music? The Sound Film and Its Spectator" from *Unheard Melodies: Narrative Film Music* (London, BFI, 1987). Reprinted by permission of Claudia Gorbman.
4. Tim Anderson, "Reforming 'Jackass Music': The Problematic Aesthetics of Early American Film Music Accompaniment" from *The Cinema Journal* 37 (1) (Austin, University of Texas Press, 1997), pp. 3–22. Reprinted by permission of University of Texas Press.
5. Jeff Smith, "Did They Mention the Music: Toward a Theory of Popular Film Music" and "Banking on Film Music: Structural Interactions of the Film and Record Industries" from *The Sounds of Commerce: Marketing Popular Film Music* (New York, Columbia University Press, 1998), pp. 1–44. Reprinted by permission of Columbia University Press.
6. Lawrence Grossberg, "Cinema, Postmodernity and Authenticity" from Frith, S. *et al.* (eds), *Sound and Vision: The Music Video Reader* (London, Routledge, 1993), pp. 187–209. Reprinted by permission of Routledge/Taylor & Francis Ltd.
8. Ian Garwood, "Must You Remember This?: Orchestrating the 'Standard' Pop Song in *Sleepless in Seattle*" from *Screen* 41 (3) (Cambridge, Cambridge University Press, 2000), pp. 282–298. Reprinted by permission of Cambridge University Press.
9. Krin Gabbard, "Whose Jazz, Whose Cinema?" from *Jammin' at the Margins: Jazz and the American Cinema* (Chicago, Chicago University Press, 1996), pp. 1–19. Reprinted by permission of Chicago University Press.
10. Philip Brophy, "The Animation of Sound" from Cholodenko, A. (ed.), *The Illusion of Life: Essays on Animation* (Sydney, Power Publications, 1991), pp. 81–104. Also available from http://media-arts.rmit.edu.ac/Phil_Brophy/soundtrackList.html. Reprinted by permission of Philip Brophy.
11. Kay Dickinson, "Pop, Speed and the 'MTV Aesthetic' in Recent Teen Films" from *Scope* June 2000 (www.nottingham.ac.uk/film/journal/). Reprinted by permission of Kay Dickinson.

12. Carl Plantinga, "Gender, Power and a Cucumber: Satirizing Masculinity in *This is Spinal Tap*" from Grant, B. and Sloniowski, J. (eds), *Documenting the Documentary: Close Readings of Documentary Film and Video* (Detroit, Wayne State University Press, 1998), pp. 318–332. Reprinted by permission of Wayne State University Press.
14. Lisa Lewis, "A Madonna 'Wanna-Be' Story on Film" from *Gender Politics and* MTV: *Voicing the Difference* (Philadelphia, Temple University Press, 1990), pp. 185–198. Reprinted by permission of Temple University Press.

Movie Music,

The Film Reader

General introduction

For a long while, there seemed to exist a custom for starting any book on film music with a complaint about the degree to which academics had overlooked the topic. In fact, Roy Prendergast even goes so far as to call his work *Film Music: A Neglected Art*. However, long gone are the days when film studies seemed a mono-sensory discipline concerned only with visual categories like "the spectator," "the gaze" and "the mirror stage." More and more, the kinds of intricate analyses which film's imagery inspires are being matched by equally rigorous research into music's place within cinema. In the past, film writers were more likely to pass over a soundtrack quickly, merely commenting in a fairly oblique way upon how it enhanced a movie's mood. Nowadays, the musical constituents might be explored for, say, their subtle appeal to the subconsious; their position within the global market place; their ability to "brand" the film and help create a kind of franchise; their registration of a string of cultural reference points; or their creation of a certain nostalgic ambience. In response to these developments, this anthology celebrates the long-awaited abundance of writing on music and film. If anything, the difficulty has been not in finding suitable material, but in pruning down what has recently become available and selecting a limited number of categories (which, sadly, means that there is no room for musicals).

Of course, this wealth of written material is a hugely selective response to the thoroughness with which music permeates the cinematic form. Almost every film in every culture features some type of music and only the very smallest fraction of it has been given serious theoretical consideration. As the scholarly literature is equally anxious to point out, even in its first thirty years, cinema was never silent. Film screenings almost always featured live accompaniment by anything from a full orchestra to a battered, out-of-tune piano. Similarly, the musicianship of the performers was as varied as the places where one could watch a film and their playing could be constrained by a fully written score or left to almost total improvisation. Some of these musicians continued the traditions of theatrical melodrama, some worked more within the rubrics of vaudeville, but all of them in their different ways shaded a greater spatial and emotional dimensionality into the flickering ghostliness of the projected film world.

During this period, accompaniment was usually continuous, providing a smoother, more encompassing feel to what might have seemed a distanced mode of expression in its earlier days. If a film was compiled out of apparently disjointed sequences, then a consistent and coherent sonic component spread over it served to make it flow past more effortlessly. It has also been said that music helped compensate for the lack of spoken dialogue in silent cinema, although this might only be partially the case. Such an argument depends on the proposition that silent cinema was an incomplete technology, merely biding its time waiting for the invention of its sonic dimension so that actors could be heard as well as seen. In fact, several films made during the transition to sound suggest that speech was not necessarily considered the obvious element to be included in this newly audio-visual media. Some producers used its potential merely to graft musical scores on to their movies and even as late as 1936 Charlie Chaplin's *Modern Times* preferred more abstract, textural sounds to those of the human voice.

If music was such an integral component of the pre-sound era and the addition of an audio track to film stock provoked so many experiments, then charting anything like the entirety of film music's history is daunting. Instead, it seems a more manageable project for this book's introduction to outline how the subject has been intellectually circumscribed. Within this body of material lie practical, theoretical and poetic writings on a range of processes which fuse the moving image with music. There is work on the specially composed score and on how film borrows already existing music of every conceivable genre. Perhaps the most popular development in recent thinking has been towards the commercial, industrial and economic means through which music and film interrelate. However, it makes more sense to start with an exploration of the topic which first attracted a number of scholars to the area: orchestral scoring for Hollywood movies, a style which has its roots in late nineteenth-century European "classical" music. Although this is by no means the only way of combining music with cinema, it became one of the dominant modes and, as such, has been the central focus for many major movie music theorists, such as Caryl Flinn, Royal Brown, Claudia Gorbman, Irwin Bazelon and Mark Evans.

Hollywood's orchestral film scores

The mid-1930s saw a set of increasingly standardized compositional practices settle into place within the established Hollywood studios. By this time, sound films had adopted the narrative potential of human speech, and music, unlike in the silent era, only appeared intermittently— mostly when it was needed to stress an important issue, to steer the audience in a particular way or to evoke an emotional response of some kind.

As ever, historical forces shaped these developments and music's place within cinema may just as well have taken an entirely different course (in some cases, as will become apparent, it did). The influx of German and Central European immigrants into California in this period bore with it not only the men who were to become the movie moguls, but also a considerable number of composers and performers. From Europe, these largely conservatoire-trained musicians brought a comprehensive understanding of the types of music which had dominated the concert halls in the late nineteenth century. Of particular importance to them were the works of such composers as Richard Strauss and Giacamo Puccini who had continued to pursue the goals of Romanticism which had been established earlier in the nineteenth century. This was a melody-driven style which favoured rich textures, dense orchestration and an emphasis on chromatic harmony. These characteristics soon found their way into the oeuvre of scorers such as Erich Korngold and Max Steiner, who both exemplified the continuation of this tradition. Another European device which soon became standard practice in Hollywood was the Wagnerian *leitmotif*—the assignment and repetition of short melodic phrases to signify key characters, places or social groups (something which Chapters 1 and 2 of this book explore in more detail).

However, although this mode of composition sprung from European high art traditions, it stood for something different and unique in its new American context. While its genealogy can be traced back to art music practices, the European avant-garde had long moved on from this kind of composition in order to embrace the rawer instrumentation and experiments in the expanded tonality of modernism. Although many of Hollywood's hired scorers yearned to explore these ideas too, they were increasingly held back by their studios' conservatism. This reveals an agenda which is typical of Hollywood at that time: to elevate films above certain other "low-brow" cultural forms, yet to remain extremely wary of the art world's more challenging developments. In this sense, classical Hollywood scoring remained neither exclusively populist nor entirely "high art," but a complex mixture of aspirations, muddled cultural pretensions, prejudices and concessions, all of which help mark out the uniqueness of cinema and point out what a communally negotiated finished product it so often is.

Another factor which significantly determined how music was to function in Hollywood cinema was the studios' assimilation of a more Fordist means of production. This meant that specialist roles were assigned to its workers and that manufacturing rolled along in a strict linear fashion. Composers were positioned near the end of this chain, receiving pretty much a final cut of a film into which, up to that point, they had more than likely had no input. They would be asked to "spot" the movie, maybe with an editor—a practice which involved suggesting places where music would function well—and then to etch out melody lines. These would usually be handed over to an arranger who would orchestrate them before they were rehearsed, recorded and, more often than not, edited down (usually without the composer having any say in the finished piece). Six weeks was the typical time period for these processes and, because they took place so late on in production, it is fair to say that the role of the composer was more to complement the already established narrative than to add anything more philosophically or thematically free-standing to the movie. It is worth contemplating what Hollywood film music might have been like had this factory system not been implemented, or even if the composer had come in at some earlier point.

Obviously, within these conditions, a scorer's authorial control was enormously compromised. Composers were often not the sole creators of the music, their work might be chopped up and rearranged without their blessing and they did not even own the copyrights to what they had written. Most importantly, all studio employees were under contracts which might be terminated at any time if they failed to meet certain requirements—a threat which evidently encouraged many of them to play safe.

In her book *Strains of Utopia*, Caryl Flinn wonders whether the sense of artistic frustration this incited might have drawn film scorers more powerfully towards the preoccupations of Romanticism, which would explain why it became such a popular style during Hollywood's classical period. For her, Romanticism, coming out of the great upheavals of the nineteenth century, is semantically resonant with the traumas of increasing industrialization, urbanization and *embourgeoisement*—concerns which evidently still trouble us today. As a musical movement, Romanticism often presents a philosophy of abstract, supra-linguistic utopianism (music functioning "above meaning"), and, simultaneously, a deeply rooted investment in individual struggle. While this latter feature was the obvious allure for the embattled scorers, the former offered a certain interpretative looseness, the kind which allows film music to be elusive and persuasive simultaneously.

Following a different path from Flinn, there are writers who analyse how such formal qualities (rather than their historical contingencies) have given rise to the enduring presence of orchestral incidental music in cinema. Gorbman highlights its potential to wallpaper over the cracks caused by the disruptive elements of film composition, while Kathryn Kalinak (1992: 101) similarly claims:

> Film is a discontinuous medium, made up of a veritable kaleidoscope of shots from different angles, distances and focal depths, and of varying duration. Romanticism, on the other hand, depends upon the subordination of all elements in the musical texture to melody, giving auditors a clear point of focus in the dense sound. Given the high value placed on the spectator's focus on, indeed absorption into, the narrative by the classical Hollywood narrative film, the romantic music idiom may be its most logical complement.

It comes as something of a surprise that the soundtrack (outwardly one of the least "realistic" elements of cinema) should be drawn upon to diminish these disorienting qualities of the film experience. This points out just how convention-based our notions of coherence and harmony are—after all, most people's everyday lives would seem far from smooth if the noise of a string section started up at random moments during their day. Thinking through simple correspondences like these allows us to open up what we take for granted about movie music, to realize that it is a richly encoded and culturally determined way of conveying a certain (political) agenda, rather than anything more commonsensical. Thanks to its long history, the Romantic tradition in orchestral music has a wealth of in-built force which might also rearrange cinema and meld new perceptual possibilities into it.

Perhaps as a result of the academic focus on studio system scoring (which was, after all, compliantly responding to completed story-lines), these more autonomous characteristics of film music are still ripe for extensive exploration. Music and cinema are two separate art practices with two distinct (although definitely interlinking) histories and, as with most interactions, meanings are exchanged rather than ever entirely swamped, with their distinctive features mutating as they journey through time and to different locations.

The diversity of musical and cinematic meaning

In response to these differences and their fluctuations, writers such as Nicholas Cook go to great lengths to accent the historical and formal distinctions between music and the moving image—their physical and spatial properties, their wildly divergent modes of reception. Of course, it is impossible truly to outline how each art form and all its generic off-shoots might be unified philosophically, linguistically or commercially, or how their meanings might not coalesce at all. It would take (and has taken) volume upon volume to pinpoint, for example, "the West's" interest in thinking of art music as ineffably transcendental, in creating the sort of attitude towards music that has, ironically, perhaps stopped scholars feeling comfortable even talking about it. In complete contradiction, there are very precise and strict visual systems of categorization which have been painstakingly described and notated and which have become central to our means of social discrimination. Both of these hegemonic deployments of sensory perception initially appear incompatible, but such ideas are constantly rubbing up against each other when music enters cinema, and these are the sorts of liaison with which Part 3 of this book will deal.

Such clefts between what the two media and all their subdivisions have come to represent are exactly what make film music fascinating. Although most good writing on orchestral composition is aware of such resonances, there is a tendency (especially when attention has been so squarely given to music composed especially to meet the needs of film narrative) to insinuate a form of musical servitude to a movie's narrative lord and master. Coming from this position, considering music (however creative) to be secondary to film (which is by no means always the case, as this book will demonstrate) is perhaps not the best vantage point from which to observe how one media might extend the other, might introduce into it by accidental association things which could be politically emancipating. There are often arguments about whether particular combinations "work," but less joy expressed in the fortuitous occurrences that a supposed "mismatch" might throw up—let alone many self-critical evaluations of how specific, hegemonically loaded cultures of taste might predetermine such judgements. Even when the one medium is seemingly trying its best to allude to the other's ideas, surely all it can offer under these terms is a rough translation or a metaphorical insinuation. But we should not forget that metaphors are both generative and interpretative, creative and reductive, with all these processes begging analysis. The potential to discover surprising new ideas from such alliances (maybe even ones which might be refreshingly liberating rather than simply ready for tired critique) is something, it is hoped, that academics will continue to pursue. And, in looking out for instances where the music does not simply retire into the background, there is much more scope for penetrating the kinds of music which have not been formulated especially to suit a certain story-line—ones which may have had a long life of their own within popular culture before ever finding their way into cinema.

Film and popular music

It is certainly true that the academic spotlight has been rather unwaveringly fixed on orchestral scoring. However, there is now a growing body of work from Jeff Smith's *The Sounds of Commerce: Marketing Popular Film Music* to Pamela Robertson Wojcik and Arthur Knight's collection *Soundtrack Available: Essays on Film and Popular Music* that look at types of music which have not been written exclusively for cinema. As these two titles indicate, the newer breed of book tends to home in on what is usually called popular music. It is never as easy as one might presume, though, to pin down and pore over any such a coherent entity as "popular music." First, there are the problems of popular for whom and when? Second, and more specific to the cinematic equation, the score and the pop song frequently evade the possibility of mutual exclusion. Soundtracks for films such as *Casablanca* (1942) and *Laura* (1944) have consisted of variations on the theme of a key song and there have also been plenty of specially commissioned scores which could be labelled as "popular music," like Simon and Garfunkel's work for *The Graduate* (1967). Here a polarization of, on one hand, more autonomous, perhaps previously circulated music and, on the other, pieces formulated in post-production does not come so easily. Again, this blurring of categories can be used to a musician's advantage. For example, in Jonathan Romney and Adrian Wootton's collection *Celluloid Jukebox*, Kodwo Eshun points out how the rise in "blaxploitation" cinema afforded established r 'n' b performers like Marvin Gaye many more spacious compositional liberties (those more common to the soundtrack) than had been granted them in their singles chart-oriented output.

However, while these minglings of popular and "standard" scoring have opened up previously unimaginable opportunities for those working in the music business, it is also vital to acknowledge the impact pre-written popular music has had on the film industry. At almost every historical juncture, its performers, its agents and its share-holders have muscled their way unapologetically and uncompromisingly into the middle of the movie world. Even at the beginnings of film history, musical accompaniment followed cue sheets which asked their performers to improvise around well-known popular tunes. Since then, all manner of films (especially musicals) have capitalized on previously released popular numbers. The sway of chart music can also be witnessed in a series of "jukebox musicals" which showcased rock 'n' roll, and, along with wide-screen and Technicolor formats (and perhaps more successfully), these helped woo a television-obsessed US demographic back to the movies. To this day, popular music has served myriad similar functions, sometimes economically carrying cinema, sometimes being borne by it, but, more often than not, serving a more complicated function. As a result of these pressures, the role in film production of the music advisers (who select tunes and balance the budgets which pay the licensing fees) has become a vital one.

With a presence this resonant it is therefore somewhat surprising that popular musical forms have been the subject of so few scholarly books. There has been a small number of theoretical writers such as Hilary Lapedis who break down songs' lyrics, their musical formation and the ways in which films incorporate them. With work of this sort, the theorist must understand the often delicate machinery of popular music and also show a sensitivity towards the collected connotations it brings with it from its old world into the new. In undertaking work of this nature, David Shumway, Jeff Smith (in Philip Brophy's collection *Experiencing the Soundtrack*) and the writers featured in *Celluloid Jukebox*—along with Lawrence Grossberg and Ian Garwood in this volume—have tracked popular music semantics back to one of its most abundant and nourishing mainsprings: nostalgia. David Sanjek's essay in Brophy's anthology *The World of Sound in Film* offers an enlightening contemplation of the role of nostalgia within the money-making schemes of the contemporary media industries. By reviewing the scavenging that takes place here, he discusses the implications of *exhuming* (his metaphor), stripping down and cleaning up American vernacular music in order to reissue it commercially via a film springboard.

The position of the popular music/cinema equation within the international market place is, justifiably, a major draw for many writers. As has become clear, the music and film industries have been financially married almost since the inception of cinema—and, indeed, many of the behemoths of the global economy have interests in both spheres. William Romanowski, R. Serge Denisoff, Alexander Doty and Gary Marmorstein are all theorists who delve into the nitty gritty of music and film synergy, but the one figure who manages to discuss these elements with a trilingual fluency in economics, musicology and film studies parlance is Jeff Smith (who appears in Chapter 5 of this reader). Throughout the histories that these academics have plotted there have been manifold alliances struck—both inspired and preposterous—in order to try to squeeze more cash out of fewer outlays. This means that certain films seem like glorified promos for songs, and hit movie tunes have been known to bankroll cinematic production—issues which severely obscure any facile belief in music's subordinate position within film. Synergy takes many forms and its coagulation of music and movie products does not always cohere around the soundtrack model. Here it seems germane to open up what "music" within cinema might imply in an increasingly broad sense and to ruminate upon what happens when other ideas on what music might mean are drawn into the body of a narrative.

Music and musicians within the narrative

Up to this point in time, most theorists in the field have upheld a rigid definition of how "music in film" might be interpreted, namely through either soundtracks or musicals (an area too vast to find a place in this book). Another, largely younger set of ideas (and perhaps one dispersed more widely throughout the domains of film and cultural studies) works with the role of music and musicians within film narratives. What might it mean to tell the story of a musician, to make the music industry the topic of a documentary or even to cast a musical performer as the star of a film? In these instances, music is neither something tacked-on in post-production nor a wilfully coherent pre-existing unit inserted into a cinematic cavity. Instead it is a prominent bearer of far-reaching cultural propositions, acting beyond the limitations of any more internal concept of musical grammar. These are all exciting areas where new writing is just beginning to trickle through and where more research would be greatly welcomed.

At the moment, a sprinkling of articles looks at the imprint that musical personalities (and the ready-made reference points they carry with them) have had on film. One such study is Thomas Carlson's essay which peruses the postmodern cinematic allusions to Elvis Presley in order to seek out the ways in which musical celebrity is constantly repackaged and the effect this might have upon fans. With such a lengthy career in the movies, Presley would appear to be a good starting point from which to talk about film and rock 'n' roll, yet the books on the subject are somewhat disappointing if one is searching for in-depth intellectual discourse. Most are biographies of Elvis with supplementary lists of film details, photos and synopses and many follow a common thread which finds its source in fan discourse: the argument that presents a "pure" expressive musical Elvis (and one with significant acting talent) who was corrupted and abused by an evil and heartless Hollywood which coerced him into making a batch of uninspired movies.

The irony of this type of narrative is that it often provokes similar retaliation from the film industry. In a large catalogue of films from *The Girl Can't Help It* (1956) and *Jailhouse Rock* (1957) to *The Harder They Come* (1973) and *That Thing You Do* (1996) the exposure of the music industry's exploitation of "authentic" yet naive talent is paramount. John Mundy and in this volume Keir Keightley prise apart these accusations of culpability, while Cory Creekmur follows them through with a meticulous analysis of how movies and music videos turn the mechanical processes of recording music into filmic spectacle.

These writings are related to another set of questions about what it means for the lives of musicians (real or imaginary) to fuel the narrative. What sorts of moral and ideological tales do they facilitate? Thus far, there has been very little exploration of, say, how musicians' life stories have been cinematically rendered, despite the bundle of musician biopics which Hollywood has churned out over the years. George Custen's more general book about biopics homes in on the amount of attention given to "entertainers"—including those in the sphere of music—stressing how horizontally integrated financial interests were woven into the genre's very fabric. More specifically, Carl Hanson explores how musicians' biopics ideologically define key social concepts such as "the ordinary" and "the extraordinary," "the amateur" and "the professional." In one of the few other examinations of the subject in the English language, Michael Atkinson (writing in

Celluloid Jukebox) investigates the constant recourses to death, decadence and the American dream in musician biopics.

In the same anthology, Jonathan Romney pulls the idea of the artist's life story away from the more radically recreated form of the biopic and into a discussion of "rockumentaries" where musicians "play themselves." Considering the popularity of such footage films as *Monterey Pop* (1969), *Gimme Shelter* (1970) and *Woodstock* (1973) and more individually centred numbers such as *In Bed with Madonna* (1991), there is (again) very little academic ink spent on the depictions of music in non-fiction cinema. Romney takes music as his starting point for looking at the concept of "backstage" in defining "self" and "performance," but most other forays into the topic wander in through the study of documentaries at large. In a series of more general books on factual cinema, one finds by chance, for example, Susan Knobloch's investigation of how Bob Dylan manipulates gender regulations in *Don't Look Back* (1967) and William Rothman's precise formal reading of the same film, both welcome (if slightly more coincidental) additions to the literature on music on film.

This shared disciplinary border also holds the phenomenon of musicians who turn their hands to film acting—another as yet under-examined topic. Although a surprisingly common occurrence with a long (albeit often undistinguished) history, few people—save journalists taking pot-shots—have felt the need to plumb this less obvious union of music and the moving image. What might this rather literal approach to synergy provoke? How might it question or reinforce notions of performance and talent within each respective industry? With performer personae as fascinating and diverse as Fats Waller, Frank Sinatra, David Bowie and Ice-T (not to mention Tommy Steele and the Spice Girls) to draw upon, this is surely an area ripe for critical exploration.

Again, for those wishing to investigate the area, a piecemeal set of readings can be scrambled together from several branches of film (rather than music) studies. In her book on working women on screen (and all the connotations of that phrase), Yvonne Tasker explores the lucrative cross-promotional presence of Janet Jackson, Whitney Houston and Cher in a series of recent movies. Houston is again the topic of an essay by Marla Shelton, although the author has more interest in her biography than the details of her musical developments and their filmic implications. One of the few writers with a sustained interest in these issues is Kevin Donnelly who has focused for a number of years on British pop stars and their relationship to cinema. Elsewhere, Henry Sullivan offers a heavily Lacanian interpretation of Paul McCartney's relation-ship with the late John Lennon in *Give My Regards to Broad Street* (1984) and Ben Thompson in his *Celluloid Jukebox* essay queries the inability of many pop stars to pull off a successful acting performance. This strangely recurrent inadequacy in translating charisma and dexterity from one medium to another (and the same can be said of most actors who try to launch musical careers) speaks volumes about the codes of professionalism in both industries and might prove a fecund starting point for anatomizing the differences between each art form's ideological underpinnings. At the same time, why is so much venom expended by critics the moment an out-of-place star slips up? Why will a fan suspend all critical judgement when a favoured performer is unanimously unconvincing to all other audience members? These moments tell us as much about how taste formations and work ethics are inscribed into film and music as they do about our devotion to and identification with stars (and the mercantile opportunism which these practices invite).

Such debates are still fledglings in the nest of film/music analysis. In an attempt to make room for these newer arrivals, this anthology has donated one of its four parts to studies of musicians within movie narratives, perhaps at the expense of showcasing more established examples of work on orchestral scoring. It is hoped that more books and articles like these which help create a much broader picture of how music and film cultures overlap and influence each other will be forthcoming in the near future.

Spaces for future development and a celebration of past achievement

However, one even more expansive area which has yet to come under full academic scrutiny is the interaction between film and music created outside the "Western" spheres of production. So far, there is a dearth of English language studies of music's place in non-English language film and, when there is a movement away from Hollywood, it tends to be a movement into European material. (This lack of material has also sadly taken its toll on the balance of contents in this anthology.)

Granted, such writers as Claudia Gorbman and Anahid Kassabian have criticized how Hollywood has often used music to drive an alienating wedge between its presumed white audience and selected oppressed social groups. Yet it would be a more enriched area of study if there were a greater number of scholars who moved more speedily through Hollywood (or bypassed it altogether) on their journeys to other film industries. In the absence of these kinds of developments, the host of books dedicated more broadly to "non-Western" cinemas luckily often incorporates a certain amount of music analysis (Lizbeth Malkmus and Roy Armes's *Arab and African Film Making* and Viola Shafik's *Arab Cinema*, for example, include sections on music). However, as yet, there has been practically no work which draws out, say, how film music formulates a set of propositions about the post/neo-colonial world or discusses such issues as hybridity, presumed local specificity, global comprehensibility or transnational domination.

Of all these might-have-beens, perhaps the most surprising is the lack of much debate of Indian film music. Aspects of music are central to Indian film narratives as diverse as *Baiju Bawra* (1952) and *The Music Room* (1958) and, more pressingly, almost every popular Hindi film is bursting with songs. *Filmi* music is recorded by play-back performers who are rarely seen on screen, it is sold in advance of the film and, in places like India, forms the backbone of the music market (76 per cent according to Thoraval, 2000: 68). It functions much more centrally and autonomously as popular music than soundtracks ever have in Europe or the United States, offering a truly fascinating model of horizontal integration within the global economy. These issues are raised in more topically ambitious books about India such as Peter Manuel's on audio cassette culture and Yves Thoraval's on cinema. However, the fleetingness with which they necessarily deal with film music has proven unsuitable for republication in the format of this particular collection.

All things considered, the neglect of Hindi film's relationship with music is startling. Ashis Nandy and Rachel Dwyer both provide fascinating insights into "Bollywood" at large, but only make scant references to music, while journals like *South Asia* and their contributors seem similarly preoccupied with different concerns. One exception to this state of affairs is the book *Soundtrack Available: Essays on Film and Popular Music* which effortlessly weaves together essays on Hollywood, Indian cinema and various other hybrid and diaspora formulations of music on film and, in doing so, offers an admirable model of practice for the future.

Another smaller area which does not seem to leap out at people working on movie music immediately is animation. For some reason, people forget that live action features are not the extent of cinema—surprising when we consider that *Snow White and the Seven Dwarfs* (1937) featured one of the first soundtracks to gain an LP release and that the "Best Song" Academy Award winner is, more often than not, drawn from an animated film.

So far, the existing scholarship has usually followed one of two pathways. The first runs through the use of pre-existing music with an emphasis on what this achieves commercially and culturally—an example would be Moya Luckett's study of the production, promotion and reception of *Fantasia* (1940). The second (which can be found in various sections of Gary Marmorstein's (1997) book) moves towards animation's anarchic tendencies, seeing them as key in encouraging the more avant-garde tendencies of composers like Carl Stalling (who scored many a Looney Toons short). Both these ideas are played out contrapuntally in a piece by Philip Brophy which is reprinted in this volume. Where sustained work is rarer is in the study of how notions of repetition, abstraction, and even sensory intoxication drawn from music have fundamentally inspired experimental film-makers working within animation (figures like Oscar Fischinger, Harry Smith and Tony Conrad) precisely through a common sense of music's peculiar "anti-realism."

Interestingly, two figures who do tackle such phenomena and are also part of the select group that has taken animation seriously are notably absent from this book: they are Michel Chion and Sergei Eisenstein. Despite producing arguably the most sustained and stimulating treatises on how sound and moving image interact (or, more likely, because of this), it is very hard to extract the kind of small morsels of their writing necessary for an anthology format. As such, their work is best read in its unedited versions. However, in an attempt to emphasize their centrality, it is only right that some justice is done to their work now.

Coming from a *musique concrete* composition background, but hopping effortlessly from academic topic to topic, Chion's written work, and particularly *Audio-Vision*, moves far beyond the idea of music as a structured and culturally recognized phenomenon and concentrates upon larger concepts such as sound and silence. Metaphorical and exuberant, ranging from art to music video to film, Chion presents ideas on how sound and image perception differ and what happens when they criss-cross each other's paths.

Eisenstein, as most readers will be aware, was also a practitioner (here within film-making) as well as a theorist. Again, his ideas are too expansive for, and would be enormously diminished by, editing—they are too excitedly digressive and to strip them of this quality would be to rob them of their vitality. In many of his writings—and, in particular, his discussions of synaesthesia—Eisenstein reveals how he sees and structures his films musically. Throughout his analyses of his own movies, he constantly and consciously reiterates musical terms such as polyphonic, contrapuntal, rhythmic and symphonic in order to expand upon how different filmic strands might structurally interlock. Eisenstein's most famous technique—montage—works like musical counterpoint by throwing up unexpected but powerful associations. It places seemingly incongruous elements next to each other, forcing us to evaluate new arrangements and to question our own learned senses of appropriate stylistic continuity. With Eisenstein, there is a sense not only that he wished to evoke a certain musicality within the silent image (for example, he discusses the drumroll effect of the shots of feet running down the Odessa Steps in *Battleship Potemkin* (1925) in his book *Nonindifferent Nature*), but also that he had a profoundly poetic ability to play sensorial evocations off one another. It is this desire to bring the cultural implications of music and the moving image into communion, to set them in conversation rather than to silence one in favour of the other, which really marks out Eisenstein.

Continuing an Eisensteinian line of thinking, David Bordwell's piece in Rick Altman's *Cinema/Sound* collection entreats us to think of cinema more musically; in essence, to break through certain literal and linear narrative traditions and search out a more multi-layered and less guided way of experiencing movies. This echoes earlier endeavours by film-makers such as Jean-Marie Straub who, in a discussion of his own oeuvre, claims: "The point of departure for our *Chronicle of Anna Magdalena Bach* was the idea of attempting a film in which the music was used not as accompaniment, nor as commentary, but as an aesthetic means" (Straub, 1967: 56).

These figures are searching for a cinema where music is not subservient to film narrative's "melody," and does not merely run alongside it holding up cue cards in a desperate attempt to heighten an audience's response to the story-line's main current. In such instances, delicate and extremely rich audio-visual associations can happen and, bearing in mind that neither medium can gain ultimate dominance, it is worth fathoming some of the ways in which music has eloquently and noisily inspired film's creative activities.

Of course, there have always been those who doubt that music truly bears "meaning" in any straightforward sense—an entrancing idea to the many who long for just one small space where such fraught concerns as import and value cannot plague them. However tempting it may seem, though, this proposition is dependent on a fairly limited understanding of "meaning," one which wishes music to live up to the more commonly shared precision of written and spoken language. All the writers in this collection, as well as theorists like Simon Frith, argue for the liveliness and variety of musical meaning and aim to open out the richness of its connotations to a wider audience. Music for them is simultaneously a vast store of resources for provoking emotional response; a shared but debated means of communication; an instrument for smoothing over the ruptures caused by film editing (as Claudia Gorbman would suggest); a lifestyle choice through which we delineate our social identities; a commodity which is fed through huge international networks; and much more besides.

By drawing on an assortment of such writings, this book endeavours to suggest a taxonomy of music in film (and indeed film in music) which includes (but also extends past) the soundtrack in order to appreciate how other uses of music might produce and replicate a certain set of cultural values. Music infiltrates, creates and informs a wealth of different social configurations— many of which have been explored in movies—and its political impact on everyday life both through these outlets and a multitude of others is immeasurable.

In trying to evoke a greater sense of what movie music might be, this book unfortunately has to speed by some fine articles on familiar topics. This kind of strategic rearrangement cannot provide us with an overview of Busby Berkeley-style regularity. The articles in the collection are too diverse in their methodological positions and too eager to move in different directions to afford that. However, the chaotic variations they display when thrust together mark out just how much potential music in cinema offers us to arrange intriguing and complex patterns of our own. Hopefully movie music scholarship will continue to flourish and the spaces for development that this introduction has exposed will soon be inhabited by all manner of eager and intrigued analysts.

PART ONE

THE MEANINGS OF THE FILM SCORE

The majority of film-goers would not be able to tell you much about movie scores. Even if you were to catch a group leaving a movie theatre and ask them about the score they had just heard, many would admit to not really having noticed it. However, if the same ensemble had been asked to sit through that material minus the music, they would probably feel frustratedly disconnected from the film and its characters precisely because of the lack of musical prompts to guide them towards a set of expected responses. Although the average movie fan would be even more baffled by the cryptic languages of composition techniques, they are (whether knowingly or not) hugely attuned to the tricks of scoring. Without musical anchoring, most would be forced to agree that the film world would be a strangely hollow place.

It has been a daunting task trying to select a mere four of the many critical excursions into scoring for this book. When almost all of the explicitly conscious "film music analysis" deals with soundtracks of the orchestral variety, it is extremely difficult to single out just a few exemplary articles. The chosen four all scrutinize formal languages, production procedures and modes of reception, while also managing to come to completely different conclusions.

The collection opens with Kalinak's lucid introduction to how music functions, both grammatically and hermeneutically, within cinema. For those under-confident about their comprehension of accepted musical vocabulary, it offers one of the most reliable and enjoyable descriptions of the nuts and bolts of scoring. Anyone unsure of how those strange tadpole-like notes that hang on stave notation sheets translate into what we hear at the movies will find this article's reference to examples from *Vertigo* (1958) extremely helpful.

Like Kalinak, Adorno and Eisler are curious about how film music is constructed—although their offering is more of a barbed reproach of the capitalist rationale propping up scoring's conventions. They pepper their chapter with such terminology as "pseudo-individualization," "culture industries" and "standardization" which readers familiar with the work of the Frankfurt School will recognize and which the uninitiated will be able to master as the chapter wears on. Their article is marked by a deep pessimism about the impact of mass production on art and it laments the utilitarian functioning of music within cinema—its lazy recourse to stock devices and its general submissiveness to the visual track. This stance derives from a heavy investment in Marxist politics and, in particular, strategies for changing the conditions of labour and production which might enable a more thought-provoking, even revolutionary way of engaging with culture. Although more *laissez-faire* readers may baulk at this chapter's bleakness, it is worth noting its authors' historical situations. Both men were political refugees who fled Germany upon the rise of the Nazis, only to find the America into which they had arrived subsumed by the very capitalist ethic they had spent their adult lives fighting.

Instead of using leftist politics to criticize the state of soundtracking, Gorbman draws upon the rhetoric of psychoanalytical theory in order to work out what makes the score so potent in the sound era, when there is no directly logical requirement for non-diegetic film music. The score's key functions for her are "semiotic *ancrage* [anchoring]" and "psychological suturing": the first subtly channelling our emotional responses in line with the story's themes, the second lulling us into a sense of being wrapped in a coherent and comfortingly resolved movie experience. While this chapter persuasively accounts for the kinds of film soundtracks which one might wish to call "background music" (as Gorbman herself does), her theories do not willingly extend into more obtrusive musical types, such as scores compiled from pop songs. However, this focus is hardly a limitation and the extract comes from a book which has rightly become a benchmark in recent movie music scholarship.

Anderson moves outside the psychological and into the social with an examination of American film accompaniment in the early part of the twentieth century. Of all the essays in this section, this is the most eager to deal with a finite amount of material rather than to propound a more encompassing theory of readership. Scouring through cue sheets, movie reviews and nickelodeon advice pamphlets, Anderson thinks through how the then youthful format—film— installed itself in certain cultural and class registers. In his examination of a medium with a precarious sense of its own prestige, Anderson discovers how the art of music infused and structured film of the time and outlines how these practices became increasingly regulated. Unlike the other chapters in this section, Anderson's concentrates less on orchestral scoring and more on improvised and vernacular music, easing us smoothly into the next part's focus on more popular idioms.

The Language of Music

A brief analysis of *Vertigo*

KATHRYN KALINAK

[. . .]

Musical language

Film music is above all music, and coming to terms with the filmic experience as a musical experience is the first step in understanding how a film's score wields power over us. I would like to offer a selective analysis of a cue from a classical Hollywood film score, Bernard Herrmann's main title for *Vertigo*, to demonstrate how one might begin to think about a film score in musical terms.

[. . .]

Music is a coherent experience, and because it is a system of expression possessing internal logic, it has frequently been compared to language. While a linguistic analogy is fraught with difficulty, it does, at least on a preliminary level, help to reveal something fundamental about how music works. Like language and other systems of human communication, music consists of a group of basic units, a vocabulary, if you will, and a set of rules for arranging these units into recognizable and meaningful structures, a grammar. The pitches themselves constitute the vocabulary of the system and harmony the grammar for organizing them. Like language, music is also a culturally specific system. The Western world, especially from the eighteenth century through the twentieth, has organized music around a single note, called the **tonic**, which serves as a focal point for its structure. "All other pitches are heard in relation to this pitch and it is normally the pitch on which a piece must end."[1] **Tonal music** or **tonality**, the system of music derived from this principle, constitutes *one* possible way of organizing music. It will, however, be the system of music explored here as it is the system which forms the basis of the classical film score.

In tonal music, the pitches or notes may be combined horizontally, that is, in succession, or vertically, that is, in simultaneity.[2] The most familiar strategy for organizing notes horizontally is **melody**, which can be defined as an extended series of notes played in an order which is memorable and recognizable as a discrete unit (hummable, if you will). One of the most distinguishing characteristics of tonal music since about the middle of the eighteenth century is the extent to which melody is privileged as a form of organization. Its presence prioritizes our listening, subordinating some elements to others and giving us a focal point in the musical texture.

How does melody, as an organizing construct, figure in the main title of *Vertigo*? It largely doesn't. One of the most identifying characteristics of *Vertigo*'s score, indeed of most of the Herrmann–Hitchcock oeuvre, is the absence of hummable melody. (Try whistling the shower scene from *Psycho* [1960] or the main title from *North by Northwest* [1959].) Herrmann begins *Vertigo* with a musical figure associated in the film with vertigo itself, alternately descending and ascending arpeggiated chords played in contrary motion in the bass and treble voices. This may sound rather technical and somewhat daunting but a quick look at Figure 1 may make this description clearer. Notice how in the top part of the composition, the **treble** voice, the musical notation moves down and then up, while in the bottom part, the **bass** voice, the musical notation moves up and then down; in other words, they move in opposite directions or in **contrary motion**. The chords here are described as **arpeggiated** because in both the treble and bass voices the notes of the chord are played in succession (or horizontally) instead of simultaneously (or vertically). Ultimately, this figure resists definition as melodic (I, for one, have trouble even humming it) in three ways: the contrary directions it incorporates defeat a sense of linearity inherent in the concept of melody; both parts are equally important musically (which one is the "melody," the treble voice or the bass voice?); and the arpeggiated chords themselves are unstable and shifting harmonic constructions.[3] Herrmann's main title for *Vertigo*, as we shall see, is unnerving in the context of tonal music. One of the reasons for the discomfort of the opening is the absence of a conventional melody, which denies the listener the familiar point of access.

Copyright 1958 Famous Music Corporation

Figure 1   Measures 1–2, *Vertigo*

Harmony is an equally important component of musical language and one which figures importantly in the *Vertigo* example. **Harmony** can be defined as a system for coordinating the simultaneous use of notes. (Generally, three or more notes sounded simultaneously are known as a **chord**.) Tonal harmony privileges those combinations of notes described as **consonant**, which do not require resolution, over those combinations described as **dissonant**, which do require resolution. Consonance and dissonance underlie tonal music's patterns of tension and resolution enacted through chordal structures that deviate from and ultimately return to the most stable and consonant of all chords in the harmonic system, the **tonic chord**, or a chord built on the tonic note. In tonal music the desire to return to the tonic chord for a sense of completion is so great that to deny it at the end of a piece of music is to constitute an intense disruption. An example of a score that exploits this desire is Michel Legrand's music for Jean-Luc Godard's *Vivre sa vie* (1962). Though tonal, the score fails to offer the tonic chord in each of the dozen times musical accompaniment occurs in the film.[4] Expectation concerning a resolution becomes so strong that at the end of the film, when the tonic chord is missing even from the music which accompanies the closing credits, a common reaction among listeners is to turn to the projector, wondering if a mechanical breakdown or faulty print is the cause of this deliberate act of musical irresolution.

Vertigo is a score which exploits harmony for disturbing effect. Its opening, as we have seen, is formed by arpeggiated chords. I'd like to return to Figure 1 and be musically specific for just a moment. These are seventh chords, which include and draw attention to the seventh and least stable note of the scale. Contributing to the dis-ease created by the seventh chords are the intervals constructed by the intersection of the bass and treble voices. An **interval** may be defined as the relationship between any two given notes, measured according to the number of notes that span the distance between them. In this example from Vertigo the opening notes in the bass and treble voices form an extremely grating interval, the major seventh, and the point at which the arpeggiated chords come closest together forms a major second, another dissonant interval. The specifics of the preceding analysis are far less important to remember than the main point: Herrmann has created a harmony to disturb tonality. Royal S. Brown has compellingly argued that the scores Herrmann composed for Hitchcock are distinguished by exactly this kind of "harmonic ambiguity whereby the musical language familiar to Western listeners serves as a point of departure." The extent of this ambiguity is almost immediately discernible to the ear. "Norms are thrown off center and expectations are held in suspense for much longer periods of time than the listening ear and feeling viscera are accustomed to."[5] There is something quite unsettling about listening to Vertigo, and at least part of that something is its harmonic structure.

Musical affect

The main title for Vertigo is disconcerting in a number of ways, musically speaking. I have been analyzing its basic structure as music, the way it avoids melody as a construct of organization and the way it bends the syntactical "grammar" of harmony. Music, however, means on a number of levels, and like other systems of human communication it is capable of producing meaning outside of itself. Expressivity is not intrinsic or essential to music: yet as any listener can attest music may and often does arouse an emotional or intellectual response.

[. . .]

One of the most demonstrable of the ways in which music can have a definite, verifiable, and predictable effect is through its physiological impact, that is, through certain involuntary responses caused by its stimulation of the human nervous system. The most important of these stimulants—rhythm, dynamics, tempo, and choice of pitch—provide the basis of physiological response.

The power of rhythm has frequently been traced to primitive origins, music "borrowing" from human physiological processes—heartbeat, pulse, breathing—their rhythmic construction. **Rhythm** organizes music in terms of time. The basic unit of rhythm is the **beat**, a discernible pulse which marks out the passage of time. Since the Renaissance, rhythm has been characterized by regular patterns of beats, usually composed of groups of twos or threes. The term **meter** refers to the way these units are used to organize the music, providing a kind of sonic grid against which a composer writes. Western art music is characterized by a high degree of regularity in terms of both rhythm, that is, the patterns themselves, and meter, that is, their organization. Regular rhythms, perhaps because of their physiological legacy, and certainly because of the way they have been conventionalized, can be lulling and even hypnotic because of the familiarity created through their repetition. Irregular or unpredictable rhythms attract our attention by confounding our expectations and, depending on the violence of the deviation, can unsettle us physiologically through increased stimulation of the nervous system.

In *Vertigo* Herrmann confuses a clear perception of rhythm. The metrical organization of the main title is a **duple** meter, or one in which there are two beats to the measure. Conventionally, such a meter would cause the primary accent to fall on the first beat of each measure, creating a rhythm of alternating accented and unaccented beats (something like a trochee in English metrical verse). And, in fact, for most of the main title, the first beat carries the accent. At certain points, however, Herrmann displaces this point of emphasis for disturbing effect. In measures 12 to 15, for instance, he begins a restatement of the arpeggiated chord in the flutes on the second beat of the measure, instead of the first, which disturbs the pattern. Notice the presence of a **rest**, the musical notation for silence, ▬▬ at the beginning of the first measure in both Figure 2 and Figure 3. Herrmann emphasizes this displacement through the use of the **sforzando** (sfz), a sudden, loud attack on a note or chord, on the second beat in the horns (Figure 3). Besides avoiding identifiable melody and flirting with tonal ambiguity, the opening moments of the score exploit the effects of an unpredictable rhythmic change which contributes to the agitation many listeners feel in hearing this cue.

The most obvious way in which music or any type of sound can elicit a direct response is through its **dynamics**, or level of sound. Volume reaches the nervous system with distinct impact, increasing or decreasing its stimulation in direct proportion to its level. Extremes in sound are the most noticeable dynamic because of their pronounced divorce from the natural

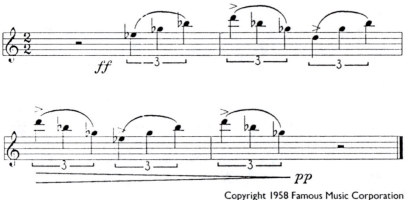

Copyright 1958 Famous Music Corporation

Figure 2   Measures 12–15, *Vertigo*

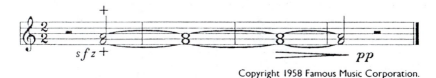

Copyright 1958 Famous Music Corporation.

Figure 3 Measures 12–15, *Vertigo*. The "+" directs the player to muffle the sound, usually by placing the hand in the bell of the instrument.

sound level of everyday life. Extremely loud music can actually hurt the listener, while extremely soft music tends to drop out of the range of human perception. **Crescendos** and **decrescendos**, or the increase and decrease in the volume of sound, respectively, help to modulate the stimulation and can be used to heighten or diminish it. Quick and unexpected changes in dynamics intensify this process.

Herrmann's main title clearly demonstrates the effect of volume. By juxtaposing **fortissimo** (very loud) and **pianissimo** (very soft) both successively and simultaneously, Herrmann creates discernible effects in us. Listen for the change in dynamics at the beginning of the main title. Measures 1–8, for instance, contain six measures (1–6) of sustained *fortissimo* (denoted *ff*) followed by only two measures (7–8) to decrease the sound level to *pianissimo* (denoted *pp*). Although this passage contains a *decrescendo* to help modulate this change, the asymmetry, if you will, of the sound dynamics keeps us off guard musically.

Tempo modulates the speed with which a piece of music is performed. Quick tempi tend to intensify stimulation of the nervous system; slow tempi tend to dissipate it. Diverging from a characteristic pace can also cause a physiological response. The **accelerando** and **ritardando**, a speeding up and slowing down of the musical pace, respectively, help to control such response, heightening, sustaining, or diminishing it.

In the main title of *Vertigo* the tempo is basically regular (Herrmann marks it "*Moderato Assai*" in his score), but it does incorporate a sudden change in its second half which has the effect of doubling the tempo. Near the end of the main title (at measure 53 to be exact) the arpeggiated chord is heard twice as fast as its previous occurrences. Herrmann has accomplished this effect by cutting each note value in half. Where the motif had initially taken a full measure to perform in the violin part (Figure 4), it can now be performed twice in the same amount of time by the harps (Figure 5).

Even choice of pitch can elicit response. Herrmann frequently manipulated pitch to create anxiety. The shower scene in *Psycho*, for instance, is scored for violins; the players execute upward *glissandi* culminating in the highest note in the pitch system. In the scene which

Copyright 1958 Famous Music Corporation

Figure 4 Measures 51–52, violin part *Vertigo*

Copyright 1958 Famous Music Corporation

Figure 5   Measures 53–54, harp part, *Vertigo*

precedes it, notes of extremely high pitch erupt out of the musical tapestry often an octave or more above the musical line which precedes or follows them. In the main title of *Vertigo* a six-note rising and falling figure is played high in the violins' register. It is set off against the extremely low pitch of the tubas, not only exploiting the effect of pitch but combining it with the dis-ease created by splitting the listener's attention between widely divergent musical registers.

Musical conventions

One of the best ways to understand the power of music is to study the conventions by which musical affect circulates through a culture. A musical convention harnesses musical affect to specific and concrete meaning through the power of association. Musical conventions which become ingrained and universal in a culture function as a type of collective experience, activating particular and predictable responses. In tonal music, for example, an **habanera** rhythm ♩♫♫ is a musical convention which summons up thoughts of Spain. Harmonic structures such as open fourths and fifths are used to represent ancient Greece and Rome. Quartal harmony, based on the interval of the fourth, suggests the Orient. To an overwhelming extent, the classical score relied upon such conventions. Composers, working under the pressure of time, used familiar conventions to establish geographic place and historical time, and to summon up specific emotional responses predictably and quickly. The fact that musical conventions are often arbitrary seems of little consequence. The *habanera* rhythm associated with Spain is actually of Cuban origin (via a French composer); the open fourths and fifths associated with the classical age are modern conjecture; quartal harmony is not used exclusively in music of the Orient. But for all their lack of authenticity, conventions are nonetheless powerful.

The classical Hollywood film score relied largely on the resources of the standard symphony orchestra with unusual instruments added for particular effects. Thus at its disposal was a veritable arsenal which could be tapped to activate specific associations. The string family, for instance, because of its proximity in range and tone to the human voice, is thought to be the most expressive group of instruments in the orchestra. For this reason strings are often used to express emotion. In particular, the violin is characterized by its ability to "sing" because its **timbre** or tonal quality is close to that of the human voice. In the opening sequence of *God Is My Co-Pilot* (1945), for example, Franz Waxman uses violins to add emotional resonance explaining, "[for a] deeply religious, emotional tone . . . I used massed violins playing in a high register to convey the feeling."[6] Herrmann, on the other hand, in *Psycho*, exploits these associations for ironic effect: the entire score of this chilling thriller, one of Hitchcock's grisliest films, is composed for a string orchestra.

Horns, with their martial heritage, are another obvious example. Because of their link to pageantry, the military, and the hunt, horns are often used to suggest heroism. Says Henry Mancini, "The most effective and downright thrilling sound is that of all of the |brasses| playing an ensemble passage." [7] Erich Wolfgang Korngold, who was known for his use of brass instruments, exploits a complement of horns for the rousing main title of *Captain Blood*. John Williams relies on horns in the epic *Star Wars* trilogy to suggest the heroic nature of this futuristic saga. Even a contemporary score like *RoboCop*'s (1987) exploits the conventional associations of the horns, using different combinations of brass instruments to accompany the death-defying deeds of the robocop.

Rhythm, like instrumentation, can also provoke specific responses. Dance rhythms, in particular, can be very evocative. Thus, when Herrmann in *The Magnificent Ambersons* charac-terizes the Ambersons with a waltz, he is employing a familiar convention to project the sense of grace and gentility that the family symbolizes. When Waxman bases the theme music for Norma Desmond in *Sunset Boulevard* (1950) on a tango, he is characterizing her as steamy, sultry, Latin, and in 1950, conspicuously out of date. Carlotta's theme in *Vertigo* exploits the fiery and passionate associations of the *habanera* rhythm, transferring to the icy exterior of Kim Novak's fragile Madeleine the sensuality of her psychic ancestor, Carlotta. Musical conventions are profuse and can even be intercepted by a personal response, but to overlook their effect is to ignore the power of collective association in human perception. Film music, when it taps this source, is appealing to a strong response that can impact spectators whether they are consciously aware of it or not.

A crucial site for the acquisition of a culture's musical conventions is the cinematic auditorium itself where musical effects are combined with visual imagery to reinforce them. In fact, for spectators who are basically unversed in art music, films are the major site for the transmission of a culture's musical conventions. The association of **tremolo** strings (the sustaining of a single note through rapid repetition) with suspense, for instance, is a response acquired, in all likelihood, not from an acquaintance with the musical idiom of the nineteenth century, where it is earlier exemplified, but from film scores which exploit it. One of the most interesting aspects of Herrmann's score for *Vertigo* is the way it avoids the most obvious musical convention for suspense, *tremolo* strings, and exploits subtler techniques for the creation of tension such as harmonic instability, shifting and unpredictable rhythm, tempo, and dynamics, and absence of conventional melody.

Music and image

|. . .|

Film music obviously does not exist in a vacuum. It shares with the image track (and other elements of the soundtrack) the ability to shape perception. Film music's power is derived largely from its ability to tap specific musical conventions that circulate throughout the culture. But that power is always dependent on a coexistence with the visual image, a relationship bounded by the limits of credibility itself. Imagine a perfectly innocuous setting, an eighteenth-century drawing room where two lovers are reunited after numerous narrative complications. But instead of a soaring melody played by an offscreen orchestra, we hear *tremolo* strings and dissonant chords. Our tendency as spectators would be to perceive that music as meaningful, specifically to read the scene as suspenseful. We might even expect some kind of narrative complication or even a visual shock because of the music. If these expectations are thwarted, most spectators would feel manipulated, even cheated. Craig Safan, a contemporary film composer, explains it in these terms: "You excite an audience in a certain way and if you betray them they won't want to see your movie. And musically, you can betray your audience. You have to be very careful about that."[8] Music and image collaborate in the filmic process. The farther music and image drift from a kind of mutual dependency, the more potential there is for the disruption or even destruction of the cinematic illusion.

The music for the main title of *Vertigo* plays out against a series of brightly colored geometric spirals which spin against a black background. Hitchcock films often give Herrmann's main title free rein by overtly drawing attention to the music through abstract visual constructions. (*Psycho* and *North by Northwest* are two other examples.) In *Vertigo* the correspondence between the circularity of these images and the film's title is obvious, but it is equally important to note the relationship between these images and Herrmann's music. *Vertigo*'s opening consists of alternately descending and ascending arpeggiated chords played in contrary motion in the bass and treble voices. At this point I would like to define it as a **motif**, a distinctive musical passage that is repeated (and varied) throughout a musical text. This motif progresses in time without establishing a clear direction (neither up nor down) or, as discussed earlier, a clear harmony (hovering dangerously close to an abnegation of tonality). It is an almost uninterrupted undulation from beginning to end. This quality of the music is, interestingly enough, reflected graphically in its very notation: It is Herrmann's mesmerizing evocation of dizziness. Spinning in time with the spiraling geometric forms, the motif reinforces and is in turn reinforced by the vertigo suggested by the images.

[. . .]

Film music is a stimulus that we hear but, by and large, fail to listen to. I hope that this brief introduction has highlighted the most important components in the mental machinery that structures our understanding of music, and offers a context through which to listen as well as to hear.[9]

Notes

1 Fred Lerdahl and Ray Jackendoff, A *Generative Theory of Tonal Music* (Cambridge, MA: MIT Press, 1983), 295.
2 Strictly speaking a pitch refers to any one of the sounds existing within a given musical system while a note refers to the visual sign for a pitch. In practice, however, such a distinction is rarely maintained, and the term "note," especially in English, is used to designate both the sound and its sign. It is this practice that I follow when I use "note" throughout the text.
3 All of the musical examples in this chapter originated as my own transcriptions. I was able to compare these against the autograph copy of the full score in the Bernard Herrmann Archive of the University of California at Santa Barbara. All future references to this score will be quoted from this copy.

4 For an insightful reading of the score for *Vivre sa vie* see Royal S. Brown, "Music and *Vivre sa vie*," *Quarterly Review of Film Studies* 5, 3 (Summer 1980): 319–33.

5 Royal S. Brown, "Herrmann, Hitchcock, and the Music of the Irrational," *Cinema Journal* 21, 2 (Spring 1982): 17.

6 Franz Waxman, "Franz Waxman," in *Film Score: The View from the Podium*, ed. Tony Thomas (South Brunswick and New York: A. S. Barnes, 1979), 55.

7 Henry Mancini, *Sounds and Scores: A Practical Guide to Professional Orchestration* (Northridge Music, 1967), 131.

8 Craig Safan, quoted in Fred Karlin and Rayburn Wright, *On the Track: A Guide to Contemporary Film Scoring* (New York: Schirmer Books, 1990), 127.

9 This final paragraph was added by the author for this reader.

Prejudices and bad habits

2

THEODOR ADORNO AND HANS EISLER

Introduction

The motion picture cannot be understood in isolation, as a specific form of art; it is understandable only as the most characteristic medium of contemporary cultural industry, which uses the techniques of mechanical reproduction. The popular messages conveyed by this industry must not be conceived as an art originally created by the masses. Such an art no longer exists or does not yet exist. Even the vestiges of spontaneous folk art have died out in the industrialized countries; at best it subsists in backward agrarian regions. In this advanced industrial age, the masses are compelled to seek relaxation and rest, in order to restore the labor power that has been spent in the alienated process of labor; and this need is the mass basis of mass culture. On it there has arisen the powerful amusement industry, which constantly produces, satisfies, and reproduces new needs.

Cultural industry is not a product of the twentieth century; however, it is only in the course of the last decades that it has been monopolized and thoroughly organized. And because of this process, it has assumed an entirely new character—it has become inescapable. Taste and receptivity have become largely standardized; and, despite the multiplicity of products, the consumer has only apparent freedom of choice. Production has been divided into administrative fields, and whatever passes through the machinery bears its mark, is predigested, neutralized, levelled down. The old distinction between serious and popular art, between low-grade and refined autonomous art, no longer applies. All art, as a means of filling out leisure time, has become entertainment, although it absorbs materials and forms of traditional autonomous art as part of the so-called "cultural heritage." It is this very process of amalgamation that abolishes aesthetic autonomy: what happens to the *Moonlight Sonata* when it is sung by a choir and played by a supposedly mystical orchestra now actually happens to everything. Art that does not yield is completely shut off from consumption and driven into isolation. Everything is taken apart, robbed of its real meaning, and then put together again. The only criterion of this procedure is that of reaching the consumer as effectively as possible. Manipulated art is consumer's art.

Of all the media of cultural industry, the motion picture, as the most comprehensive, most clearly displays this tendency to amalgamation. The development and integration of its technical elements—pictures, words, sound, script, acting, and photography—have paralleled certain social tendencies to amalgamation of traditional cultural values that have become commodities. Such tendencies were operative earlier—in Wagner's music dramas, in Reinhardt's neo-romantic theater, and in the symphonic poems of Liszt and Strauss; later they were consummated in the motion picture as the amalgamation of drama, psychological novel, dime novel, operetta, symphony concert, and revue.

Critical insight into the nature of industrialized culture does not imply sentimental glorification of the past. It is no accident that this culture thrives parasitically on the products of the old individualistic age. The old individualistic mode of production should not be set up against it as necessarily superior to it, nor should technology as such be held responsible for the barbarism of the cultural industry. On the other hand, the technical advances, which are the triumphs of the cultural industry, must not be accepted under all circumstances. Which technical resources should be used in art should be determined by intrinsic requirements. Technology opens up unlimited opportunities for art in the future, and even in the poorest motion pictures there are moments when such opportunities are strikingly apparent. But the same principle that has opened up these opportunities also ties them to big business. A discussion of industrialized culture must show the interaction of these two factors: the aesthetic potentialities of mass art in the future and its ideological character at present.

The following pages are intended as a partial contribution to this task. In them we have dealt with a strictly delimited segment of the cultural industry, namely the technical and social potentialities and contradictions of music in relation to motion pictures.

[. . .]

The character of motion-picture music has been determined by everyday practice. It has been an adaptation in part to the immediate needs of the film industry, in part to whatever musical clichés and ideas about music happened to be current. As a result, a number of empirical standards—rules of thumb—were evolved that corresponded to what motion-picture people called common sense. These rules have now been made obsolete by the technical development of the cinema as well as of autonomous music, yet they have persisted as tenaciously as if they had their roots in ancient wisdom rather than in bad habits. They originated in the intellectual milieu of Tin Pan Alley; and because of practical considerations and problems of personnel, they have so entrenched themselves that they, more than anything else, have hindered the progress of motion-picture music. They only seem to make sense as a consequence of standardization within the industry itself, which calls for standard practices everywhere.

Furthermore, these rules of thumb represent a kind of pseudo-tradition harking back to the days of spontaneity and craftsmanship, of medicine shows and covered wagons. And it is precisely this discrepancy between obsolete practices and scientific production methods that characterizes the whole system. The two aspects are inseparable in principle, and both are subject to criticism. Public realization of the antiquated character of these rules should suffice to break their hold.

Typical examples of these habits, selected at random, will be discussed here in order to show concretely the level on which the problem of motion-picture music is dealt with today.

The leitmotif

Cinema music is still patched together by means of leitmotifs. The ease with which they are recalled provides definite clues for the listener, and they also are a practical help to the composer in his task of composition under pressure. He can quote where he otherwise would have to invent.

The idea of the leitmotif has been popular since the days of Wagner.[1] His popularity was largely connected with his use of leitmotifs. They function as trademarks, so to speak, by which persons, emotions, and symbols can instantly be identified. They have always been the most elementary means of elucidation, the thread by which the musically inexperienced find their way about. They were drummed into the listener's ear by persistent repetition, often with scarcely any variation, very much as a new song is plugged or as a motion-picture actress is popularized by her hair-do. It was natural to assume that this device, because it is so easy to grasp, would be particularly suitable to motion pictures, which are based, on the premise that they must be easily understood. However, the truth of this assumption is only illusory.

The reasons for this are first of all technical. The fundamental character of the leitmotif—its salience and brevity—was related to the gigantic dimensions of the Wagnerian and post-Wagnerian music dramas. Just because the leitmotif as such is musically rudimentary, it requires a large musical canvas if it is to take on a structural meaning beyond that of a signpost. The atomization of the musical element is paralleled by the heroic dimensions of the composition as a whole. This relation is entirely absent in the motion picture, which requires continual interruption of one element by another rather than continuity. The constantly changing scenes are characteristic of the structure of the motion picture. Musically, also, shorter forms prevail, and the leitmotif is unsuitable here because of this brevity of forms which must be complete in themselves. Cinema music is so easily understood that it has no need of leitmotifs to serve as signposts, and its limited dimension does not permit adequate expansion of the leitmotif.

Similar considerations apply with regard to the aesthetic problem. The Wagnerian leitmotif is inseparably connected with the symbolic nature of the music drama. The leitmotif is not supposed merely to characterize persons, emotions, or things, although this is the prevalent conception. Wagner conceived its purpose as the endowment of the dramatic events with metaphysical significance. When in the *Ring* the tubas blare the Valhalla motif, it is not merely to indicate the dwelling place of Wotan. Wagner meant also to connote the sphere of sublimity, the cosmic will, and the primal principle. The leitmotif was invented essentially for this kind of symbolism. There is no place for it in the motion picture, which seeks to depict reality. Here the function of the leitmotif has been reduced to the level of a musical lackey, who announces his master with an important air even though the eminent personage is clearly recognizable to everyone. The effective technique of the past thus becomes a mere duplication, ineffective and uneconomical. At the same time, since it cannot be developed to its full musical significance in the motion picture, its use leads to extreme poverty of composition.

Melody and euphony

The demand for melody and euphony is not only assumed to be obvious, but also a matter of public taste, as represented in the consumer. We do not deny that producers and consumers generally agree in regard to this demand. But the concepts of melody and euphony are not so self-evident as is generally believed. Both are to a large extent conventionalized historical categories.

The concept of melody first gained ascendancy in the nineteenth century in connection with the new *Kunstlied*, especially Schubert's. Melody was conceived as the opposite of the "theme" of the Viennese classicism of Haydn, Mozart, and Beethoven.[2] It denotes a tonal sequence, constituting not so much the point of departure of a composition as a self-contained entity that is easy to listen to, singable, and expressive. This notion led to the sort of melodiousness for which the German language has no specific term, but which the English word "tune" expresses quite accurately. It consists first of all in the uninterrupted flow of a melody in the upper voice, in such a way that the melodic continuity seems natural, because it is almost possible to guess in advance exactly what will follow. The listener zealously insists on his right to this anticipation, and feels cheated if it is denied him. This fetishism in regard to melody, which at certain moments during the latter part of the Romantic period crowded out all the other elements of music, shackled the concept of melody itself.

Today, the conventional concept of melody is based on criteria of the crudest sort. Easy intelligibility is guaranteed by harmonic and rhythmic symmetry, and by the paraphrasing of accepted harmonic procedures; tunefulness is assured by the preponderance of small diatonic intervals. These postulates have taken on the semblance of logic, owing to the rigid institutionalization of prevailing customs, in which these criteria automatically obtain. In Mozart's and Beethoven's day, when the stylistic ideal of filigree composition held sway, the postulate of the predominance of an anticipatable melody in the upper voice would scarcely have been comprehended. "Natural" melody is a figment of the imagination, an extremely relative phenomenon illegitimately absolutized, neither an obligatory nor an *a priori* constituent of the material, but one procedure among many, singled out for exclusive use.

The conventional demand for melody and euphony is constantly in conflict with the objective requirements of the motion picture. The prerequisite of melody is that the composer be independent, in the sense that his selection and invention relate to situations that supply specific lyric-poetic inspiration. This is out of the question where the motion picture is concerned. All music in the motion picture is under the sign of utility, rather than lyric expressiveness. Aside from the fact that lyric-poetic inspiration cannot be expected of the composer for the cinema, this kind of inspiration would contradict the embellishing and subordinate function that industrial practice still enforces on the composer.

Moreover, the problem of melody as "poetic" is made insoluble by the conventionality of the popular notion of melody. Visual action in the motion picture has of course a prosaic irregularity and asymmetry. It claims to be photographed life; and as such every motion picture is a documentary. As a result, there is a gap between what is happening on the screen and the symmetrically articulated conventional melody. A photographed kiss cannot actually be synchronized with an eight-bar phrase. The disparity between symmetry and asymmetry becomes particularly striking when music is used to accompany natural phenomena, such as drifting clouds, sunrises, wind, and rain. These natural phenomena could inspire nineteenth-century poets; however, as photographed, they are essentially irregular and nonrhythmic, thus excluding that element of poetic rhythm with which the motion-picture industry associates them. Verlaine could write a poem about rain in the city, but one cannot hum a tune that accompanies rain reproduced on the screen.

More than anything else the demand for melody at any cost and on every occasion has throttled the development of motion-picture music. The alternative is certainly not to resort to the unmelodic, but to liberate melody from conventional fetters.

Unobtrusiveness

One of the most widespread prejudices in the motion-picture industry is the premise that the spectator should not be conscious of the music. The philosophy behind this belief is a vague notion that music should have a subordinate role in relation to the picture. As a rule, the motion picture represents action with dialogue. Financial considerations and technical interest are concentrated on the actor; anything that might overshadow him is considered disturbing. The musical indications in the scripts are usually sporadic and indefinite. Music thus far has not been treated in accordance with its specific potentialities. It is tolerated as an outsider who is somehow regarded as being indispensable, partly because of a genuine need and partly on account of the fetishistic idea that the existing technical resources must be exploited to the fullest extent.[3]

Despite the often reiterated opinion of the wizards of the movie industry, in which many composers concur, the thesis that music should be unobtrusive is questionable. There are, doubtless, situations in motion pictures in which the dialogue must be emphasized and in which detailed musical foreground configurations would be disturbing. It may also be granted that these situations sometimes require acoustic supplementation. But precisely when this requirement is taken seriously, the insertion of allegedly unobtrusive music becomes dubious. In such instances, an accompaniment of extra-musical sound would more nearly approximate the realism of the motion picture. If, instead, music is used, music that is supposed to be real music but is not supposed to be noticed, the effect is that described in a German nursery rhyme:

> Ich weiss ein schönes Spiel,
> Ich mal' mir einen Bart,
> Und halt mir einen Fächer vor,
> Dass niemand ihn gewahrt.
>
> |I know a pretty game:
> I deck me with a beard
> And hide behind a fan
> So I won't look too weird.|

In practice, the requirement of unobtrusiveness is generally met not by an approximation of nonmusical sounds, but by the use of banal music. Accordingly, the music is supposed to be inconspicuous in the same sense as are selections from La Bohème played in a restaurant.

Apart from this, unobtrusive music, assumed to be the typical solution of the problem, is only one and certainly the least important of many possible solutions. The insertion of music should be planned along with the writing of the script, and the question whether the spectator should be aware of the music is a matter to be decided in each case according to the dramatic requirements of the script. Interruption of the action by a developed musical episode could be an important artistic device. For example, in an anti-Nazi picture, at the point when the action is dispersed into individual psychological details, an exceptionally serious piece of music occupies the whole perception. Its movement helps the listener to remember the essential incidents and focuses his attention on the situation as a whole. It is true that in this case the music is the very opposite of what it is conventionally supposed to be. It no longer expresses the conflicts of individual characters, nor does it persuade the spectator to identify himself with the hero; but rather it leads him back from the sphere of privacy to the major social issue. In pictures of an inferior type of entertainment—musicals and revues from which every trace of dramatic psychology is eliminated—one finds, more often than elsewhere, rudiments of this device of musical interruption, and the independent use of music in songs, dances, and finales.

Visual justification

The problem relates less to rules than to tendencies, which are not as important as they were a few years ago, yet must still be taken into account. The fear that the use of music at a point when it would be completely impossible in a real situation will appear naive or childish, or impose upon the listener an effort of imagination that might distract him from the main issue, leads to attempts to justify this use in a more or less rationalistic way. Thus situations are often contrived in which it is allegedly natural for the main character to stop and sing, or music accompanying a love scene is made plausible by having the hero turn on a radio or a phonograph.

The following is a typical instance. The hero is waiting for his beloved. Not a word is spoken. The director feels the need of filling in the silence. He knows the danger of nonaction, of absence of suspense, and therefore prescribes music. At the same time, however, he lays so much stress in the objective portrayal of psychological continuity that an unmotivated irruption of music strikes him as risky. Thus he resorts to the most artless trick in order to avoid artlessness, and makes the hero turn to the radio. The threadbareness of this artifice is illustrated by those scenes in which the hero accompanies himself "realistically" on the piano for about eight bars, whereupon he is relieved by a large orchestra and chorus, albeit with no change of scene. In so far as this device, which obtained in the early days of sound pictures, is still applied, it hinders the use of music as a genuine element of contrast. Music becomes a plot accessory, a sort of acoustical stage property.

Illustration

There is a favorite Hollywood gibe: "Birdie sings, music sings." Music must follow visual incidents and illustrate them either by directly imitating them or by using clichés that are associated with the mood and content of the picture. The preferred material for imitation is "nature," in the most superficial sense of the word, i.e. as the antithesis of the urban—that realm where people are supposed to be able to breathe freely, stimulated by the presence of plants and animals. This is a vulgar and stereotyped version of the concept of nature that prevailed in nineteenth-century poetry. Music is concocted to go with meretricious lyrics. Particularly landscape shots without action seem to call for musical accompaniment, which then conforms to the stale programmatic patterns. Mountain peaks invariably invoke string tremolos punctuated by a signal-like horn motif. The ranch to which the virile hero has eloped with the sophisticated heroine is accompanied by forest murmurs and a flute melody. A slow waltz goes along with a moonlit scene in which a boat drifts down a river lined with weeping willows.

What is in question here is not the principle of musical illustration. Certainly musical illustration is only one among many dramaturgic resources, but it is so overworked that it deserves a rest, or at least it should be used with the greatest discrimination. This is what is generally lacking in prevailing practice. Music cut to fit the stereotype "nature" is reduced to the character of a cheap mood-producing gadget, and the associative patterns are so familiar that there is really no illustration of anything, but only the elicitation of the automatic response: "Aha, nature!"

Illustrative use of music today results in unfortunate duplication. It is uneconomical, except where quite specific effects are intended, or minute interpretation of the action of the picture. The old operas left a certain amount of elbow room in their scenic arrangements for what is vague and indefinite; this could be filled out with tone painting. The music of the Wagnerian era was actually a means of elucidation. But in the cinema, both picture and dialogue are hyperexplicit. Conventional music can add nothing to the explicitness, but instead may detract from it, since even in the worst pictures standardized musical effects fail to keep up with the concrete elaboration of the screen action. But if the elucidating function is given up as superfluous, music should never attempt to accompany precise occurrences in an imprecise manner. It should stick to its task—even if it is only as questionable a one as that of creating a mood—renouncing that of repeating the obvious. Musical illustration should either be hyperexplicit itself—over-illuminating, so to speak, and thereby interpretive—or should be omitted. There is no excuse for flute melodies that force a bird call into a pattern of full ninth chords.

Geography and history

When the scene is laid in a Dutch town, with its canals, windmills, and wooden shoes, the composer is supposed to send over to the studio library for a Dutch folk song in order to use its theme as a working basis. Since it is not easy to recognize a Dutch folk song for what it is, especially when it has been subjected to the whims of an arranger, this procedure seems a dubious one. Here music is used in much the same way as costumes or sets, but without as strong a characterizing effect. A composer can attain something more convincing by writing a tune of his own on the basis of a village dance for little Dutch girls than he can by clinging to the original. Indeed, the current folk music of all countries—apart from that which is basically outside occidental music—tends toward a certain sameness, in contrast to the differentiated art languages. This is because it is grounded on a limited number of elementary rhythmic formulas associated with festivities, communal dances, and the like. It is as difficult to distinguish between the temperamental characters of Polish and Spanish dances, particularly in the conventionalized form they assumed in the nineteenth century, as it is to discern the difference between hill-billy songs and Upper Bavarian *Schnaderhüpferln*. Moreover, ordinary cinematic music has an irresistible urge to follow the pattern of "just folk music." Specific national characteristics can be captured musically only if the musical counterpart of beflagging the scene with national emblems like an exhibition is not resorted to. Related to this is the practice of investing costume pictures with music of the corresponding historical period. This recalls concerts in which hoop-skirted elderly ladies play tedious pre-Bach harpsichord pieces by candlelight in baroque palaces. The absurdity of such "applied art" arrangements is glaring in contrast with the technique of the film, which is of necessity modern. If costume pictures must be, they might be better served by the free use of advanced musical resources.

Stock music

One of the worst practices is the incessant use of a limited number of worn-out, musical pieces that are associated with the given screen situations by reason of their actual or traditional titles. Thus, the scene of a moonlight night is accompanied by the first movement of the *Moonlight Sonata*, orchestrated in a manner that completely contradicts its meaning, because the piano melody—suggested by Beethoven with the utmost discretion—is made obtrusive and is richly underscored by the strings. For thunderstorms, the overture to *William Tell* is used; for weddings, the march from *Lohengrin* or Mendelssohn's wedding march. These practices—incidentally, they are on the wane and are retained only in cheap pictures—correspond to the popularity of trademarked pieces in classical music, such as Beethoven's E-flat Concerto, which has attained an almost fatal popularity under the apocryphal title *The Emperor*, or Schubert's *Unfinished Symphony*. The present vogue of the latter is to some extent connected with the idea that the composer died before it was finished, whereas he simply laid it aside years before his death. The use of trademarks is a nuisance, though it must be acknowledged that childlike faith in the eternal symbolic force of certain classical wedding or funeral marches occasionally has a redeeming aspect, when these are compared with original scores manufactured to order.

Clichés

All these questions are related to a more general state of affairs. Mass production of motion pictures has led to the elaboration of typical situations, ever-recurring emotional crises, and standardized methods of arousing suspense. They correspond to cliché effects in music. But music is often brought into play at the very point where particularly characteristic effects are sought for the sake of "atmosphere" or suspense. The powerful effect intended does not come off, because the listener has been made familiar with the stimulus by innumerable analogous passages. Psychologically, the whole phenomenon is ambiguous. If the screen shows a peaceful country house while the music produces familiar sinister sounds, the spectator knows at once that something terrible is about to happen, and thus the musical accompaniment both intensifies the suspense and nullifies it by betraying the sequel.

As in many other aspects of contemporary motion pictures, it is not standardization as such that is objectionable here. Pictures that frankly follow an established pattern, such as "westerns" or gangster and horror pictures, often are in a certain way superior to pretentious grade-A films. What is objectionable is the standardized character of pictures that claim to be unique; or, conversely, the individual disguise of the standardized pattern. This is exactly what happens in music. Thus, for example, throbbing and torrential string arpeggios—which the guides to Wagner once called the "agitated motif"—are resorted to without rhyme or reason, and nothing can be more laughable to anyone who recognizes them for what they are.

Such musical conventions are all the more dubious because their material is usually taken from the most recently bygone phase of autonomous music, which still passes as "modern" in motion pictures. Forty years ago, when musical impressionism and exoticism were at their height, the whole-tone scale was regarded as a particularly stimulating, unfamiliar, and "colorful" musical device. Today the whole-tone scale is stuffed into the introduction of every popular hit, yet in motion pictures it continues to be used as if it had just seen the light of day. Thus the means employed and the effect achieved are completely disproportionate. Such a disproportion can have a certain charm when, as in animated cartoons, it serves to stress the absurdity of something impossible, for instance, Pluto galloping over the ice to the "Ride of the Walkyries." But the whole-tone scale so overworked in the amusement industry can no longer cause anyone really to shudder.

The use of clichés also affects instrumentation. The tremolo on the bridge of the violin, which thirty years ago was intended even in serious music to produce a feeling of uncanny suspense and to express an unreal atmosphere, today has become common currency. Generally, all artistic means that were originally conceived for their stimulating effect rather than for their structural significance grow threadbare and obsolete with extraordinary rapidity. Here, as in many other instances, the motion-picture industry is carrying out a sentence long since pronounced in serious music, and one is justified in ascribing a progressive function to the sound film in so far as it thus has discredited the trashy devices intended merely for effect. These have long since become unbearable both to artists and to the audience, so much so that sooner or later no one will be able to enjoy clichés. When this happens there will be both need and room for other elements of music. The development of avant-garde music in the course of the last thirty years has opened up an inexhaustible reservoir of new resources and possibilities that is still practically untouched. There is no objective reason why motion-picture music should not draw upon it.

Standardized interpretation

The standardization of motion-picture music is particularly apparent in the prevailing style of performance. First of all, there is the element of dynamics, which was at one time limited by the imperfection of the recording and reproduction machinery. Today, this machinery is far better differentiated and affords far greater dynamic possibilities, both as regards the extremes and the transitions; nevertheless, standardization of dynamics still persists. The different degrees of strength are levelled and blurred to a general mezzoforte—incidentally, this practice is quite analogous to the habits of the mixer in radio broadcasting. The main purpose here is the production of a comfortable and polished euphony, which neither startles by its power (fortissimo) nor requires attentive listening because of its weakness (pianissimo). In consequence of this levelling, dynamics as a means of elucidating musical contexts is lost. The lack of a threefold fortissimo and pianissimo reduces the crescendo and decrescendo to too small a range.

In the methods of performance, too, standardization has as its counterpart pseudo-individualization.[4] While everything is more or less adjusted to the mezzoforte ideal, an effort is made, through exaggerated interpretation, to make each musical motif produce the utmost expression, emotion, and suspense. The violins must sob or scintillate, the brasses must crash insolently or bombastically, no moderate expression is tolerated, and the whole method of performance is based on exaggeration. It is characterized by a mania for extremes, such as were reserved in the days of the silent pictures for that type of violinist who led the little movie-house orchestra. The perpetually used espressivo has become completely worn out. Even effective dramatic incidents are made trite by oversweet accompaniment or offensive overexposition. A "middle-ground," objective musical type of interpretation that resorts to the espressivo only where it is really justified could by its economy greatly enhance the effectiveness of motion-picture music.

Notes

1 A prominent Hollywood composer, in an interview quoted in the newspapers, declared that there is no fundamental difference between his methods of composing and Wagner's. He, too, uses the leitmotif.
2 As a matter of fact, the modern concept of melody made itself felt as early as within Viennese classicism. Nowhere does the historical character of this apparently natural concept become more manifest than in the famous Mozart critique by Hans Georg Naegeli, the Swiss contemporary of the Viennese classicists, which is now made accessible in a reprint edited by Willi Reich. Musical history generally recognizes as one of the greatest merits of Mozart that he introduced the element of cantability into the sonata form, particularly the complex of the second theme. This innovation, largely responsible for the musical changes that led to the crystallization of the later *Lied* melody, was by no means greeted enthusiastically in all quarters. To Naegeli, who was certainly narrow-minded and dogmatic but had rather articulate philosophical ideas about musical style, Mozart's synthesis of instrumental writing and cantability appeared about as shocking as advanced modern composition would to a popular-music addict of today. He blames Mozart, who is now regarded by the musical public as the utmost representative of stylistic purity, for lack of taste and style. The following passage is characteristic: "His |Mozart's| genius was great, but its defect, the overuse of contrast, was equally great. This was all the more objectionable in his case because he continuously contrasted the non-instrumental with the instrumental, cantability with the free play of tones. This was inartistic, as it is in all arts. As soon as continuous contrast becomes the main effect, the beautiful proportion of parts is necessarily neglected. This stylistic fault can be discovered in many of Mozart's works" (Hans Georg Naegeli, *Von Bach zu Beethoven*, Benno Schwabe & Co., Basel, 1946, pp. 48–9).
3 In the realm of motion pictures the term "technique" has a double meaning that can easily lead to confusion. On the one hand, technique is the equivalent of an industrial process for producing goods: e.g. the discovery that picture and sound can be recorded on the same strip is comparable to the invention of the air brake. The other meaning of technique is aesthetic. It designates the methods by which an artistic intention can be adequately realized. While the technical treatment of music in sound pictures was essentially determined by the industrial factor, there was a need for music from the very beginning, because of certain aesthetic requirements. Thus far no clearcut relation between the factors has been established, neither in theory nor in practice.

4 "By pseudo-individualization we mean endowing cultural mass production with the halo of free choice or open market on the basis of standardization itself" (T. W. Adorno, "On Popular Music," in *Studies in Philosophy and Social Science*, vol. IX, 1941, p. 25).

Why Music? The Sound Film and its Spectator

CLAUDIA GORBMAN

[. . .]

According to different writers, music was used to accompany films in the silent era because:

1   It had accompanied other forms of spectacle before, and was a convention that successfully persisted.
2   It covered the distracting noise of the movie projector.
3   It had important semiotic functions in the narrative: encoded according to late nineteenth-century conventions, it provided historical, geographical, and atmospheric setting, it helped depict and identify characters and qualify actions. Along with intertitles, its semiotic functions compensated for the characters' lack of speech.
4   It provided a rhythmic "beat" to complement, or impel, the rhythms of editing and movement on the screen.
5   As sound in the auditorium, its spatial dimension compensated for the flatness of the screen.
6   Like magic, it was an antidote to the technologically derived "ghostliness" of the images.
7   As music, it bonded spectators together.

In this chapter we shall consider which of these arguments help us understand the persistence of music into the narrative sound film—or whether the sound film has its own distinct reasons for using music. The nagging question remains: what might help to explain the return of background music to the soundtrack of a cinema whose diegetic codes had become strongly consolidated? Nondiegetic music simply does not logically belong in a diegetic film. Max Steiner states that sound film producers before 1932 considered background music unacceptable, fearing that spectators would demand to know where the music was coming from. French cine-semiotician Michel Marie likewise points out the "radically" nonrealistic nature of soundtrack music:

> Film music is the only sound that does not issue from the visually produced diegesis, but the film's spectator conventionally accepts it. Its arbitrary manifestation is radical. This naturalized arbitrariness is particularly revealing of the degree of convention the

spectator will accept, and it structures all the rules that determine the functioning of filmic listening.[1]

[. . .]

The multifaceted evolution of cinema during the transition to sound revealed (1) demands for both illusionism and spectacle underwent rapid changes; (2) the introduction of sound effected shifts in what was read as "realistic"; (3) background music was implicated in those shifts.

Thus, while it is necessary, it is not sufficient to recognize that the musical score persisted as a convention because it had been there before. The continuity-of-conventions thesis cannot stand alone. A specious argument in illustration: if all could be explained by continuity of conventions, we might also expect intertitles (other than dialogue titles) to persist too. After all, both titles and music have informative and expressive functions, and, historically, both titles and music did persist into the era of the part-talkies.

The continuity-of-conventions thesis may be inadequate, but even worse, Comolli's ideological model, as it stands, avoids the issue entirely. He mentions the role of music in silent films as sonic compensation for lack of actual diegetic sound; but he does not return to the problem of nondiegetic music in the sound film, whose presence can no longer be explained as a substitute for sound and speech. In fact, virtually all theorists of sound cinema—with rare exceptions such as Marie—disavow the nondiegetic music problem, limiting their concerns to diegetic sound and, occasionally, the voiceover.

Let us briefly probe [. . .] into the John Gilbert phenomenon [. . .] Articles and reviews published in 1928–1929 indicate that not only Gilbert in his first sound feature but others as well—for example, Charles Farrell, in *Sunny Side Up* (October 1929)—were being received with whistles and laughter (signs of male embarrassment?) for love scenes whose dialogue was overly "mushy." In fact, placing it in historical context, we may surmise that this "overexplicit" dialogue violated the viewing contract then in effect. Instead of heightening a spectator's involvement in the story, it only threatened to break the contractual terms that made involvement possible in the first place. It is almost as if the silence of intertitles had acted as a form of psychic censorship, and reintroducing the spoken word itself was too concrete an outlet of libidinal energy. A *Variety* review of autumn 1929 takes up the issue of some dialogue films' treatment of romantic love:

> Studios have found that the hooey going over in |inter-|titles won't go over in talkers. Someone in the audience titters and it's all off. Hereafter the love passages will be suggested with the romantic note conveyed by properly pitched music. Metro, the first to learn by experience, is heading that way: others will follow for their own protection.[2]

What precise terms of the filmic viewing contract might this anonymous reviewer be suggesting? Either he advocates a recorded music sequence (in the style of *Don Juan*) acting as a dialogue "overlay"—a part-talkie solution—or he might be proposing that the characters not directly declare their passion in their dialogue, and that simultaneously playing nondiegetic music should indicate this passion instead (a solution, we recall, that was not technically feasible until 1931 or 1932). Whatever the reviewer has in mind, his example illustrates features central to film music accompanying emotional scenes. Music removes barriers to belief; it bonds spectator to spectacle, it envelops spectator and spectacle in a harmonious space. Like hypnosis, it silences the spectator's censor. It is suggestive; if it's working right, it makes us a little less critical and a little more prone to dream.

Music has persisted as an integral part of the sound film because it accomplishes so many things at once. Its freedom from the explicitness of language or photographic images, its useful denotative and expressive values easily comprehended by listeners raised in the nineteenth-century orchestral tradition, its malleability, its spatial, rhythmic, and temporal values, give it a special and complex status in the narrative film experience. If the advent of diegetic sound narrowed the possibilities of temporality into a sort of relentless linearity, music could return as the one sound element capable of freeing up that temporal representation (thus music normally accompanies montage and slow-motion sequences, initiates flashbacks, and so on). Film music is at once a gel, a space, a language, a cradle, a beat, a signifier of internal depth and emotion as well as a provider of emphasis on visual movement and spectacle. It bonds: shot to shot, narrative event to meaning, spectator to narrative, spectator to audience. In the rest of this chapter I shall discuss these aspects of music's behavior in film. Overall, the two overarching roles of background music may be characterized as semiotic (as *ancrage*) and psychological (as suture or *bonding*).

Functional music

While film music functions differently from autonomous music, it is commonly held that well-conceived and well-written music for film will be better than "hack" scores, all other things being equal. This position, tenable as it might be, often leads scholars to dismiss serious consideration of the utilitarian functions of film music. After all, it is more acceptable to write about the work of such film composers as Sergei Prokofiev, George Antheil, Arthur Honegger, Hanns Eisler, and Bernard Herrmann than to tackle the question of the efficacy of sweet violins during a romantic scene or bass pizzicati mickey-mousing the footsteps of a thief through an abandoned warehouse.

For the moment, though, let us consider some purely functional aspects of music as it is set in the classical narrative film, by comparing film music to an extreme case, the most functional kind of music—background or "easy-listening" music. The age of mechanical/electronic reproduction, and of the commodification of music, has fundamentally changed the meaning of music, the ways in which we listen to it and hear it.[3] It is impossible to ignore that film music also participates in this transformation of listening.

Film music and easy-listening music have much in common. They are both utilitarian; both are received in a larger, nonmusical context; neither is designed to be closely attended to. (This latter feature does not obviate the possibility of their having "inherent" aesthetic worth. A Bach harpsichord sonata piped in through loudspeakers to a pastry and espresso shop is functioning as easy-listening music, as is rock or country music on the car radio as one drives along a city freeway.)

[. . .]

What does this utilitarian music do? It relieves anxiety, irritability, tension.[4] Music is good in traffic and on long drives. In the waiting room it allays fears about the imminent drilling or pulling of teeth, or the airplane's departure. It loosens shoppers' purse strings. For such reasons, music has been inserted into every public place where it is economically advantageous to alleviate consumer anxiety. It fills silences (or covers other sounds) that would allow us to dwell on such anxiety, or the "pain of existence" itself.[5]

Easy-listening music at its most standardized is barely discernible as music, and does not call attention to itself with surprising harmonies or dynamics. Extremes of volume or instrumentation, any departure from the most conventional harmony and the most regular rhythm, detract from the "ease" of listening. Such music signifies little but a general *pleasantness*. It has as its purpose to lull the individual into being an *untroublesome social subject*.

As I have suggested, the parallels to be drawn between easy-listening and film music are numerous. Music in film is electronically regulated, and generally rendered subservient to the denotatively signifying elements of narrative discourse. Its effectiveness often depends upon its not being listened to. While certainly not always signifying "pleasantness," it is nonetheless programmed to match the mood or feelings of the narrative scene of which it is a part, to bathe it in affect. Unlike the dentist's office, though, the narrative cinema (and the concert, too, for that matter)[6] is an institution that channels psychic energies in patterns of tension and relaxation; *the way* to the satisfaction of narrative closure (or musical resolution) is paved with anticipation and conflict. Thus the expressive range of functional music is broader in a film score. All the same, the overall purpose of film music is very much like easy-listening music: it functions to lull the spectator into being an *untroublesome* (less critical, less wary) *viewing subject*. Utilitarian music may be seen as an "intellectual or cerebral anesthetic." "Music will always have this influence," asserts Roger Tallon, "because it does not pass through the same control circuits, because it is almost directly plugged into the psyche."[7]

Easy-listening reduces the displeasure engendered by the economic tensions of shopping and the physical fear of dentists' drills. Film music also helps to ward off displeasure—a displeasure of two sorts connected with the film experience.

First [. . .] music serves to ward off the displeasure of uncertain signification. The particular kind of music used in dominant feature films has connotative values so strongly codified that it can bear a similar relation to the images as a caption to a news photograph. It *interprets* the image, pinpoints and channels the "correct" meaning of the narrative events depicted. It supplies information to complement the potentially ambiguous diegetic images and sounds. It cues the viewer in to narrational positions: for example, the menacing 'shark' theme, heard even before the camera in *Jaws* reveals the deadly shark closing in on the unsuspecting swimmers, gives the viewer advance knowledge of the narrative threat. It creates on one hand an ironic distance between viewer and characters, and, on the other, a complicity with the film's narrative voice.

Further, standard film music efficiently establishes historical and geographical setting, and atmosphere, through the high degree of its cultural coding. The *signification* attained through the use of this music (freshness of springtime, the seventeenth century, menacing. evil) wards off the displeasure of the image's potential ambiguity, which Barthes characterized "the terror of uncertain signs." This primarily semiotic functioning of music, then, is what Barthes called *ancrage* in connection with the photograph caption. Music, like the caption, anchors the image in meaning, throws a net around the floating visual signifier, assures the viewer of a safely channeled signified.

A second kind of displeasure that music helps to ward off is the spectator's potential recognition of the technological basis of filmic articulation.[8] Gaps, cuts, the frame itself, silences in the soundtrack—any reminders of cinema's materiality which jeopardize the formation of subjectivity—the process whereby the viewer identifies as subject of filmic discourse—are smoothed over, or "spirited away" (recall Eisler and Adorno's view of music as magical "antidote to the picture") by the carefully regulated operations of film music. (In this light, it is possible to see that both "parallel" and "counterpoint" aesthetics of film music ultimately serve the same impulse, i.e., to have the spectator identify as subject with a certain production of meaning and expression.) The loss of identification which filmic discourse constantly threatens, via the very means that carry the narrative (cutting, the frame, etc.)—this loss of pleasure is countered in part by the particular ways in which the classical film takes advantage of music.

Needless to say, background music functions according to a larger sphere of reference than musical syntax itself. Like the supermarket music whose volume drops in deference to an announcement, film music is normally subordinated to more "directly" significant sounds on the soundtrack, and to the demands of "the narrative itself." Soundtrack music will drop in volume when characters speak, because the intelligibility of dialogue is more important in the narrational hierarchy. Likewise, musical form is normally subject to the temporal and dramatic conditions of narrative segmentation. The bath or gel of affect in which music immerses film narrative is like easy-listening music in that it rounds out the sharp edges, smooths roughnesses, masks contradictions, and masks spatial or temporal discontinuity with its own sonic and harmonic continuity. Film music lessens awareness of the frame, of discontinuity; it draws the spectator further into the diegetic illusion. The playwright Elmer Rice characterized this effect of movie music quite vividly—in fact he emphasized its oneiric power to the point of caricature—in his novel Voyage to Purilia, which originally appeared in The New Yorker during 1929. Here he describes the planet Purilia, a thinly disguised conceit of movieland:

> It is difficult to convey to the terrestrial reader, to whom music is an accidental and occasional phenomenon, the effect of living and moving in a world in which melody is as much a condition of life as are light and air. But let the reader try to fancy himself lapped every moment of his existence, waking or sleeping, in liquid, swooning sound, for ever rising and falling, falling and rising, and wrapping itself about him like a caressing garment. The effect is indescribable. It is like the semi-stupor of an habitual intoxication: an inebriety without intervals of either sobriety or complete unconsciousness . . . the sensitive reader will catch echoes and overtones of that omnipresent harmony; now pathetic, now gay, now ominous, now martial, now tender, but always awakening familiar memories, always swellingly mellifluous, and always surcharged with a slight but unmistakable tremolo.[9]

Rice's satire may not be much of an exaggeration. Psychoanalytic critics, as we shall see, would agree with his view of music as a sort of sonic/psychic bridge between "sobriety" and "unconsciousness," being tied in with "familiar memories."

Music and pleasure

> Describing [film music's] functions is
> rather like describing a beautiful woman—
> there's no way of doing it adequately.[10]

Underlying the arguments I have put forth are notions, taken from aestheticians and scholars of music and film, that music enjoys a direct line to the "soul." Exactly what this soul is, and why music has privileged access to it, has long inspired debate. Clearly music consists of a discourse—an organized series of units understood (in some way or other) by human beings, and involving the transfer or circulation of energy, of tension and release. But it is a discourse without a clear referent, and certainly a nonrepresentational discourse; consequently, its affective powers and its association with pleasure have remained elusive.

Theories abound regarding why music gives pleasure and emotion. Plato, in prescribing the study of harmony to liberate the soul from the tyranny of the senses, inaugurated a major line of thought which holds that musical pleasure depends on an intellectual ability to perceive structure. Most traditional aestheticians do not venture much beyond describing the satisfaction gained from witnessing music's organic unity and form. An opposing aesthetic argument roots musical pleasure precisely in the senses, claiming that rhythm, harmony, and melodic movement stimulate sensual responses which we call aesthetic experience.

In this century, structuralism has flirted with the issue; Claude Lévi-Strauss likened the role of music to—what else?—myth:

> A myth coded in sounds instead of words, the musical work furnishes a grid of signification, a matrix of relationships which filters and organizes lived experience; it substitutes for experience and produces the pleasurable illusion that contradictions can be overcome, and difficulties resolved.[11]

For their part, some Freudians point out homologies between the structure and processes of the unconscious and those of musical discourse: both are sites where energies circulate and whose manifestations are regulated by a limited number of processes—for example, condensation and displacement characterize both—and whose overall guide is the pleasure principle (the resolution of tension). Others emphasize that music is a nonreferential language which stimulates a temporary regression; it is a "safe" language in evading verbal logic and articulation, and it short-circuits the defenses and thus gains access to deep emotions.[12] Some claim that we may speak of a sort of "music-work" analogous to the dream-work, whereby melodic, rhythmic, and harmonic structures embody the manifest content of the composer's (and the responding listener's) unconscious desires.

These theories do little to shed light on the emotive effects of music in *film*, however. The pleasure they describe is based on the notion of formal structure, of a "whole" piece of music with no reference outside itself. Narrative film music often lacks this closed and sustained formal structure, but even in its "formlessness," it obviously has emotive effects (in fact, these effects are the major part of its mission).

In nineteenth-century Germany, Helmholz and Fechner were among the first to attempt to bring physics, physiology, and aesthetics together to understand responses to the basic musical elements. Such work blossomed into a century of empirical research on the psychology of music. For many psychologists, "musical emotion" is due to physiological responses to pitch, rhythm, tempo, timbre, and so on. This approach might be seen as a scientific extension of the traditional sensualist aesthetic. Today, researchers in this area regard pleasure in terms of arousal of the autonomic nervous system, and measurable via heart rate, EEG readings of brain waves, and respiration. Others, however, prefer to view musical emotion purely as the effect of repetition and association in culture; maintaining that it consists largely of a set of learned responses, they study tonal memory and the effects of repetition.[13]

Psychoanalytic theory provides a particularly compelling framework for considering not only musical emotion and pleasure, but the oft-cited quality of "depth," "inner feeling," the "dramatic truth" which music brings to the film scene. Psychoanalysts studying music tend to agree that musical response is related to the very earliest periods of development. Some comment on the "oceanic feeling" experienced by the music listener—feeling that the sounds of music come not only from outside but from within their own emotions—and trace it to the pre-Oedipal, preverbal period when the boundary between self and other does not exist. As early as 1917, Frieda Teller wrote that for the adult listener, music "causes the censor to weaken;"[14] it breaks down normal ego defenses and makes the listener more receptive to phantasy. Other writers have elaborated on the ideas that music relaxes the censor and has a hypnotic effect, and that it causes a temporary, benign regression, transporting the subject to the pleasurable realm of early phantasies.

More recent psychoanalytic work on the auditory dimension in general which has contributed to the understanding of film sound may also shed some light on film music. Guy Rosolato and Didier Anzieu theorize the role of sound in the development of the subject.[15] Auditory space, they claim, is the first psychic space. Even before birth, sounds such as the mother's heartbeat, digestion, and voice—and why not voices outside the mother's body?—constitute the sonic environment. Anzieu speaks of a "sonorous envelope" in which the infant exists, "bathed in sounds," and as yet unaware of distinctions between self and other or inside/outside the body. The sonorous envelope consists of sounds originating both in the infant and in its environment. One may reasonably link the melodic bath of the sonorous envelope to the oft-cited oceanic feeling of adult musical listening; this pleasure of music invokes the (auditory) imaginary.

Rosolato attributes prime importance to the formulation of originary phantasies based on auditory perceptions. "Sonorous omnipotence": the infant's psychic auditory space does not know the limits to be imposed later by the realities of psychomotor development; it can project its voice into space, it can hear and be heard in the dark, through walls and around corners. Also, the voice is both emitted and heard, sent and received, by the same body. This reciprocal movement carries with it the potential for a confusion of exit and entry, of exterior and interior.

> Because one can hear sounds behind oneself as well as those with sources inside the body (sounds of digestion, circulation, respiration, etc.), two sets of terms are placed in opposition: exterior/front/sight and interior/back/hearing. And "Hallucinations are determined by an imaginary structuration of the body according to these oppositions . . ."[16]

The imaginary longing for bodily fusion with the mother is never erased; the terms of the original illusion of fusion are largely defined by the voice. Thus for Rosolato, Anzieu, and others, the voice of the mother is fundamental to the later development of the auditory unconscious; it is understood psychoanalytically as an "interface of imaginary and symbolic, pulling at once toward the signifying organization of language and its reduction of the range of vocal sounds to those it binds and codifies, and toward original and imaginary attachments."[17] In an earlier phase it is the rise and fall of her voice, its rhythm and timbre, that is a "good object" for the child as yet uninitiated into language.

> At the same time that she nurtures, the mother speaks, a speech charged with rhythm, pitch, timbre, tempo, and intensity, an imprint; word/sounds anchored to her body like the mouth to the breast . . . Thus the amazement, the incomprehension colored with anxiety, then the still doubting integration by a 15-month-old who discovers, in the morning, the word for a fly (*mouche*), and who in the evening hears mother say "Come let mommy wipe your nose (viens que maman te *mouche*)". Speech from which, if you take away the signified, you get *music*—which holds there the acoustical image, before "language restores in the universal |the child's| function of subject."[18]

The mother's voice is central in constituting the auditory imaginary, before and also after the child's entry into the symbolic. From this—and from even earlier auditory perceptions and hallucinations—musical pleasure may be explained. Of course, music is subsequently a highly coded and organized discourse; but its freedom from linguistic signification and from representation of any kind preserve it as a more desirable, or less unpleasurable discourse. It is therefore a "safe" language, it circumvents defenses and provides easier access to the unconscious. Dominique Avron reiterates this view:

> in the case of music, the organism is exposed to external excitations with whose direction and nature it is acquainted. It can let them penetrate to the deepest layers of the psychic apparatus without risk of feeling attacked . . . This opportunity to let oneself be invaded in all safety figures into our pleasure in listening to music. As in the very beginning, the good thing is to be swallowed. Introjection of the good object; "good" less in the sense of its aesthetic qualities than its nonthreatening character.[19]

Rosolato, for his part, suggests that the pleasure of musical harmony is itself a nostalgia for the original imaginary fusion with the mother's body. "It is therefore the entire dramatization of separated bodies and their reunion which harmony supports."[20]

Bonding

For Jean-Louis Baudry the classical cinema is an institution that places its spectator-subject in a state of regression. The film spectator is like the dreamer in the dark, in a submotor, hyperreceptive state. During the course of a narrative film the spectator occupies a psychic register which mimes infantile and dream states. The classical narrative film encourages the film subject's return to a primitive narcissism, in which there are no boundaries between active and passive, body and environment, self and other. This cinema simulates not reality but *a condition of the subject*. In fact, Baudry makes the crucial point that the cinematic apparatus simulates a *subject-effect* of regression and identification, not *reality*:[21]

> The impression of reality that the spectator has in the cinema, and the consequent form of identification, has less to do with a successful rendering of the real than with the reproduction and repetition of a particular condition, a "fantasmatization of the subject."[22]

Nancy Wood develops Baudry's thesis to argue that the auditory realm as well as the visual is caught up in the circle of desire, which derives from the earliest memories of auditory pleasure. Cinema brings an artificial regression to a narcissistic hallucination wherein the subject was "bathed in sounds."

From these considerations the pervasive role not only of the voice, but, even more, of music in films, becomes clear. The underlying pleasure of music can be traced to originary hallucinations of bodily fusion with the mother, of nonseparation prior to the Oedipal crisis of language and interdiction. If music plays in a film—"secondarily" to the register of language, of narrative—if it is in the background, it works on the spectator-subject most effectively, fusing subject to film body, bypassing the usual censors of the preconscious. In practical terms this means a deeper sleep, a lowered threshold of belief, a greater predisposition for the subject to accept the film's pseudo-perceptions as his/her own.

During the course of a fiction film, the belief in the fiction, or to use Baudry's term, the subject-effect, ebbs and flows. Metz notes that the degree of this diegetic effect "is inversely proportional to that of wakefulness." Music |. . .| lessens the spectator's degree of wakefulness. Were the subject to be aware (fully conscious) of its presence as part of the film's discourse, the game would be all over. Just as the subject who resists being hypnotized might find the hypnotist's soothing language silly or excessive, the detached film spectator will notice the oversweet violin music in a romantic scene. Like the good hypnotic subject, on the other hand, the cinematic subject receptive to the film's fantasy will tend not to notice the manipulations of the background score.

|. . .|

Summary

In addition to historical explanations for the presence and workings of background music in narrative films, this chapter has offered some arguments that take into account psycho-analytically and ideologically oriented theories of the film spectator-subject's positioning.

In the process of questioning why one does not normally notice background music in films, we ought to bear in mind that the work of cinematic discourse *in general* is to efface itself, in the service of "the narrative," as Christian Metz stated in *The Imaginary Signifier*:

The fiction film is the film in which the cinematic signifier does not work on its own account but is employed entirely to remove the traces of its own steps, to open imme-diately on to the transparency of a signified, of a story, which is in reality manufactured by it but which it pretends merely to "illustrate," to transmit to us after the event, as if it had existed previously (= referential illusion): another example of a product which is its own production in reverse . . . |T|he fiction film represents both the negation of the signifier (an attempt to have it forgotten) and a certain working regime of that signifier, a very precise one, just the one that is required to get it forgotten (more or less forgotten, according to whether the film is more or less submerged in its script). Hence what distinguishes fiction films is not the "absence" of any specific work of the signifier; but its *presence in the mode of denegation*, and it is well known that this type of presence is one of the strongest there are.[23]

Background music *should* be less invisible than other registers of the cinematic signifier, since it is not as directly a part of the fictional world. The returns on the investment of a musical score are enormous, considering that the film normally "gets it forgotten." Music greases the wheels of the cinematic pleasure machine by easing the spectator's passage into subjectivity.

Narrative cinema's "dispositions of representation" fluctuate constantly; the contractual terms setting the ratio between identification and spectacle change according to genre, directional style, and a host of historical conditions. But globally speaking, music remains in the dramatic film as the hypnotic voice bidding the spectator to believe, focus, behold, identify, consume. One could imagine a narrative cinema that did not deploy music, but would it be as successful on all fronts?

Notes

1 Michel Marie, "Comment parler la bouche pleine?" (How can you talk with your mouth full?) *Communications* 38 (1983), 56.

2 *Variety*, October 31, 1929. Quoted in Alexander Walker, *The Shattered Silents: How the Talkies Came to Stay* (New York: William Morrow, 1979), 171.

3 See, for example, the argument of T. W. Adorno's 1938 essay, "On the Fetish Character in Music and the Regression of Listening," in Andrew Arato and Elke Cebbart, eds, *The Essential Frankfurt School Reader* (New York: Urizen, 1978), 270–299.

4 Richmond Cardinell comments on music's effect of relieving nervous tension: "This has been noted in several plants by a reduction of strife between employees. A Red Cross Blood Doning Center installed a musical program and stopped all post-transfusion fainting." Cardinell, *Music in Industry: Principles of Programming* (New York: American Society of Composers, Authors and Publishers, 1944).

5 "Played in public places or supermarkets, its purpose is to put to sleep [.] put what to sleep? *Painfulness*: it's a response to pain. When peasants sing while planting rice, they're counteracting pain." Roger C. Tallon, interviewed, "La Musique utilitaire," *Musique en jeu* 24 (September 1976), 72.

6 See Dominique Avron, "Notes pour introduire one métapsychologie de la musique," *Musique en jeu* 9 (November 1972), 102–110.

7 Tallon, see n. 5. His formulation comes dangerously close, of course, to suggesting that musical listening is somehow a wholly unmediated phenomenon, as if music is more natural than other discursive registers.

8 This helps explain why the noise of the projector needed to be drowned out by live music in the days of the silent film.

9 Elmer Rice, *A Voyage to Purilia* (New York: Cosmopolitan Book Corp., 1930), 32.

10 Tony Thomas, *Music for the Movies* (S. Brunswick and New York: A. S. Barnes, 1973), 17.

11 Claude Lévi-Strauss, "Boléro de Maurice Ravel," *L'Homme* 11, 2 (April–June 1971), 5–14. (p.5.) Leonard B. Meyer also invokes myth, in specifying the difficulty of pinning down any particular connotations of a piece of music: "the flexibility of connotation is a virtue. For it enables music to express what might be called the disembodied essence of myth, the essence of experiences which are central to and vital in human experience." Meyer, *Emotion and Meaning in Music* (Chicago: University of Chicago Press, 1956), 265.

12 See I. H. Coriat, "Some Aspects of a Psychoanalytic Interpretation of Music," *Psychoanalytic Review* 32 (1945), 408–418. For an excellent digest of the psychoanalytic literature on music to 1965, see Pinchas Noy, "The Psychodynamic Meaning of Music," in five parts in the *Journal of Music Therapy* 3, 4 (Dec. 1966), 126–134; 4, 1 (March 1967), 7–23; 4, 2 (June 1967), 45–51; 4, 3 (September 1967), 81–94; 4, 4 (December 1967), 117ff.

13 See, for example, John Booth Davies, *The Psychology of Music* (London: Hutchinson, 1978).

14 F. Teller, 'Musikgenuss und Phantasie" *Imago* 5 (1917), 8–15.

15 Guy Rosolato, "La Voix: Entre corps et langage," *Revue française de psychanalyse* 38, 1 (Jan. 1974), 75–94; Didier Anzieu, "L'enveloppe sonore do soi," *Nouvelle revue de psychanalyse* 13, (Spring 1976), 161–179.

16 Mary Ann Doane, "The Voice in the Cinema: The Articulation of Body and Space," *Yale French Studies* 60 (1980), 44.

17 Doane, 45.

18 Francis Hofstein, "Drogue et musique," *Musique en jeu* 9 (November 1972), 111–115.

19 Avron, "Notes pour one métapsychologie," 104. See also H. Racker, "Contribution to Psychoanalysis of Music," *Am. imago* 8 (1951), 129–163, linking music with the primary infant–mother relationship.

20 André Michel, echoing ego psychologists such as Heinz Kohut, suggested in a 1951 study that music's primary appeal is that of "whistling in the dark" for fear of silence. It provides a reassuring language of rhythm and sound. Or perhaps the child fears "being abandoned by his auditory world, at first indistinguishable from the mother." *Psychanalyse de to musique* (Paris: Presses Universitaires de France, 1951), p. 30.

21 See Jean-Louis Baudry, "The Apparatus," *Camera Obscura* 1 (December 1976), 104–126; and Constance Penley, "The Avant-Garde and Its Imaginary," *Camera Obscura* 2 (Fall 1977), 3–33.

22 Penley, 15.

23 Christian Metz, *The Imaginary Signifier* (Bloomington: Indiana University Press, 1982), 40.

Reforming "Jackass Music"

The problematic aesthetics of early American film music accompaniment

TIM ANDERSON

[...]

The relationship between the performance of live music and film has appeared in a variety of forms, including a contemporary interest in the production of atypical forms of film music. For example, within the Chicago area improvisational musicians such as Ken Vandermark and Jim O'Rourke have begun to rethink the practice of accompanying film with music by establishing a series of group improvisations during the screening of narrative and experimental films. Vandermark is not interested in accompanying the film with a different narrative music per se. Instead, he says, "I [am] more interested in creating that weird parallel—like when you watch TV with the sound off and other music playing—where the visuals and sound connect, even though they aren't really intended to. I [don't] really care about plinking and plonking along to the action of the films."[1]

Despite the fact that the above scenario may appear as a seemingly novel practice within an avant-garde context, this form of film music accompaniment is not without a popular precedent, let alone a significant place within American film history. I hope to help recover a portion of this history by examining the issues involved in early film music accompaniment in the United States to embellish our understanding of some of the general issues involved in silent film music. In this sense, the essay is a historico-theoretical piece wherein I hope to illustrate a few of the practices and issues involved in the sound and musical accompaniment of early American film by highlighting some of the complaints and advice given in the periodical *Moving Picture World* (MPW) between 1907 and 1915. It is through recognizing this long-running debate that I wish to amplify how some of these practices were positioned as nuisances that needed to be eradicated for the formation of both a "proper" narrative cinema and site of exhibition. By concentrating on the suggested aesthetic functions, and performative parameters of film music and sound accompaniment within nickelodeon spaces, I will discuss some of the theoretical underpinnings driving the desire to reform both the sound and musical accompaniment of film from a potentially excessive, "music hall" aesthetic of collective performance into a more formalized, theatrical regime of film exhibition whose elements are dedicated to the needs of the master narrative. Thus, I hope to make clear that nickelodeons existed as potentially disruptive and heterogeneous spaces of spectacle and distraction not only at the level of the filmic image but also in the possible musical aspects involving audiences and employees. And as exhibitors moved further away from nickelodeon spaces toward a new set of standards and practices throughout the 1910s to establish the successful presentation of a developing narrative cinema, these aesthetic disruptions became formulated as "problems" that needed to be solved. Specifically, audiences and musicians needed to be educated and reformed to respect a less spectacular, more narrative-oriented cinema. As film style began to develop its own formal narrative system to gain both an economic and cultural means of legitimacy, these spaces and practices of exhibition needed to follow accordingly to satisfy the desires of film's new exhibitors, producers, critics, and, most importantly, audiences.[2]

Although recent scholarship has utilized numerous approaches and disciplines to understand the various issues involved in film exhibition, the need to understand the perfomative aspects of exhibition has been sorely underestimated. Most film criticism and scholarship continue to focus narrowly on the benefits of textual analysis, thus forgetting (and sometimes seemingly dismissing) the particular circumstances and forces exerted at the site of reception in the production of both meanings and pleasures.

[. . .]

Though the exhibition of early American film took place in sites as diverse as Chautauquas, vaudeville stages, and local fairs, the emerging art discovered its initial mainstream success in the development of the nickelodeon. The swift increase in nickelodeons between 1905 and 1910 not only provided the United States with its first spaces specifically devoted to film exhibition, but it also provided an opportunity for the reformation and relative formalization of exhibition practices.[3] To be sure, these spaces were able to succeed partially due to their architectural flexibility: a nickelodeon could exist just about anywhere. With the exception of strict fire safety codes, governmental requirements such as zoning laws and taxes were, for the most part, not applied to the earliest nickelodeons.[4] As a result, nickelodeon owners and management took advantage of this scenario by creating makeshift exhibition spaces from converted storefronts and restaurants.[5] The informal status of the nickelodeon makes it difficult to know where these spaces were or even how many existed on a nationwide basis. Nevertheless, there were numerous estimates. In 1907 Variety offered a "conservative estimate" of 2,500 nickelodeons in the nation, while Moving Picture World stated that the number was between 2,500 and 3,000 during the same year. One year later an Oakland newspaper estimated that the country had close to 8,000 nickelodeons.[6] The nickelodeon boom peaked by 1910, and by 1911 it was evident that theatrical spaces, specifically picture palaces, would become the desired spheres for film exhibition through the remainder of the teens and into the twenties.[7]

While the informality of these spaces meant that numerous sites could be considered to be nickelodeons, this lack of uniformity allowed for an abundance of aesthetic and exhibitionary practices. As Tom Gunning has argued, cinema before 1908 presented diverse terrain where style and aesthetics were employed not only to deliver stories but also to *display* attractions that escaped the demands of formal narrative structures.[8] But 1908, the development of the Motion Picture Patents Company (MPPC) and other elements of film production were stitched together in such a manner to have significant effects on film style. Gunning's thesis is primarily concerned with early film style and how it operated as a "nonunified" system of narrative presentation. Yet, modes of narrative presentation can never be completely extricated from the terms of exhibition. Not only were systems of cinema in early film assorted, but methods of exhibition and reception were just as eclectic, as a brief overview of the questions and testimonials which comprise MPW illustrate. The most widely read, nationally distributed periodical devoted solely to the needs of exhibitors, the MPW also attempted to maintain a modicum of objectivity by taking no position in the struggle between the MPPC trust and the nickelodeon exhibitors. Most importantly, the MPW advanced a definite belief in the importance of "uplifting" aesthetic norms of film style and exhibition and in how the terms of "uplift" would eventually attract the middle class as a new mass audience for film. As perceived by many, the lack of aesthetic standards posed problems in placing many aspects of the exhibition process into a more theatrical, less spectacular model of presentation.[9] Although these problems ranged from issues involving projectionists to exhibition staff and film programmers, the journal produced a considerable amount of copy addressing what it felt was one of the more deplorable elements involved in the exhibition of film: inadequate musical accompaniment.

"Better music means better patronage and more of It"

[. . .]

What we know about the function of narrative film music is significant, to say the least. But when it comes to early film music scholars are typically reduced to, at best, educated guesses. Perhaps the best, most concise description of both the possible functions and reasons for music in silent cinema is offered by Claudia Gorbman. According to Gorbman, music in silent cinema had accompanied other forms of spectacle before and was a convention that successfully persisted; it covered the distracting noise of the movie projector; it had semiotic functions in the narrative; and it provided a rhythmic "beat" to complement, or impel, the rhythms of editing and movement on the screen. As sound in the auditorium, its spatial dimension compensated for the flatness of the screen, and, like magic, it was an antidote for the technologically derived "ghostliness" of the images. Finally, it bonded spectators together.[10]

With the exception of the final hypothesis, music is described within a particular set of aesthetic relationships with the on-screen image. To be sure, Gorbman's final hypothesis—that music could "bind" an audience—is intriguing. The thesis posits a focused analysis of the performance of a film music that embraces a dialogical relationship between the desires of the "film" and the moment-to-moment pleasures of the audience. As a result, this thesis questions the almost-always assumed dominance of the visible text as the primary determinant in the reception and interpretation of narrative film. Through this mode of exhibition both audiences and musicians actively create and listen to a film music (or "noise") that is contingent on the relationship that each performer assumes vis-à-vis the master narrative and the manner in which it is presented. The possibilities of the triangulated relationship between the space of exhibition, the audience, and the performer are by no means "naturally" deducible. To be sure, among the many factors forging these possibilities is vocal criticism, of which there was no lack where discussions of nickelodeon spaces and the performance of music were concerned. In at least one 1907 case it was claimed that the constant clamor of music from a nickelodeon caused significant physical damage to a patron. The MPW reported that the steady repetition of a theme to The Holy City had been named in a lawsuit as the prime cause behind one woman's case of "nerves."[11] Less hyperbolic in tone, a 1908 MPW column titled "Hints to Exhibitors" claimed that the sound and music in nickelodeons could have specific effects, some desirable, others not. "No picture could not be improved by music and effects," the author proclaimed, and, in fact, a good piano player was seen as "essential to the success of the progressive and successful electric theater." Unfortunately, not every musical portion of the nickelodeon was viewed as holding such reformatory promise. For example, the popular nickelodeon practice of the illustrated song slide, an opportunity for combining the musical performances of both musicians and audience, was continually regarded by some critics as a potential problem. According to these reports, sing-alongs were all too often led by a "breed of 'singers' in the cheaper theaters that in many cases |called| for suppression by either the police or the board of health, or both." To paraphrase the same critic, so uncivilized were these singers that the performance of just one verse from any song would promise to scare the proverbial wolf back into the forest.[12] In other cases, complaints about the music/noise that these spaces yielded were not limited to those sounds within the walls of the nickelodeon. Phonographs and small bands providing "outside music" to attract crowds in front and, eventually, into the nickelodeons themselves sometimes created "a horrid din" if too many five-cent theaters were located on the same thoroughfare, a 1907 MPW article reported. The sound of the bands and phonographs that had been placed in these streets to attract crowds was not only a nuisance but reminded "the average man of the midways and pikes or trails of the world's fairs,"[13] another site designed to blur the borders between public and exhibition space.

Nickelodeon musicians and their accompaniment of films were not exempt from criticism, as countless complaints were voiced over inappropriate performers and performances. In 1909 an MPW editorial noted that, while there were plenty of nickelodeon musicians who could "strike the keys |of the piano| with something like accuracy and precision, if not violence, |they| cannot play music, or, if |they| can, |they do| not," and, in general, the article found the musical end of the motion picture house programs unsatisfactory.[14] This type of complaint was best expressed in 1911 with Louis Reeves Harrison's MPW article titled "Jackass Music." Aggressively asserting the need for the expanding industry to reconcile musical accompaniment within the needs of a "proper" filmic narrative, Harrison argued that a new, moneyed clientele could be cultivated with a developed attention to the musical aesthetics of exhibition:

> Ten thousand dollars a day is spent to *produce* the moving pictures and it would be impossible to say how much more to keep going the ten thousand motion-picture theatres throughout the country. These pictures are not all masterpieces, many of them are very crude, but the whole art is in a primitive state, is constantly improving, and the exhibitions are kept alive by their production. People go every day to see the pictures, once in a while for the variety entertainment, and it is not only asinine but unbusinesslike to lower the grade of musical accompaniment when the lights are turned down. Inappropriate music may "do" for the unintelligent part of the audience, but what is the use of driving away the intelligent portion? Better music means better patronage and more of it, and superior patronage means a demand for superior photoplays. Suitable music is an essential.[15]

With several illustrations depicting the typical "jackass music" maneuvers (i.e., playing to members of the audience, instead of playing to the film, musicians leaving their post during the most dramatic portion of the film, etc.), the article made a case that these actions stemmed from no specific source per se but were common indiscretions made by players who were irresponsible, inadequate, or both.

By naming no specific culprits, Harrison's article addresses the entire industry through generalizations made from years of nickelodeon attendance and, as a statement, firmly fits within a dominant rhetoric of reformation, uplift, and aesthetic betterment. This rhetoric was not unfamiliar to discussions regarding music in early-twentieth-century America. As Lawrence Levine points out, during the nineteenth century the United States witnessed great cultural reformation when the aesthetic divisions between "high" and "low" were established, as were standards of professional behavior, presentation, and repertoire. This reformation affected not only how Americans viewed theater and literature but music in particular. This is especially true in the case of opera. Though throughout the nineteenth century opera held popular/low connotations, during the same century the musical form became culturally refined into a classical category.[16] Many of the critics concerned with film exhibition held similar viewpoints regarding the "uplift" of film music. In many cases these critics perceived musical betterment as an unmistakable "herald of progress."[17] Yet this "progress" was not solely cultural. As Harrison's article notes, the desire to develop music in the same manner that film style was being transformed was part of a larger industrial movement that anticipated sizable profits. Indeed, Gunning has illustrated how film style was fostered to "articulate the narrative elements and involve the audience in their unfolding," with middle-class audiences kept directly in mind.[18] To accomplish this improvement readers and critics publishing throughout the music columns of MPW identified four areas of film music accompaniment as problematic and in need of betterment: (1) the aesthetic reformation of music vis-à-vis film narrative; (2) the propriety and limits of musical performance; (3) the professionalization of the musician; and (4) the undefined site of exhibition/participation.

[. . .]

A few "refinements" for a "polite theater"

[. . .]

Maintaining this rationale, MPW advised that dramatic film genres should be accorded both specific music and tones that would remain subordinate and underline the needs of the master narrative. Tragedy, farce, melodrama, drama, light comedy, burlesque, fairy tales, and mythological, biblical, and historical films were categorized as dramatic subdivisions that could and should be made easily recognizable through complementary and sympathetic musical selections and/or improvisations. Although there was a need to contain improvisational possibilities, bad, repetitive, or limited improvisation could act as a threat to deaden the picture through too much boredom and predictability. This was especially true if the accompanying musician was not the most adept improvisor. His reliance on "impromptu stuff" for his accompaniment could make him "apt to fall into a rut, and that spells 'monotony,'" the MPW warned.[19] As a general rule, the player had to be aware of the on-screen situation and understand all the possible combinations between the music and picture that could be made to make the picture as lively as possible.

[. . .]

For most nickelodeon exhibitions these pointers were more concerned with the mood of specific segments of the film and less so with which compositions to play. A convenient illustration of this is a program suggestion of cues that appeared in a 1912 edition of MPW for the accompaniment of Pathé's film *For the Papoose.*

(1)   Indian music ("Os-ka-loo-sa-loo") till man seizes girl, then:
(2)   Short agitato till "That Same Night."
(3)   Mysterious till Indian kills sleeping man.
(4)   Hurry till "Next Morning."
(5)   Indian sentimental till man throws cloth over Indian girl's head.
(6)   Agitato till "Be Not Afraid, My Sister."
(7)   Mysterious agitato till struggle.
(8)   Hurry till man is seen dead.
(9)   Indian pathetic till end of picture.[20]

These cue sheets may appear to be something of mystery, and to be sure not much is known about the nature and practice of improvising to cue sheets in early cinema. Yet the practice has a popular theatrical precedence, as highly skilled, professional vaudeville performers had already made playing to cue sheets something of a science.

[. . .]

A "polite vaudeville" was one that included a variety of restraints, one of which was an understandable system of performative parameters placed on professional musicians. Although it is not clear if urban nickelodeon spaces, many of which lacked professional musicians, could have simply adopted *any* system of cue sheets, the proposal that musicians should use cue sheets signaled an escalating interest in altering the methods of performance and the performers themselves.

The admission of "professional standards" for musical performance and aesthetics negotiates a number of relationships between sound and image, the first of which concentrates on matching the ambiguities of sound and music with the specific needs of the on-screen narrative.

[. . .]

Critics interested in uplifting early cinema not only decided that [the earlier forms] of musical accompaniment were too great a distraction from the primary text, but that this practice had to be eliminated in order to shelter the master narrative from the flood of semiotic deviations it could release.

Yet no matter how important the need to uplift film music was perceived to be, critics continually argued that this transformation had to ensure that the pleasures of the audience were retained in any reorganization and containment of the semiotic possibilities involved in musical accompaniment. Indeed, many reformers continually affirmed the necessity of diverse and heterogeneous material in playing for the pictures. Nowhere is this desire for diversity better exhibited than in the call for a balance between classical and popular musics. For example, in his "Suggestions for Pianists" column, C. K. Aiken noted that Pathé's weekly newsreel offered an interesting musical challenge for both musicians and audiences alike. Since Pathé's newsreel would likely include a number of assorted images and topics, ranging from the most bizarre and fantastic elements of society to the most mundane, Aiken claimed that "every class of music is needed from the popular to the severely classical." As the column noted, after the accompanying musician started off with "a little something brilliant to arouse the attention of the audience," each of the subsequent narrative events should be accompanied appropriately. The suggestions included many examples and stylistic variations, ranging from Beethoven and Mendelssohn to national sentiments and "music which makes your audience hum" so that the spectators would have an opportunity to take part in finding a pleasing note before they left the pictures.[21]

The desire to please the entire audience was sincere, if for no other reason than to secure the return and inclusion of working-class audiences in these spaces of exhibition. Certainly, the search for middle-class legitimacy involved raising the price of admission, but it also involved distinguishing these new spaces as primarily theaters for the exhibition of narrative film. Throughout these processes new standards for attentiveness and overall decorum were continually emphasized, yet there still was no wish to lose cinema's initial audiences and their consistent profits in the reformatory process.

[. . .]

Certainly, a booming and quickly changing American film industry needed to recognize the diversity of the audience's tastes as it expanded into new venues and acquired new spectators. Though narrative demands were to be the primary consideration, the industry was compelled to continue serving the needs of the audience, no matter if the musical selections were popular, provincial, or contradictory. But the musical program could not be *too* contradictory.

[. . .]

On the other hand, musicians who went after the laughs by playing to the audience were continually acknowledged and appreciated. These musicians were "the only fellows who seem to receive any audible praise . . . They play comic songs in classical pictures (the spectators often join in singing these), the drummer injects some fool noise in a serious scene and your 'jackass audience' is delighted." The author continues to note that this kind of behavior was commonplace, as he had not only seen it in Chicago and other neighboring towns but had heard that New York had similar problems.[22]

The noisy conduct of these urban audiences and their effect on the nature of musical performances within these spaces reveal quite a bit about the potential power of the audience in early cinema. Not only could these audiences influence what selections the musician made, but they could alter the meanings found in the dominant narrative of the film.

[. . .]

Indeed, the performative nature of live film music may have been a means by which a variety of marginalized audiences were able to gain pleasure in the exhibition of both narrative and early film styles. Given this as a legitimate, perhaps even encouraged, possibility of exhibition in some communities, we can see how earlier forms of cinema may have operated as an alternative public sphere. According to Miriam Hansen, the exhibition of early cinema offered a particular "public sphere for particular social groups, like immigrants and women, by providing an inter-subjective horizon through—and against—which they could negotiate the specific displacements and discrepancies of their experience."[23] The use of improvised music and sound effects assisted in the mediation of the on-screen imagery by offering, at minimum, "a sense of collective presence" and, at its most radical, acted as a force that "allowed for locally and culturally specific acts of reception, opening up a margin of participation and unpredictability."[24]

In these cases early cinema may have employed one of the basic tropes involved in nineteenth-century music hall performances. Invoking Peter Bailey's work on the music hall, Simon Firth notes that these spaces involved "a kind of *knowingness*, a *collusion* between performer and (implied) audience, between audience and (implied) performer, which was both inclusive and exclusive, worrying and reassuring." Through "a mode of address which both flattered the audience's social competence and acknowledged its social wariness, its feeling that it might *get things wrong*," the best music hall performers "constructed their own audiences, their own colluders.[25]

[. . .]

Certainly, the unruly and unpredictable potential of musical performance is due to the excessive semiotic possibilities which can be employed by the skillful orchestration of musical systems. Though they operate within definite historical contexts, the disruptive possibilities of music are not necessarily historical but systemic. Music operates as a closed system of referentiality, whereby these systems, as Umberto Eco has pointed out, have, unlike systems of language, no clear semantic values to reference.[26] As John Corbett has argued, music's ability to call forth meaning is one with a complex history of metalinguistically affixing meaning to musical tropes and codes, best illustrated in the discipline of musicology.[27] But, for Corbett, the arbitrary nature of musical meanings does not eradicate semantic possibilities in music. Rather, "music is not anti-semantic or non-semantic. It has polyvalent semantics."[28]

This polyvalency carries with it the potential to create numerous meanings that are neither firm nor arbitrary but rather contingent on multiple performative contextualities. In classical rhetoric these specific performative contextualities are typically understood as *elocutio* (style) and *actio* (body language). But if *actio* can be understood as the effects of the performer's gestures on the inflection and configuration of meaning, then *elocutio*, as Allen Weiss has argued, can be seen as *musication*, "the purest figure of elocution, which underlies all rhetorical figuration." By understanding that "speech is 'worked' by metaphysics, and 'played' at the other hand by music, "Weiss argues that the separation between logocentrism and melo-centrism can be best comprehended. The discipline of musicology adheres to a logocentric purpose, whereby its systems of meaning attempt to fasten meaning firmly to a number of operational tropes (i.e., musical keys, leitmotifs, effects, etc.). Improvisational performers, on the other hand, propose a melocentric goal of executing new and differing meanings and pleasures that are produced and offered through multiple methods of "meaning fastening." Indeed, the excessive possibilities in performance for "meaning making" exists as a continual threat to all systems of meaning. This being the case, one can recognize that all systems of meaning, whether they be on- or off-screen narrative elements, are a fortiori musical and can be played.[29] This is, of course, where the essential semantic threat and power of music exist. Not only does music have the ability to reinforce meaning(s) through the containment of semantic possibilities, but through numerous musical tropes, techniques, and figurations music and musicians can also offer narrative interruptions, disorder, and sidetracks that exhaustively investigate, discover, and create new meanings and spectacles. In short, the hazard and the pleasure of improvisation lies in how the practice is precisely *not* invested in preserving a standard set of meanings or pleasures. As a result of this potential semiotic anarchy, those persons invested in creating film music that held a specific allegiance to the master narrative were forced to contain signifying possibilities. One method of containment was to restrain those improvisational opportunities by criticizing "inappropriate" improvisations and musical selections while suggesting "appropriate" or "proper" codes and significant performative parameters.[30]

According to those involved in reforming film music accompaniment, improvisation needed to be limited or at least tamed and identified as a possible obstacle that could hinder the development of a narrative cinema.

[. . .]

This problem continued to plague theatrical orchestras that provided insensitive accompaniment, instead of recognizing the "dramatic possibilities of the picture." These orchestras would "fill up the time with waltzes, rags, medleys and popular stuff generally selected at random and totally without regard to the fitting of the play.[31] MPW critics continued to recommend that orchestras begin to recognize when they were "spoiling a tender scene with boisterous music or vice versa" and respect the film as an orchestra would a play with "real" actors.[32]

The betterment of these nickelodeons, however, required much more than the simple application of these suggestions to the practice of exhibition. For many exhibitors, the problem was not unruly musicians but rather a lack of professional musicians. The demands made by critics for flexible, highly skilled players who could call on a large repertoire of appropriate musical pieces were consistently voiced throughout this period of industrial and aesthetic transformation. Yet it is uncertain how quickly exhibitors and professional musicians became attuned to this process of exhibition. Indeed, a large portion of resistance to hiring professional players arose from many nickelodeon managers. The first line of resistance arrived out of a specific perception of nickelodeon audiences as "uncivilized" and uninterested in narrative film music. Typically these claims were made regarding urban nickelodeons such as those operating in Chicago. But a second logic also helped keep professional musicians outside nickelodeons. While many theaters may have wanted to uplift their film music accompaniment, the contesting desire to maximize profits may have acted as a deterrent significant enough to keep most professional elements of labor away from exhibition sites, particularly the guilded and unionized professional musician.

Even from its earliest inception, the MPW kept a close eye on urban centers, with a special focus on the development of Chicago nickelodeons, and offered numerous criticisms concerning the manner in which these nickelodeons and theaters exhibited their films. Alternately, the MPW was always quick to praise those theaters that took seriously the task of offering quality musical accompaniment. Mentioned most often by MPW critics was

Chicago's Orpheum, whose celebrity must have been enhanced by the fact that the MPW's most prominent music critic, Clarence Sinn, was also a former music director at this theater. Overall, however, the city's nickelodeons were roundly denounced as one bad example after another. After reading a few of these complaints, one self-identified Chicago nickelodeon patron stated that he thought the critics were correct: the music was, for the most part, carelessly managed and inappropriate.

> I believe that if the managers of the downtown picture houses of Chicago were thoroughly impressed with the importance of proper musical accompaniment for the films, they would insist upon more careful work upon the part of the pianists along this line. I am interested in moving pictures and have visited nearly all of the larger picture houses throughout the city of Chicago and, I am sorry to say, have found general disregard for proper accompaniment for the films.[33]

These larger theaters also had the distinction of receiving the negative connotations of being known as "quantity houses" among patrons and critics. One such Chicago theater, the Superba, was known not only for its speedy efficiency in providing an extraordinary number of reels (five) for a dime but also for the overall poor quality of these exhibitions, particularly the projections. Not surprisingly, the emphasis on quantity was reflected in the "low" quality of musical accompaniment, with the Superba often providing "awful parodies" masquerading under the name of music, as at least one reviewer noted.[34] In most cases, the locus of responsibility was clearly identified as poor management, which was to blame for providing musical accompaniment that was not only negligent but ignorant. As another MPW article noted, the nickelodeon managers' so-called lack of pride placed Chicago alongside New York as one of the worst places in the nation to see motion pictures.[35]

Of course this type of judgment could only have been made by audiences once they began to recognize the performative limitations that distinguished "proper" musicians from "jackass" musicians, the roles defining audiences from musicians, and the sonic boundaries between acceptable music and distracting noise. It is unclear exactly when these distinctions were beginning to be made by a majority of film spectators, but we can at least begin to recognize that film music underwent such an aesthetic transformation. This transformation not only affected music, but it also helped define the relationships that audiences would have with the on-screen image. These relationships are continually cultivated and reinforced not only when an usher chides an unruly spectator, but when other stylistic devices such as a soundtrack are designed to amplify specific portions of the narrative. In this sense, this particular aesthetic transformation, although hardly sufficient, was necessary to fulfill the needs of the classical narrative film. This process occurred within a larger context involving the development of other narrative film style techniques during the teens. It is a technique with a history, as well as a historical process. But no matter how normative these processes have become, their conventional status can always be renegotiated, if only for an instant. It is precisely this threat that the "betterment" of musical accompaniment wished to check. Of course, this aim became only as meaningful as the contradictory threat involved, the "nonsense" that arose from those particular restrictions and the limits defining the site of exhibition that these stylistic elements desired to erect. In a way, the system of meaning that developed "proper" musical accompaniment gave birth to the "noise" that can always be articulated and rearticulated to criticize and reveal the arbitrary nature of these designs. If establishing the theatrical exhibition of film necessitated the reformation of "jackass music" as well as "jackass audiences" in order to prosper, then these same alterations also conceded that the above social compositions were exceptionally dynamic methods of mobilizing popular critical pleasures.

Notes

This chapter owes much to the incisive and probing remarks and conversations that Larra Clark, Derek Kompare, Marc Giordano, Priya Jaikumar-Mahey, Nina Martin, Jim Lastra, J. A. Lindstrom, Richard Maxwell, Jim Schwoch, and Barbara Willinsky were willing to share with me concerning both the exhibition of cinema and popular music. Focus was provided by the editors of *Cinema Journal* and the 1995–96 Student Writing Award committee, who demanded that obscured thoughts became defined. Essential to this research is Tom Gunning, who sat through numerous classes and one-on-one conversations where these ideas were less than developed. His patience, intellect, and good humour were essential in shaping this essay.

Lastly, this chapter is dedicated to the loving memory of Margaret Arlene Anderson. She, more than anyone else in my family, always made a point to teach her grandchildren that the power of a good laugh (preferably made in public) could carry one through the toughest times and ease the most difficult tasks. To my grandmother, here's a funny face.

1 Ben Kim, "Raw Material: Loose Sprockets, Vandermark's Post-Original Soundtracks," *New City*, September 21, 1995, 21.

2 Tom Gunning, "Weaving a Narrative: Style and Economic Background in Griffith's Biograph Films," in Thomas Elsaesser, ed., *Early Cinema: Space, Frame, Narrative* (London: British Film Institute Publishing, 1992), 338.

3 It would be a mistake to believe that exhibition practices have been at any time strictly formalized at a national level. Nevertheless, part of what this paper argues is that some of the "problems" of exhibition do become national and, in some fashion, standard in the terms of their discussion throughout the emergent film industry between 1910 and 1915.

4 Douglas Gomery, *Shared Pleasures: A History of Movie Presentation in the United States* (Madison: University of Wisconsin Press, 1992), 21.

5 Ibid., 18.

6 Eileen Bowser, *The Transformation of Cinema 1907–1911: History of the American Cinema*, Vol. 2 (Berkeley: University of California Press, 1990), 4.

7 Ibid., 121.

8 Tom Gunning, "'Now You See It, Now You Don't': The Temporality of the Cinema of Attractions," *Velvet Light Trap* 32 (fall 1993): 4.

9 I do not want to enter into a discussion about the all-too-typical claim that forms of classical film narrative are "less theatrical" and more "real" or "spatial" than primitive film, because this would be wholly unproductive for this essay. For an elaborate discussion of this debate, see Tom Gunning, *D. W. Griffith and the Origins of American Narrative Film: The Early Years at Biograph* (Urbana: University of Illinois Press, 1991), 34–39.

10 Claudia Gorbman, *Unheard Melodies: Narrative Film Music* (Bloomington: Indiana University Press, 1987), 53.

11 "'Holy City' Got on Her Nerves," MPW, November 9, 1907, 578.

12 Stephen W. Bush, "Hints to Exhibitors," MPW, October 24, 1908, 317.

13 "When 'Music' Is a Nuisance," MPW, December 28, 1907, 702.

14 "The Musical End," MPW, July 3, 1909, 7.

15 Louis Reeves Harrison, "Jackass Music," MPW, January 21, 1911, 125.

16 Lawrence W. Levine, *Highbrow/Lowbrow: The Emergence of Cultural Hierarchy in America* (Cambridge, Mass.: Harvard University Press, 1988), 83–168.

17 Emmah Williams, "Music for the Picture: Playing for Pictures," MPW, April 6, 1912, 33.

18 Gunning, "Weaving a Narrative," 340.

19 Clarence E. Sinn, "Music for the Picture," MPW, December 3, 1910, 1285.

20 Clarence E. Sinn, "Music for the Picture," MPW, June 8, 1912, 922.

21 C. E. Aiken, "Suggestions for Pianists," MPW, June 8, 1912, 922.

22 Clarence E. Sinn, "Music for the Picture," MPW, July 1, 1911, 1509.

23 Miriam Hansen, *Babel & Babylon: Spectatorship in American Silent Film* (Cambridge, Mass.: Harvard University Press, 1991), 43–44.

24 Ibid., 43.

25 Simon Frith, *Performing Rites: On the Value of Popular Music* (Cambridge, Mass.: Harvard University Press, 1996), 209.

26 Umberto Eco, in John Corbett, "On the Musical Subject: Sound Politics and the Body of the Performer in the Era of Recorded Music," Ph.D. diss., Northwestern University, 1994, 143.

27 Ibid., 144.

28 Ibid., 151.

29 Allen Weiss, *The Aesthetics of Excess* (Albany: State University of New York Press, 1989), xi–xii.

30 I am using the notion of "performative parameters" as a direct invocation of Stuart Hall's essay, "Encoding, Decoding." According to Hall, "dominant" or "preferred" readings of text are mapped and ordered, "*through* the codes, the orders of social life, of economic and political power and of ideology. Further, since these mappings are 'structures in dominance' but not closed, the communicative process consists not in the unproblematic codes, but of *performative rules*—rules of competence and use, of logics-in-use—which seek actively to *enforce* and *prefer* once semantic domain over another and rule items into and out of their appropriate meaning-sets. Formal semiology," according to Hall, "Encoding, Decoding," in Simon During, ed., *The Cultural Studies Reader* (New York: Routledge, 1994), 98–99.

31 Clarence E. Sinn, "Music for the Picture," MPW, March 27, 1915, 1917.

32 Ibid.

33 John W. Raymond, "The Music to Suit the Picture," MPW, April 23, 1910, 562.

34 "Chicago Notes," MPW, October 1, 1910, 755.

35 "Vaudeville—Music—Uniforms," MPW, November 19, 1910, 1166.

PART TWO

THE PLACE OF THE SONG

Very few of us live a life without songs of one variety or another. Regardless of their age or genre, there is something particularly powerful about how songs fuse words with music. This is reflected not only in the value we place on the songs which soundtrack our lives (the ones we repeatedly sing in our heads), but also in the amount of time many of us spend seeking out more permanent versions of these tunes (on CD, vinyl or minidisc, for instance). A good deal of us define our pasts, structure our leisure time and choose our friends on the basis of our tastes in pop songs, and large amounts of our spare cash is spent making these delineations clear.

Accordingly, this second section of the book concerns itself with cinema's love of lyrical, popular music and its position amid film's industrial pressures and aesthetic prejudices. It also delves into specific film audiences' literacy in popular music's generic formations and the incalculable impact of popular songs upon quotidian experience. Moreover, it has to be stressed that popular music is a mammoth business, accounting, for example, for more of the UK's export trade than does its once powerful steel industry.

With similar financial implications at the forefront of his mind, Smith provides a detailed map of how the film and music industries interlock and how even seemingly throwaway musical references in films are caught up in big business mechanisms such as licence-fee negotiations. Smith's piece moves beyond the casual assumptions many writers make about cross-promotion and into a detailed historical analysis of the specific mergers and strategic alliances which have shaped the market place as we know it today. In his book *The Sounds of Commerce*—from which this is an extract—Smith blends this economic and historical precision with an adroit facility in engaging in filmic and musicological interpretation. Although these skills are less evident in this particular selection (and readers are strongly recommended to search out the source text), Smith's role within this collection is to provide a rigorous example of industrially based research, something which is still rather underdeveloped in most other writing in this field.

Maintaining an interest in the financial workings of music within cinema, but with more of an eye on sociological factors, Grossberg contemplates what one specific type of music—rock—might offer the film text and its viewers. By concentrating on the youth market, he studies how the connotations of rock are constantly rewritten. For him, rock is not just a musical genre, but a plethora of social practices which are scattered across our perceptions of personal and shared history and our notions of class, age, consumerism, rebellion and authenticity (to name but a few categories). Writers like Grossberg can consequently argue that musical references bear far-reaching implications which are extremely readable to a broad cross-section of the film-going public. It has to be noted that this chapter, before it was edited, focused more on music videos, and any readers who are inquisitive about how MTV features in this arrangement of music and cinema are advised to search out the original and peruse it in its entirety.

In considering the social ramifications of popular song, Valassopoulos's chapter on *The Silences of the Palace* (1992) adopts a project similar to Grossberg's, but takes it more into the realm of post-colonial thinking. Proving just how potent popular song references can be, Valassopoulos scrutinizes the reinscription of a body of material popularized by Umm Kalthoum into a female-directed Tunisian film of the last decade of the twentieth century. Kalthoum's biography is wrapped up in Egyptian independence struggles and any reference to her immediately evokes (to audiences in the know) a history of Arab nationalism and empowerment which is cherished throughout the Middle East.

Lastly, Garwood's chapter is less caught up in specific social or economic legacies and more engaged in formal analyses. His is an extremely close reading of how films deploy a variety of techniques to capitalize upon the richness of meaning encapsulated in chosen musical moments. With an interest in romantic comedies—*Sleepless in Seattle* (1993) in particular—Garwood investigates the prismic effect of popular song on cinematic signification, tracing the numerous guided responses which might be bred from one single film's use of song.

In their varied commitments to the historical, the social, the cultural and the linguistic, the writings in this section of the volume display just how replete with interpretative possibilities popular music can be. The time when popular music was thought unworthy of study is now long gone.

Banking on Film Music

Structural interactions of the film and record industries

JEFF SMITH

Since the 1950s, the production of motion picture soundtrack albums has flourished both as an important tool of film promotion and as an aesthetic and cultural phenomenon in its own right. The remarkable success of the *Wayne's World* soundtrack during the early nineties is a case in point. The album was not only a best-seller on *Billboard*'s charts but also revived interest in the rock group Queen, spurring sales of the group's greatest hits package and bringing the single "Bohemian Rhapsody" heavy radio play more than fifteen years after its initial release. The latter's success came in large measure from the way it was featured in the film. With the art-rock chestnut booming out their car stereo, Wayne, Garth, and friends bopped their way down suburban streets in a comic set piece that is in many ways the equivalent of the song and dance numbers of classical Hollywood musicals.

The *Wayne's World* example is particularly interesting not only because the film itself pokes fun at Hollywood promotional practices like product placement, but also because it offers a view of the mall culture that is so important to the contemporary filmgoer's experience. Whereas a previous generation's exploitation of a film's soundtrack involved setting up special display cases in theater lobbies or making special agreements with local record merchants, modern film patrons, upon leaving the mall multiplex, can simply go to the mall record store and, more than likely, purchase the soundtrack album for the film they have just seen. The spatial contiguity of theaters and record stores suggests the extent to which such reciprocal arrangements between corporate interests have institutionalized what was once an expensive and time-consuming aspect of film marketing. The "one-stop shopping" concept makes the mall a haven for film promoters with soundtrack albums available at record stores, novelizations purchasable at bookstores, posters on display at video stores, T-shirts on sale in department stores, and the film itself playing at the mall multiplex.

Such interlocking business arrangements between film and music interests are, of course, nothing new. Hollywood has long used music to sell films and vice versa.[1] Yet, as Irwin Bazelon notes, what makes these last forty years since the 1950s somewhat different is the development of an "organized machinery behind the manufacture of hit songs in films."[2] The development of this "machinery" came in response to a number of industrial, historical, and sociological factors in the 1950s and early 1960s, including the trend toward diversification and conglomeration in film distribution, the emergence of studio-owned record labels, the establishment of radio and records as important ancillary markets, and changes in popular music tastes and consumption patterns.

Over the years, Hollywood's investment in music subsidiaries has yielded several economic benefits. First of all, film companies earn millions of dollars in ancillary revenues from the outright sale of records and sheet music. Second, through their ownership of publishing and record ventures, film companies also derive additional monies from their control of various copyrighted materials. Generally speaking, these revenues come from two sources—synchronization licenses and master licenses. The *synchronization license* is negotiated with the publishers of a particular song, and this entitles the licensee to use the notes and lyrics to a particular piece of music. The *master use license*, on time other hand, is negotiated within a record company, and it enables licensees to use a particular recording. To use "Bohemian Rhapsody" in *Wayne's World*, filmmakers paid both kinds of licensing fees, one to the song's publisher and one to Queen's record company. To license the song "Mickey" in the same film, however, producers paid only a synchronization fee since they used just the song rather than Toni Basil's recording of it. ("Mickey" is briefly sung by Wayne and Cassandra as they ride in his car.) Finally, with the growth of radio and records as important ancillary markets, theme songs and soundtrack albums became valuable cross-promotional tools. Through its repeated airplay, a title song effectively becomes a kind of free three-minute advertisement for its accompanying film. Similarly, though valued more for their sales than for their promotional value, soundtrack albums serve as an effective means of circulating a film's title and imagery through rack sales and retail displays.

[. . .]

In this chapter, I will examine the emergence of the soundtrack album as a vehicle for cross-promotion. To do this, however, we must first situate film music more generally within its economic, industrial, and historical context. The reasons for such contextualization are simple; theories of film music can explain certain aspects of film music's form and function, but they cannot account for everything. One must also consider the economic and cultural factors that engendered its development. In this instance, such factors include both the economic structures of the film and music industries, and the emergence of radio and records as the most important means of circulating film music.

[. . .]

Creating kingdoms of song: the film and music industries unite

The 1950s were a period of moderate upheaval for both the film and music businesses. After lengthy terms of oligopoly control, the major companies of both industries faced changes in corporate organization and market structure. They also confronted the challenges of new lifestyles and new entertainment technologies. In the case of the film industry, many of these industrial changes were precipitated by the Supreme Court's *Paramount* decision of 1948, which ended unfair distribution practices, such as block booking, and forced time divestiture of the studios' theater holdings. By effectively ending Hollywood's system of vertical integration, the *Paramount* decision helped to weaken the Production Code Administration, renewed an emphasis on foreign markets, and encouraged the rise of independent film production.

Not coincidentally, the strengthening of independent production also became important within the music business. Between 1948 and 1955, the record industry was dominated by four firms: Capitol, Columbia, Decca, and RCA Victor. After 1955, however, this oligopoly was challenged by a major influx of new artists and independent record labels.[3] Much of this new competition was linked to the emergence of rhythm and blues and rock 'n' roll. Atlantic, Chess, Monument, Sun Records, and other labels utilized these new forms to break the majors' stronghold on the record charts. Between 1955 and 1959, aggregate record sales increased by 261 percent, and by the end of the decade retail record sales totaled more than a half billion dollars. These independent labels accounted for approximately 60 percent of the total sales of 45-rpm singles and for about 75 percent of the tunes that made it onto *Billboard*'s most important sales charts.[4]

While several factors contributed to the soundtrack album's emergence in the late fifties and early sixties, the most important was the trend toward diversification and conglomeration that followed the *Paramount* decree. Beginning with the takeover of Universal Pictures by Decca Records in 1952, several motion picture producers and distributors became subsidiaries of huge conglomerates with active and interrelated entertainment divisions.[5] Through such diversification, companies could spread their risks by creating additional "profit centers" to amortize production costs and exploit various kinds of cross-promotional marketing practices.[6]

Historically, music subsidiaries have traditionally served as prime sources of cross-promotion and diversification. A relatively recent instance of this is the idea of *synergy*. The term, coined by music supervisor Danny Goldberg, became a marketing buzzword during the 1980s. According to R. Serge Denisoff and George Plasketes, the strategy of synergy held that the common cross-promotion of films and records could benefit both industries in almost equal measure. For a film company, sales of soundtrack albums could amortize production costs while radio airplay of film themes served as a cheap and practical form of advertising. For a record company, on the other hand, the link to a film gave a soundtrack album needed name recognition in a highly competitive market. When all cogs of the promotional machine were smoothly functioning, interest in one component "synergistically" fed off interest in the other until both film and soundtrack album reigned supreme over box offices and record charts.[7]

Although the term *synergy* is of more recent vintage, the idea that film music played an important economic function within the industry goes back at least to the early 1910s. For the most part, this economic function operated at the level of live exhibition during this period of silent films. As Chuck Berg points out, one way that exhibitors could differentiate themselves was by promoting the musicians themselves as a kind of special attraction. Musicians typically earned their reputations either through the quality of their performances or through the character of their personality. According to Berg, some accompanists were known as "film funners" for the humor they displayed in their performances:

> The film funner would, for example, accompany a dramatic scene where burglars are craftily entering the heroine's home with the strains of the romantic love song, "Meet Me in the Shadows." Such a performer often became a distinct feature of the house for which he played and was sure of an audience of his own which came largely "to see what he would do with the pictures."[8]

Other musicians became known for their ability to ply the audience with familiar melodies. Satisfying a particular audience sometimes meant soliciting requests, playing currently popular songs, or matching the musical accompaniment to the specific composition of the audience, such as playing Italian pieces for a predominantly Italian crowd.

Most of these early cross-promotional efforts concerned the sale of sheet music, which by 1910 had surpassed thirty million in annual aggregate sales. To capitalize on this emerging new market, several exhibitors included song slides and singers as special attractions in their programs. The singers were frequently employed by music publishers for the express purpose of "plugging" a particular tune. In exchange for the plug, the exhibitor typically sold copies of sheet music in the theater and retained a small percentage of the monies from such sales. Both publishers and exhibitors benefited from these kinds of arrangements. Publishers gained increased promotion for their music which exhibitors enjoyed greater attendance and received the services of top-notch singers for little or no cost.[9]

The heightened awareness of music in cinema led to several tie-ins between the film and music industries. In 1914, for example, songwriters created a minor fad for tunes about serial heroines. One of the earliest was "Kathlyn," a hesitation waltz honoring two-reeler star Kathlyn Williams, and it was swiftly followed by the similarly themed "Zudora," "Runaway June," "Lucille Love," and "Poor Pauline," a spoof of Pearl White's classic *The Perils of Pauline*. In fact, the vogue for "serial" music nearly overshadowed two other cinematically inspired tunes published in 1914: "Those Charlie Chaplin Feet" and "He's Working in the Movies Now," the latter a comic ditty depicting an indolent father's transformation into an industrious movie stuntman.[10]

Sales of all sheet music exploded between 1910 and 1918, much of it driven by the opening of music counters in "five and dime" stores like Woolworth's, Kresge, and McCrory. With more than one thousand stores, Woolworth's became the largest retailer of sheet music, selling some two hundred million copies in 1918 alone. With a standard selling price of ten cents and a wholesale price of six cents, Woolworth's made a tidy 40 percent profit on every piece of sheet music that it sold.[11]

This same period also witnessed the rise of the "musical illustration" as a specific film genre. According to Berg, these films were a variation of the song slide principle as they were not only created to go with a specific song but also illustrated that song dramatically. Interest in this genre culminated in the late 'teens with two series of song illustrations produced by Harry Cohn and Carl Laemmle, respectively. By featuring song slides and filmed "illustrations" of music, movie theaters joined department stores, music shops, and vaudeville as important venues for song-plugging and as hubs of a multimillion-dollar industry.[12]

The practice of using song slides gradually died out in the 1920s when composers began writing specific theme songs for films. Although sheet music sales for film themes were generally modest in the early twenties, the music industry nonetheless took note of the promotional possibilities tendered by a specially composed or compiled film score. In 1920, for example, Columbia Records advised their retailers that "each week the tune studded talking picture leaves customers of yours with impressively presented theme songs echoing in their ears."[13]

According to Russell Sanjek, the first attempt at coordinated cross-promotion occurred in 1918 when Marshall Neilan commissioned a title song for Mabel Normand's *Mickey* that went on to become an unlikely hit. Written and published by Kansas City songwriter Charles N. Daniels, the sales of "Mickey" were undoubtedly boosted by a featured photograph of

Normand and ad copy that called attention to her role in the film. Still, the unforeseen fortunes of "Mickey" were clearly the exception rather than the rule. For the most part, the stiff opposition of the American Society of Composers, Authors, and Publishers (ASCAP) served as an unassailable obstacle to the regular use of Tin Pan Alley songs as film promotion.[14]

Late silent and early sound films reversed this trend, however, with the estimable success of "Charmaine" from *What Price Glory?* (1926) and "Diane" from *Seventh Heaven* (1927). The introduction of prerecorded musical soundtracks not only wrested away the last element of film presentation that was under the exhibitor's purview, but it also undermined ASCAP's putative control over silent film music. For years, ASCAP had battled with theater owners over licensing fees for ASCAP-owned music used in silent film accompaniment. Exhibitors countered with lesser-known tunes and original compositions, which were often provided by production companies and studios. However, these efforts were ultimately thwarted by the relative paucity of high-quality, unlicensed music. This became especially evident when ASCAP's reorganization precipitated the sudden withdrawal of huge lists of previously unlicensed music. Much of this music was prepared for the 13,000 members of the Motion Picture Theater Owners Association, but ASCAP's new copyright control made it virtually untouchable. Both factions reached a compromise in 1926 when some 11,000 theater owners became ASCAP licensees and paid over a half million dollars in fees, a figure that comprised more than 50 percent of the association's income that year.[15]

The coming of sound altered this balance of power as Hollywood invested in songwriters, composers, and music publishing houses. Since filmmakers could now be assured that the same music would be played during every showing of an individual film, the new technology had, in effect, standardized the film score. More importantly, by commissioning original songs and scores, producers were able to free themselves from the dependence on ASCAP-owned music. This did not necessarily help exhibitors, who continued to pay a dime-per-seat licensing fee, but it did shift ASCAP's attention away from theater owners and toward the film studios themselves.

Despite Warner Brothers' initial protestation that it was protected under the mechanical licensing provision of copyright law, ASCAP's control over licensed music threatened to halt Warner's production of vaudeville and musical shorts before it even got started. Recognizing its vulnerable position, Warner signed an agreement with ASCAP that obliged the studio to pay a $100,000 minimum annual royalty for recorded or synchronized music rights. RCA Photophone and the East Coast Sonoraphone Company soon followed suit, and in 1928 it was announced that ASCAP and the Music Publishers Protective Association (MPPA) would receive at least a million dollars per year in royalties in exchange for the synchronization rights to their music.[16]

Hollywood soon realized that the film industry had to control a large enough number of music copyrights to make it totally independent of any combine of music publishers and songwriters.[17] Although Paramount and Loew's were the first to buy their own publishing houses, it was Warner Brothers' purchase of the original Tin Pan Alley house, M. Witmark & Sons, in January 1929 that signaled Hollywood's more aggressive stance toward ASCAP. Five months later, Warner added to its newly formed music division when it took control of Max Dreyfus's music publishing holdings, which included the Harms Music Publishing Company, a 50 percent interest in the Remick Music Corporation, a smaller share of DeSylva, Brown, and Henderson, and a host of smaller music houses. By mid-1929, Warner's music division alone commanded a major share of the music publishers' vote in ASCAP policymaking. As studios either bought or formed their own music publishing subsidiaries, Hollywood not only freed itself from the threat of outrageous synchronization fees but was also now in a position to generate added revenues from the songs it featured in original musicals.[18]

It is important to note, however, that these revenues came in two forms. There was the actual monies earned from music publishing royalties and licensing fees. In 1935, for example, Warner estimated that it would earn more than a million dollars a year from its music publishing interests.[19] And from 1937 to 1939, the thirteen music houses affiliated with Hollywood earned about two-thirds of the total monies distributed to publishers by ASCAP. Second, there was the added box office revenues generated by the successful exploitation of a film's theme song or featured music. According to a 1939 estimate, a combination of radio airplay, record sales, and sheet music plugging added as much as a million dollars to an individual film's box office gross.[20]

Between 1930 and 1943, Hollywood's control of the music publishing industry and its employment of the industry's top songwriters prompted the film song's greatest period of success. Although the bulk of these songs were culled from original movie musicals (especially those written by Irving Berlin, Rodgers and Hart, and George and Ira Gershwin), notable film songs also came from westerns, romances, and melodramas. Between 1936 and 1942, film songs were regularly found atop Variety's weekly roster of the twenty-five most-played songs. Additionally, a Peatman survey showed that Hollywood and Broadway together accounted for more than 80 percent of the most-performed songs in 1942.[21]

Although during the Depression radio had gradually replaced sheet music as the film industry's most important ancillary market, World War II brought renewed prosperity to the printed music business. The combination of gas rations and luxury taxes encouraged families to stay home for their entertainment, a factor that greatly boosted sheet music sales during the early part of the war. Annual aggregate sales of sheet music rose to forty million copies in 1943. By the end of the war, the music publishing industry anticipated a $10 million gross from ASCAP distributions and royalties on sheet music and record sales.[22]

The resurgence in sheet music sales was also abetted by the emergence of the music rack business as an important new distribution outlet. After a deal was struck between the MPPA and the Hearst Corporation in 1940, sheet music display racks were installed in some five hundred newsstands across the country. So-called rack jobbers were employed to stock these new display units, which customarily carried two copies each of the twenty best-selling new songs. By 1944 the number of racks had grown to about 13,000, a number that guaranteed each best-seller an initial order of at least 93,000 copies. In addition, because of its portability, music racks made sheet music available in more different kinds of retail outlets than ever before. Places like barber-shops, newsstands, and stationery stores, which had never before carried sheet music, were now selling it to their customers.

In the years that immediately followed the war, however, film songs no longer reigned supreme over radio and sheet music markets. According to the Peatman survey, Hollywood's and Broadway's share of the most performed songs declined to a total of about 40 percent between 1944 and 1951. Publishers blamed this downturn on three different factors: (1) the failure of films adequately to highlight new songs; (2) the changing tastes of film producers and directors; and (3) a decline in the overall quality of songwriters' outputs.[23]

Perhaps the most important factor, however, was one that publishers did not wish to acknowledge—the growth of the market for recorded music. With the advent of the LP (long-playing record), the 45-rpm single, and the transistor radio, the downward spiral continued over the next several years. Initial orders for sheet music racks dropped to about 75,000 copies, and most songs were unable to sell out even this amount. The top sheet music tune of 1958, "Volare," sold less than 250,000, a far cry from the 3.5 million copies of "Till We Meet Again" that were sold some forty years earlier. By the end of the 1950s, the number one song on the weekly *Your Hit Parade* averaged only 15,000 copies in print form. As the market for sheet music declined, publishers soon realized that their revenues would come from royalties and licensing fees rather than outright sales. By the late fifties, the music racks that had once stocked thousands of copies of sheet music were selling record albums instead.

Establishing a "sound track" record: the majors and their record subsidiaries

The weakening of the sheet music marker, however, did not mean that Hollywood had given up on the idea of film and music cross-promotion. Rather, the majors simply redirected their efforts toward the burgeoning market of recorded music. According to figures released by the Recording Industry Association of America (RIAA), the total sales of all types of records increased dramatically between 1946, during which eight million disks were sold, and 1951, during which eight million disks were sold, and 1951, during which some 180 million disks were sold.[24] Furthermore, this upward trend continued steadily, if less spectacularly, throughout the 1950s. Between 1951 and 1959 the annual sum of records' retail sales had grown from $191 million to $514 million. Of course, Hollywood's investment in the record industry goes back at least to 1930 when Warner Brothers followed its purchase of several music publishing houses by acquiring Brunswick Records. At the time, Warner had envisioned the possibility of not only owing the music in its films but also releasing it on records. Warner's initial involvement in the record business was short-lived, however, as the studio sold its Brunswick subsidiary to the American Record Company about a year later.[25] After Warner's dalliance, Hollywood had little involvement in the record industry until MGM started up its own subsidiary in the mid-1940s.

After Decca's landmark purchase of Universal, the five other Hollywood majors sought to start up or acquire record subsidiaries between 1957 and 1958. Their activity was prompted by several causal mechanisms, among them the overall climate of diversification and conglomeration, the shrinking sheet music market, and the sudden boom in record sales. Besides the opportunities for cross-promotion, these studios hoped to create subsidiaries that were profitable ventures in themselves. As *Variety* noted in January 1958, "The film companies want in to the record business for more than just pic tie-in reasons. They realize it's a booming business and they want a share."[26]

Paramount was the first to take the plunge in early 1957 with its buyout of Dot Records, one of the most successful of the current crop of indie labels. Paramount paid a fairly high price for the label, some $2 million and a hefty chunk of company stock. By purchasing Dot, the film company not only gained a label with a 12 percent share of the singles market, they also profited from the expertise of Dot's rising young executive, Randy Woods. Under Woods' careful management, the label grossed over $10 million in its first year as a subsidiary, and earned back its parent company's initial investment within five years.[27]

In October 1957, United Artists followed Paramount's lead by launching two new subsidiaries, the UA Records Corporation and the UA Music Corporation. Unlike Paramount, however, United Artists did not purchase existing companies but started their own from the ground up. As Sanjek notes, UA Music began largely as a "desk-drawer operation" that controlled only about fifty copyrights.[28] With virtually no artists or repertoire, UA Records set up distribution agreements similar to that of its parent company. In its first year of operation, UA Records did not produce any of its own music but instead leased masters from outside sources. UA Records offered financing, distribution, and a 50 percent share of a record's net profits on a production-to-production basis. Although these terms brought some proven songwriter–producer teams to UA Records, the label's most important assets were undoubtedly the soundtracks leased from films distributed by its parent corporations. Using these film scores as the centerpiece of its sales and distribution program, UA Records set a rather ambitious goal of grossing $10 million within two years.

By the middle of 1958, Warner Brothers, 20th Century-Fox, and Columbia Pictures had all leapt into the disk business with companies that were, like UA Records, started from scratch. The film companies benefited from the growing stature of the record business as well as the added exploitation angles for studio product and increased exposure for contracted performers. Since none of these companies was able to purchase established labels, the studio's film exchanges provided ready-made promotional outlets for its own record subsidiaries' product.[29] Such arrangements had an obvious disadvantage in that film distributors knew little about record marketing. However, it did allow these newly formed subsidiaries to overcome an enormous barrier to entry and maintain the close coordination of film and soundtrack sales programs.

Ironically, the hopes of these new labels were boosted by the somewhat mixed fortunes of one of their competitors. In February 1958, Loew's Inc. issued its annual financial statement and reported some rather surprising news. Although firms were undoubtedly the company's bread and butter, the firm's most profitable enterprises were its music and broadcast subsidiaries. In fact, although the company had lost almost $7.8 million from its motion picture production and distribution operations, its fortunes were salvaged by the $4 million earned by Loew's theaters and the $5.5 million income from MGM Records, its subsidiary the Big Three Music Company, and WMGM Radio in New York City. All told, Loew's realized a net profit of $1.3 million in 1957, which the firm largely attributed to its disk and music publishing ventures.[30] Moreover, in an attempt to maximize its resources, MGM named Arnold Maxin the new president of its disk label and announced in early 1958 that the studio was instituting a stronger program of coordinated disk and film promotion, one that emphasized both musicals and nonmusicals alike.[31]

As *Variety* reported in early 1958, the sudden influx of film companies into the disk market had subtly altered the industry's geographical balance of power. New York City, the site of Columbia, Decca, and RCA Victor's corporate headquarters, had long been the center of the disk business. However, with Capitol Records as the solid nucleus of a flourishing new industrial sector, Hollywood had suddenly emerged as a significant rival to New York's dominance. In the face of Hollywood competition, a number of record companies and music publishers sought to upgrade their West Coast operations and improve their fortunes in the film music market. RCA Victor, for example, revamped its entire West Coast setup in order to compete with the new labels for soundtrack product. Additionally, the Harry Fox office, a music publishing agent and trustee, set up a Los Angeles branch in late 1957 for specific purpose of collecting mechanical royalties and synchronization fees.[32]

By the end of 1960, *Variety* had proclaimed the sales of soundtrack albums one of the most significant commercial trends of the year:

> Along with comics and percussion, motion picture music had one of its most successful years in 1960. It was a throwback to the time when every film had a title song, even if it came out like "Woman Disputed, I Love You." This year, the titles were no block to the pic songs and scores being cut in bulk and hitting with a remarkably high average.[33]

Billboard added, "The record and motion picture industries are working in closer and more effective harmony today than they have since the golden days of movie musicals."[34]

By the middle of 1961, however, industry analysts also proclaimed an end to the "era of the high flying indie diskers."[35] A number of independent labels had made significant inroads into the pop singles market, but the huge volume of releases, approximately a hundred a week during the late fifties, had oversaturated the market and thinned out the sales potential of all but a few genuine hits. More importantly, small independents were severely hurt by the payola scandal that erupted in the latter part of the decade. With major market stations receiving some five thousand new releases each year, small indies were deprived of an important weapon for influencing disk jockeys and radio airplay, and consequently many of them were unable to get their disks even auditioned. Lacking established artists, durable distribution, and consistent operational patterns, small independent labels scrambled for the scraps of a risky, hit-or-miss business. And with the pop singles trade returning to the control of a dozen major labels, a number of independent record companies simply fell by the wayside.

The film-owned labels were among the independent survivors, but they experienced varying degrees of success. Warner Bros. Records, for example, floundered during its first three years of operations and racked up a $2 million deficit by the middle of 1961. The company considered shutting its doors, but changed its mind when it uncovered a large number of unpaid distributors' accounts. After signing such artists as the Everly Brothers, Bob Newhart, Allan Sherman, and Peter, Paul, and Mary, Warner's fortunes experienced a rapid turnaround and the firm was solidly in the black by May 1963.[36] With the company's prospects more secure, Warner then renewed its efforts at soundtrack promotion in late 1963 with André Previn's *Dead Ringer* (1964), Manos Hadjidakis' *America, America* (1963), and Neal Hefti's *Sex and the Single Girl* (1964), which featured performances by Count Basie and his Orchestra.[37]

Columbia's subsidiary, Colpix Records, experienced slow but steady growth in its first five years of operations. Under the management of Paul Wexler and Jonie Taps, Colpix developed a number of teen idols as singles artists, such as James Darren and Shelley Fabares, but generally failed to exploit the potential of the album and film music markets.[38] That changed in the middle of 1962 when Columbia Pictures made a series of moves to consolidate its various music subsidiaries. First of all, Columbia Pictures announced that it was minimizing its ties with ASCAP firm Shapiro-Bernstein in favor of BMI subsidiary Gower Music and its own publishing house, Colpix Music. According to Leo Jaffe, the executive vice president of Columbia Pictures, the parent company also named Marvin Cane as vice president and general manager of both Gower and Colpix in an effort to consolidate and strengthen the firm's music publishing activities.[39]

This announcement was followed some six weeks later by the news that Columbia was also planning a major buildup of its disk subsidiary. According to Colpix head Jerry Raker, the label would now concentrate on the album market with a bevy of LPs that equaled almost 25 percent of the company's output over the previous four years. Among these were a number of film and television soundtrack packages, including *The War Lover*, *The Interns*, *Damn the Defiant*, *Barabbas*, *The Flintstones*, and *Top Cat*.[40] The fruits of this new policy would be realized the next year when the label scored a major hit with its *Lawrence of Arabia* soundtrack. By far the most important move, however, was Columbia's $2.5 million purchase of Al Nevins and Don Kirshner's budding publishing and record empire. In the deal, Kirshner received Colpix's top managerial slot and a $75,000 annual salary while Colpix obtained Kirshner's Dimension record label, all the copyrights of the duo's Aldon Music, and future services of the brilliant group of songwriters known as "Brill Building Pop," which included such notable teams as Carole King and Gerry Goffin, Jeff Barry and Ellie Greenwich, and Neil Sedaka and Howard Greenfield.[41] By late 1963, Colpix was ambitiously broadcasting its intentions of entering the ranks of the major labels.[42]

With new management and talent in place, Screen Gems-Columbia's Creative Music Group specifically directed its employees to concentrate on the company's television and motion picture products. The idea, according to *Billboard*, was to "get music written which is applicable for commercial recordings."[43] In the months that followed, Columbia put its promotional muscle behind the scores of six upcoming films, including *Ship of Fools*, *Cat Ballou*, *Major Dundee*, and *Lord Jim*, all due for release in 1965. The latter film was especially important to Columbia's plans since it hoped to sell some 500,000 copies of the soundtrack on its Colpix label over the next eighteen months. Unfortunately, neither *Lord Jim* nor any of the other five scores performed up to Columbia's expectations.[44]

20th Century-Fox Records struggled throughout its first five years of operations, and clearly made the poorest showing of the four so-called "movie babies." After a period of shuffling and reorganization, the label reined in its operations in 1962 and announced plans to coordinate closely all music activities with 20th Century-Fox Film Corporation. According to Ted Cain, 20th Century-Fox's director of musical affairs, virtually all aspects of the label's enterprise, from selecting and building artists to developing a back catalog, would be governed by the parent company's film and television output. This new mandate meant that performers were now chosen not only for their disk appeal but also for their potential as film and television stars. Moreover, greater emphasis in marketing would now be placed on the label's soundtrack packages and on the title tunes culled from 20th Century-Fox's film productions.[45] Unfortunately, the new policy paid very few dividends and the record company's only sign of encouragement came in 1963 with the release of Alex North's *Cleopatra* score.

In 1965, 20th Century-Fox's artists and repertoire chief, Bernie Wayne, tried to upgrade the label's moribund soundtrack sales by adopting changes in its album format. The label announced that all film scores would be edited such that no individual track would exceed a maximum length of two and a half minutes. According to Wayne, this would give each band on the album the same running time as a pop song, and would thus encourage airplay for 20th Century-Fox's film music by pop disk jockeys. A second change involved exploiting both a film's dialogue and its background score. Fox had already successfully experimented with this approach on *Zorba the Greek* (1964), which featured Anthony Quinn's spoken introductions to each musical track, and Fox executives planned on a wider application of this format wherever it was appropriate. According to Wayne, *The Agony and the Ecstasy* (1965) and *Those Magnificent Men in Their Flying Machines* (1965) were among the upcoming Fox releases to get the dialogue-music treatment, and the album for *Flying Machines* even included dialogue in the middle of the album's music tracks in order to "inject the film's comedy flavor into the LP."[46] Wayne added that the label was also considering the release of straight dialogue soundtracks. Interest in this genre, however, proved to be very short-lived and soon the label returned to its concentration on title tunes, dramatic scores, and screen musicals.[47]

UA Records quietly inaugurated its release schedule in 1958 with the soundtrack of the Bob Hope/Anita Ekberg vehicle, *Paris Holiday*.[48] Though the album flopped, it nonetheless signaled UA's staunch commitment to exploiting its library of film music, not only for promotional purposes but also as a means of sustaining the label's own sales and distribution activities. Sales were slack during UA's first two years of operations, but vice president and general manager Art Talmadge remained optimistic at the company's first annual distribution meeting in July 1960. At the assembly, Talmadge unveiled UA's new "selective album" policy, which called for a cutback in the label's general album output to concentrate on established artists and soundtrack packages. The policy was designed to cut down on costs and allow the company's promotional staff to focus their efforts on a smaller number of potential LP hits. Talmadge admitted that UA Records had very little proven talent on its roster, but stressed that the label's film alliances offered more than a million dollars' worth of product to carry them through this rebuilding period. To demonstrate the new "selective album" strategy, Talmadge announced that UA's upcoming releases included soundtrack packages for *Inherit the Wind*, *West Side Story*, *The Misfits*, and *The Alamo*.[49]

Within six months, UA's "selective album" policy began to bear fruit, but it did so, ironically, in the singles market. The themes from *Never on Sunday*, *Exodus*, *The Apartment*, and *The Magnificent Seven* emerged as chart-topping singles, a phenomenon that *Billboard* credited to the careful planning of film and record executives during these films' preproduction stages. According to David Picker, who served as a liaison between parent company and subsidiary, UA Records was working "closer than ever with UA's indie film producers," and was using these consultations to discuss which types of composers and styles offered the best potential in the singles and album markets. As an example, Picker noted his own success in convincing the producers of *Paris Blues* to add three new Duke Ellington songs to the four classics that were already featured in Ellington's film score.[50]

By March 1961, UA's "selective album" program was fully in place and sales of all types of records were booming. Spurred by the million-selling *Exodus* single and the *Great Motion Picture Themes* LP, which went on to rack up over 450,000 in sales, UA's gross billings for January and February were 300 percent higher than that of the previous year.[51] As the year wore on, UA's sales dipped slightly from its early peak, but continued to be very strong. The label's fall sales program spotlighted fifteen new albums and pulled in nearly $1.7 million in billings.[52] UA's gross sales for 1961 topped $5 million, a figure more than double the amount of the previous year. Among the label's big hits were *Great Motion Picture Themes*; the *Never on Sunday* soundtrack, which sold over 350,000 copies; and Ferrante and Teicher's *West Side Story* LP, which attained a more modest 150,000 in sales.[53]

During this time, UA also sought to upgrade its image in foreign markets because, before 1961, the company's disks were released in Europe under a variety of different regional labels. Under a new agreement between UA and its foreign distributors, the firm's records would now be released under the UA stamp. As Talmadge noted, this arrangement offered the record label a number of advantages. The foreign offices of United Artists Pictures offered a ready-made corps of salesmen who could be utilized to market the label's European output.

...ʋreover, UA Records could also better exploit its movie tie-ins. This factor was particularly important in foreign markets since radio exposure for new releases was scarce, and theaters thus became the central outlet for promoting film music abroad. Lastly, UA Records could eliminate administrative problems that arose when UA's foreign distributors also handled competing products. An example of this occurred when British Decca, UA Record's English distributor, not only released UA's smash Ferrante and Teicher recording of the Exodus theme, but also its own version performed by Mantovani.[54]

Over the next years, UA Records expanded into the jazz, country, and children's music markets, but continued to plumb its film resources with great success. In March 1962, UA announced two rather ambitious spring sales programs, one that spotlighted eight new album releases and one highlighting nineteen different movie music LPs. The latter program, dubbed "All Out for Oscar," was timed to coincide with the presentation of the Academy Awards and gave special emphasis to the soundtrack packages of all UA nominees.[55] The effort to expand its stable of artists and repertoire, combined with its film music sales, drove UA Records' gross billings to a $7 million peak in 1962, and as Tino Balio notes, by 1964 the subsidiary could legitimately call itself "the foremost record company in the film music field."[56]

Despite the expansion, however, the fortunes of UA Records remained closely tied to its parent company's films. In 1966, for example, Variety reported that the label's immediate future was pegged to a slate of thirteen new soundtrack albums. Among these were the scores for Hawaii, The Russians Are Coming, the Russians Are Coming, Lord Love a Duck, Duel at Diablo, and After the Fox.[57] While none of these titles managed to dent Billboard's album charts, UA returned to form a year later with smash soundtracks from A Man and a Woman, You Only Live Twice, and The Good, the Bad, and the Ugly.

Still, while the new film-owned labels sought to establish themselves, MGM once again demonstrate just how valuable a film company's existing music subsidiaries could be.[58] According to a 1965 financial report, MGM Records and its subsidiary the Big Three Music Company together grossed some $21 million during the previous fiscal year. This figure not only yielded a $2 million profit for the conglomerate, it also accounted for nearly 13 percent of the firm's total income during that period. Moreover, as label executive Robert H. O'Brien noted, MGM's record division, which had enjoyed one of its most profitable years since its inception, would continue to aggressively broaden its scope through "new artists, new lines of production, and new channels of distribution."[59]

Such optimism was undoubtedly buoyed by continuing reports of the music industry's general economic health. A ten-year study by the CBS/Columbia group, for example, showed that total record sales had grown from $250 million to $650 million between 1956 and 1966. Moreover, the annual number of new record releases had also swelled from 6,157 to 10,662. While these releases catered to a variety of tastes, including classical, jazz, country and western, and folk music, consumers clearly indicated a preference for pop and rock music, which accounted for nearly half of all album purchases.[60] In sum, the record industry enjoyed unprecedented prosperity in the mid-sixties, and the film-owned subsidiaries were quite keen on riding the coattails of this success.[61]

The period of growth that dominated the record industry between 1964 and 1969 was, however, gradually replaced by a trend to market concentration and corporate conglomeration.[62] During the latter half of the decade, five major companies—MGM, Columbia, Capitol-EMI (Electrical and Musical Industries), RCA Victor, and Warner/Seven Arts—

controlled over half the record market. The film-owned record labels were greatly affected by this development as either they or their parent companies found themselves taken over by larger disk companies or highly diversified conglomerates.[63]

In 1966, Columbia signaled this new drift when it negotiated a distribution deal with RCA Victor for its newly formed Colgems label. According to the agreement, RCA Victor would distribute and promote Colgems' products in hopes of expanding its share in the singles market, but would cede the responsibility for producing records and scouting talent to Don Kirshner, who would function as both the creative director of Colgems Records and head of Columbia-Screen Gems' music division. In creating this new label, Columbia also decided to deactivate its Colpix disk operations, which had limped along in recent years under a series of managerial changes and distribution difficulties.[64]

Shortly after the Colgems move, Hollywood's other foundering record label, 20th Century-Fox, had its distribution and merchandising ventures taken over by ABC Records. Though 20th Century-Fox's music director, Lionel Newman, insisted that the merger would not affect either label's autonomy, ABC nonetheless made the deal to give itself access to a number of forthcoming film and television soundtracks, an area that it had heretofore not pursued. Soon after, ABC proudly announced that its first slate of 1966–67 20th Century-Fox releases would include the albums for *Batman*, *The Bible*, *Modesty Blaise*, *How to Steal a Million*, and *Doctor Dolittle*.[65]

With fewer worries about distribution, 20th Century-Fox's music operations began a surprisingly ambitious program of expansion some six months after the ABC merger. 20th Century-Fox severed its longstanding "favored outlet" status with MGM's Big Three and purchased the Bregman, Vocco, & Conn (BVC) music publishing house for some $4.5 million. In addition to gaining control over BVC's catalog, 20th Century-Fox intended to funnel all of its film scores and soundtracks into its newly acquired publishing interest.[66] With hits from *Doctor Dolittle* (1967) and *The Poseidon Adventure* (1972), 20th Century-Fox's music operations enjoyed moderate success under this arrangement until it was chased by Warner Communications in 1982 at a cost estimated between $16 million and $18 million.

Like its competitors, Warner Bros. Records also found itself caught up in the fervor of mergers and acquisitions. Unlike its film-owned brethren, however Warner took a much more aggressive stance toward the issue of rate expansion. The label asserted itself early on when it merged with Frank Sinatra's Reprise label in 1963. Under the terms of this deal, Warner yielded a one-third share of the company to Sinatra in exchange for Reprise's $3 million library of master tapes and its stable of recording artists, which included Dean Martin, Trini Lopez, and the Chairman himself.

Both labels experienced short-term gains after the merger, but within three years Warner's music subsidiaries were once again on the brink of financial ruin. The record company experienced a sudden reversal of fortune, however, when Jack Warner negotiated a merger with the Seven Arts Corporation in November 1966. The move immediately placed the revamped Warner-Reprise label among the frontline of disk manufacturers and distributors, a position that was only strengthened by its parent corporation's bold policy of expansion. In 1967, for example, Warner/Seven Arts purchased Atlantic Records for some $17 million and emerged as perhaps the largest combine in the music industry. Under the WB-7 umbrella were several major recording labels, including Reprise, Atlantic, Atco, a host of smaller affiliates, and an impressive assemblage of music publishing interests. The latter included three Atlantic publishing subsidiaries (Cotillion, Pronto, and Walden Music); Seven Arts Music, which published Warner's film and television music; and the Music Publishers Holding Corporation, an ASCAP firm that was then the industry's largest publishing entity.[67]

With each of these components in place, Warner/Seven Arts' disk operations flourished between 1968 and 1975. In the first nine months of 1968, the record division netted approximately $5.3 million on an anticipated $50 million gross, a figure that comprised about 76 per cent of WB-7's consolidated corporate profit during that same period.[68] Moreover, even in its subsequent incarnations as part of Kinney National Service and Warner Communications, the Warner-Reprise and Atlantic groups continued to be the most profitable part of their parent corporation's enterprises. In the early seventies, Warner's record division, which now also housed Elektra and Asylum Records, garnered over 25 percent of the slots on Billboard's charts and increased the firm's pretax earnings by almost 50 percent.[69] As the company entered the second half of the decade, Warner's stood well above its Hollywood rivals as the only firm with strong market shares in both the record and sheet music industries.

For Paramount and UA, the reorganization of their disk subsidiaries was directly attributable to the entry of huge outside interests into the film and entertainment industries. Gulf & Western took over Paramount Pictures in October 1966 and attempted to consolidate Paramount's disk and publishing interests under one umbrella. In doing so, Gulf & Western hoped to push Dot more aggressively into the pop singles market. The label had a long string of successes with artists like Billy Vaughan and Lawrence Welk, but it had not been particularly active in acquiring indie-produced masters which could be sold to a thriving market of teenage consumers.

Gulf & Western also wished to renew Dot's efforts in the soundtrack field. The conglomerate's management noted a large number of Paramount releases scheduled for early 1967, but they were disappointed to learn that the scores for these films had already been farmed out to other record labels. Gulf & Western sought closer ties between its film and disk operations, and restructured its music subsidiaries on the model of Metro-Goldwyn-Mayer's Big Three and MGM Records' empire.[70] The Paramount and Dot subsidiaries, however, enjoyed little prosperity over the next several years, and when Gulf & Western retrenched in 1974, the labels were sold off to ABC Records for a $55 million price tag.

Like Gulf & Western, Transamerica hoped to make huge inroads in the entertainment industry when it took over United Artists in 1967. Transamerica added to its empire the following year when it bought the Liberty and Blue Note labels for over $25 million and merged the former with its already existing record subsidiary to create Liberty/United Artists Records. The union produced the sixth largest enterprise in the record industry, but Liberty/UA rapidly became a financial drain only two years after the buyout. After losses of $9 million in 1970 and 1971, Transamerica reorganized its disk subsidiary, renamed it United Artists Records, and gradually began to sell off chunks of its Liberty operation. United Artists Records continued to have occasional successes with its Rocky (1976) and James Bond soundtracks, but the revenue from United Artists' music operations remained a steady 25 percent between 1966 and 1976, and as Tino Balio put it, UA "remained primarily a motion picture distribution company throughout its history."[71]

By the end of the sixties, the film-owned labels were firmly ensconced in the record industry either as surviving independents or as subsidiaries of one of the major labels. When Hollywood entered the record industry in the late fifties, film companies shared two general goals for their subsidiaries: (1) to use records and radio as promotional vehicles for their film scores and songs; and (2) to diversify their business interests by creating self-sufficient, ancillary profit centers. The subsidiaries' long-term performance, however, suggests that Hollywood ultimately attained only one of these two goals. The efforts of the film companies to sustain a market for film music proved far more successful than their efforts to sustain their own labels.

When the sheet music market collapsed in the late 1950s, Hollywood shrewdly shifted its interests in cross-promotion from music publishing to records and radio. Collections of movie music had long served a small market of connoisseurs, but the albums now became promotional vehicles for a growing audience of record buyers and radio listeners.[72] By buying or creating their own labels, the studios could generate record sales to complement the sizable licensing and performance fees garnered by their longstanding publishing interests. Soundtrack albums were especially apt in this regard in that they were both cheaply produced—their negative costs were already incurred and accounted for by the filmmakers— and offered obvious name recognition for the primary products of their parent companies. When both film and music operations functioned in concert, they not only enhanced a film's box office returns, but they also contributed as much as 25 percent of a film company's total revenues.

Between 1960 and 1969, however, the film companies came to understand that they needed much more than their film scores to survive in an exceedingly costly and competitive record industry. By 1970 the total sales of the record trade surpassed the $1 billion mark, but production expenditures for albums had risen at a comparable rate. As only 40 percent of all albums recovered their initial production costs, labels soon realized that the only way to spread their immense financial risks was by producing enough records to cover the whole spectrum of pop music tastes and thereby increase the likelihood of scoring a gigantic hit.

During their first years of operations, the film-owned independents relied on their financial muscle and cross-promotional resources to subsist in an environment where other indies were rapidly folding. Yet most film subsidiaries never developed enough talent or repertoire to maintain their status as independent labels. When companies like Dot, 20th Century-Fox, and UA faced financial troubles, they retrenched by containing costs and emphasizing their film-related products. Such strategies fulfilled the promotional interests of the parent companies but hurt the long-term fortunes of the labels themselves. Many labels were swallowed up in the late sixties trend toward mergers and conglomeration. Warner was the only film-owned label to pursue an aggressive program of expansion. By purchasing talent in its takeovers of Atlantic, Atco, and other companies, Warner was able to survive the industry's reconcentration of resources.

Yet Hollywood's inability to maintain its long-term position in the record market should not be deemed a failure. Although the film-owned labels were the victims of rising costs and huge outside investment, their status as part of larger record groups offered their parent companies the best of both worlds. Film companies could now concentrate their resources on cross-promotion without the worries of record distribution or talent acquisition. Of more importance, film companies were still guaranteed outlets for their film songs and scores, and still could realize the benefits of "synergy," which would shortly thereafter serve as a rallying cry for both industries. The soundtrack album continues to be the most common and vital form of film music exploitation; indeed this may be the most important legacy of Hollywood's entry into the record business.

Notes

1 See Douglas Gomery, *The Hollywood Studio System*; and Alexander Doty, "Music Sells Movies: (Re) New (ed) Conservatism in Film Marketing," *Wide Angle* 10, no. 2 (1988): 70–79.

2 Irwin Bazelon, *Knowing the Score: Notes on Film Music*, 30.

3 For a concise overview of the record industry's economic structure, see Richard A. Peterson and David G. Berger, "Cycles in Symbol Production: The Case of Popular Music," in Frith and Goodwin, eds., *On Record*, 140–59.

4 See Sanjek, *American Popular Music and Its Business* 3:333–66.

5 Doty, "Music Sells Movies," 72.

6 See Tino Balio, ed., *The American Film Industry*, 439–47.

7 R. Serge Denisoff and George Plasketes, "Synergy in 1980s Film and Music: Formula for Success or Industry Mythology?" *Film History* 4, no. 3 (1990): 257–76.

8 Charles Merrell Berg, *An Investigation of the Motives for and the Realization of Music to Accompany the American Silent Film, 1896–1927*, 244.

9 Berg, *An Investigation of the Motives*, 254.

10 Jim Walsh, "Fads, Foibles, and History Reflected in Pop Songs of 50 Years Ago," *Variety*, March 25, 1964, 54.

11 See Russell Sanjek, *Pennies from Heaven: The American Popular Music Business in the Twentieth Century*, 34–35.

12 Berg, *An Investigation of the Motives*, 255.

13 Quoted in André Millard, *America on Record: A History of Recorded Sound*, 160.

14 See Sanjek, *American Popular Music and Its Business* 3:47; and Sanjek and Sanjek, *The American Popular Music Business*, 35. It should be noted here that although Sanjek identifies Neilan as the person responsible for commissioning the title song for *Mickey*, the author also mistakenly credits Neilan for the film's direction. Most reference works cite Richard Jones as the director of *Mickey*.

15 See Sanjek, *American Popular Music and Its Business* 3:47–50.

16 Sanjek, *American Popular Music and Its Business* 3:52–54.

17 Ibid., 55.

18 See Sanjek, *American Popular Music and Its Business* 3:91–114; and Gomery *The Hollywood Studio System*, 106–10.

19 Sanjek and Sanjek, *The American Popular Music Business*, 43.

20 See Sanjek, *From Print to Plastic*, 19.

21 As cited in Sanjek, *American Popular Music and Its Business* 3:317–18.

22 See Sanjek, *Pennies From Heaven*, 251–53.

23 Ibid.

24 See Sanjek, *American Popular Music and Its Business* 3:245. As the author notes, this spectacular jump in sales was at least partly due to the development of new formats and technologies. In 1946 the 78-rpm record offered the only kind of format available. In 1951, however, 78-rpm records were competing with 45-rpm singles 33⅓-rpm LPs, and all three carved up a market comprised of the owners of some twenty-two million record players of all types.

25 See Millard, *America on Record*, 161–67.

26 Mike Gross, "Indies' Inroads on Major Diskeries' Pop Singles; $400,000, Record Mark," *Variety*, January 8, 1958, 215.

27 See Sanjek, *American Popular Music and Its Business* 3:344–47; and Gross, "Indies' Inroads," *Variety*, 215. Paramount's acquisition of Dot should not be confused with the already existing ABC–Paramount label. About two years earlier, United Paramount Theaters had joined with the American Broadcasting Company to form ABC-Paramount Records. This venture was part of a larger merger between UPT and ABC in 1953, and it had nothing to do with Paramount Pictures' production and distribution wings.

28 See Sanjek, *American Popular Music and Its Business* 3:346.

29 "20th Century-Fox in Disk Field; Onorati Quits Dot to Head Subsid," *Variety*, February 12, 1958, 53.

30 "Time to Grow Up," *Variety*, February 12, 1958, 53.

31 "MGM Records and Metro Pix Getting Real Chummy; Maxin's 'All Family,'" *Variety*, February 5, 1958, 53.

32 Herm Schoenfeld, "New Big Street—B'Way and Vine," *Variety*, February 5, 1958, 53.

33 Herm Schoenfeld, "R'n'R and Payola Still with the Music Biz: ASCAP Hassles; Diskeries' All 33-RPM Move," *Variety*, January 4, 1961, 207.

34 June Bundy, "Film Themes Link Movie, Disk Trades," *Billboard*, December 24, 1960, 8.

35 "End of the Indie Disker Era," *Variety*, June 7, 1961, 51 and 54.

36 See Sanjek, *American Popular Music and Its Business* 3:388–89; and Bob Rolontz, "They Laughed When Film Firms Sat Down . . .," *Billboard*, May 11, 1963, 1 and 6.

37 "WB Label Gets 'Track LPs to 3 Upcoming Pix," *Variety*, December 18, 1963, 45.

38 Rolontz, "They Laughed When," 6.

39 "Columbia Pix' Buildup of BMI Subsid Strains Ties with Shapiro Bernstein," *Variety*, June 27, 1962, 39.

40 "Raker Cooking Major Buildup of Colpix Label," *Variety*, August 1, 1962, 37; "Colpix Steps Up Soundtrack Ties with Columbia," *Billboard*, September 1, 1962, 6; and "Colpix and Parent Film Co. Hiking Cross-Promo Sked on Track LP's," *Variety*, September 5, 1962, 43.

41 See Sanjek, *American Popular Music and Its Business* 3:387; and Rolontz, "They Laughed When," 6.

42 "SG-Col Music Rolls Big Campaign to Build Colpix into Major Label Status," *Variety*, September 25, 1963, 55.

43 "SG-Col Music's Creative Group Places Songs with Top Artists," *Billboard*, January 23, 1965, 10.

44 See "'Lord Jim' LP Gets Royal Promotion," *Billboard*, February 20, 1965, 12; and "Col. Films Looks to Disks as Promotion," *Billboard*, March 13, 1965, 3.

45 "20th-Fox Label Blueprints Closer Ties with Parent," *Variety*, February 14, 1962, 45.

46 "20th-Fox Label Tests New Slant on Track LPs," *Variety*, April 21, 1965, 49.

47 See "20th-Fox Is Making Giant Track Strides," *Billboard*, December 18, 1965, 1. *Billboard* notes that 20th Century-Fox's winter sales program was organized around some thirteen scores, including *Our Man Flint*, *The Sand Pebbles*, and *The Blue Max*.

48 For a concise history of UA's various music operations, see Tino Balio, *United Artists: The Company That Changed the Film Industry*, 112–16.

49 "UA Sets First Distrib Meets," *Billboard*, June 20, 1960, 4; and "UA Stresses Pic Ties at Its First Annual Conclave," *Variety*, July 27, 1960, 109.

50 Bundy, "Film Themes Link Movie, Disk Trades," 8 and 10.

51 "UA Label Booming 300 Percent Over Last Year," *Variety*, March 1, 1961, 75.

52 See "UA Fall Sales Program Eyes $1,700,000 Billings," *Variety*, August 30, 1961, 44; and "UA & Its Diskery in Joint Push on 3 Oct. Film Bows," *Variety*, October 4, 1961, 59.
53 "UA's 1961 Gross Hits $5,000,000, a 100 Percent Increase Over Last Year," *Variety*, December 13, 1961, 47.
54 "Talmadge Shapes Strong Global UA Image, Toting Label's Name," *Billboard*, March 13, 1961, 4.
55 "UA Goes All Out for Sales Keyed to Oscar Awards," *Billboard*, March 17, 1962, 14.
56 See "UA Records Preps Film Score Projects; Formats to Include a Jazz Tie," *Variety*, August 15, 1962, 41; "UA Adds 3rd Soundtrack Album," *Billboard*, September 15, 1962, 5; "Report UA Net Off Despite Peak $7-Mil Biz in '62," *Variety*, January 2, 1963, 35; and Balio, *United Artists*, 114.
57 "UA Label Pegs Future to Flock of Film Tracks," *Variety*, April 6, 1966, 51.
58 Like other Hollywood subsidiaries, MGM Records maintained close contact with its parent company and frequently participated in the promotion of its film products between 1958 and 1965. For more on MGM's soundtrack interests, see "MGM Label Promoting Two Metro Pic Scores," *Variety*, July 13, 1960, 46; *Variety*, March 18, 1961, 58; "MGM Bountiful on 'Mutiny' Disks," *Variety*, September 5, 1962, 41; "'Bounty' Disks Get Big Push," *Billboard*, September 8, 1962, 5; "MGM & Its Pub, Disk Affils Join in Big Push on 'West,'" *Variety*, February 13, 1963, 53; "MGM in Summer Soundtrack Ride," *Variety*, June 10, 1964, 4; "MGM to Bow Six Soundtracks," *Billboard*, July 18, 1964, 35; and "MGM Records Rolls Big Push on 'Zhivago' Theme," *Variety*, December 22, 1965, 46.
59 O'Brien, quoted in "MGM Records, Big Three Annual Gross Hits $20,900,000; Net Over $2,000,000," *Variety*, December 8, 1965, 53.
60 As cited in *Time*, October 7, 1966, 56.
61 See "1965 a Boom Year in Disk Merchandising," *Billboard*, January 29, 1966, 1 and 8; "Retail Disk Sales Up 14 Percent; All-Time High," *Billboard*, June 4, 1966, 1 and 16; "$1.1 Bil. in Sales Racked Up in '67," *Billboard*, July 20, 1968, 3; "U.S. Record Survey," *Billboard* supplement, August 30, 1969, 9–13; and "Recorded Sales Put at $1.7 Bil. for '70," *Billboard*, November 7, 1970, 3.
62 Peterson and Berger, "Cycles in Symbol Production," 153–55. Some record executives recognized this trend toward market concentration much earlier than 1970. In 1967, Liberty Records' Al Bennett predicted that various mergers and acquisitions would consolidate the industry around a group of eight to ten corporate giants. The end result would be a larger oligopoly than that which had reigned during the fifties, but, according to Bennett, the ten labels dominating the market would constitute an oligopoly as powerful as the one in the film industry. See "Disk Mergers to Create 10 Industry Giants, Predicts Liberty's Al Bennett," *Variety*, December 13, 1967, 49.
63 See "Film Trade Powerplays—Its Effect on Industry," *Billboard*, December 16, 1966, 8.
64 "Victor's Col-SG Deal Accents Anew Indie Producer's Role in Disk Biz," *Variety*, June 22, 1966, 47. See also Herm Schoenfeld, "BMI's Fastest Growing Pub," *Variety*, April 13, 1966, 55; and "Col Pix-SG Disk Division Beefs up Exec Wing in Broad Expansion Move," *Variety*, December 6, 1967, 43.
65 See "ABC to Distrib 20th-Fox Disks," *Variety*, July 6, 1966, 39; and "ABC in Soundtracks with 20th-Fox Pact," *Billboard*, July 9, 1966, 4.
66 "20th-Fox Buyout of BVC Setting Stage for Big Move in Publishing and Disks," *Variety*, February 1, 1967, 57.

67 Herm Schoenfeld, "WB-7 Arts Music Empire," *Variety*, October 25, 1967, 41.

68 "Third Quarter Snappy for W7 Both in Sales, Profits; Big Eye on Disks," *Variety*, May 22, 1968, 30.

69 Sanjek, *American Popular Music and Its Business* 3:510–11.

70 "Gulf & Western to Shuffle Par's Music, Disk Cos. to Beef up Their Operations," *Variety*, December 21, 1966, 43.

71 Balio, *United Artists*, 116.

72 See Karlin, *Listening to Movies*, 227. Among the earliest albums of movie music were Miklós Rózsa's *The Jungle Book* (1942), Victor Young's *For Whom the Bell Tolls* (1943), and Alfred Newman's *The Song of Bernadette* (1943).

References

Balio, T. (1987) *United Artists: The Company that Changed the Film Industry*. Madison: University of Wisconsin Press

Balio, T. (ed.) (1985) *The American Film Industry*. Madison: University of Wisconsin Press

Bazelon, I. (1975) *Knowing the Score: Notes on Film Music*. New York: Van Nostrand Reinhold

Berg, C. (1976) *An Investigation of the Motives for and the Realization of Music to Accompany the American Silent Film 1986–1927*. New York: Arno

Frith, S. and Goodwin, A. (eds) (1990) *On Record: Rock, Pop and the Written Word* New York: Pantheon

Gomery, D. (1986) *The Hollywood Studio System*. New York: St Martin's

Karlin, F. (1994) *Listening to Movies: The Film Lover's Guide to Contemporary Film Scoring*. New York: Schirmer Books

Millard, A. (1995) *America on Record: A History of Recorded Sound*. Cambridge and New York: Cambridge University Press

Sanjek, R. (1983) *From Print to Plastic: Publishing and Promoting America's Popular Music (1900–1980)*. Brooklyn: Institute for Studies in American Music

Sanjek, R. (1988) *American Popular Music and Its Business 1900–1984*. New York: Oxford University Press

Sanjek, R. (1996) *Pennies from Heaven: The American Popular Music Business in the Twentieth Century*. New York: De Capo

Sanjek, R. and Sanjek, D. (1991) *The American Popular Music Business in the Twentieth Century*. New York: Oxford University Press

Cinema, Postmodernity and Authenticity

6

LAWRENCE GROSSBERG

The media economy of rock culture

It has often been repeated that rock is the soundtrack of the lives of postwar youth. As charming as this description may be, it is inaccurate for at least two reasons. First, the sound-track of the postwar years is also replete with bits and pieces of the history of television, not merely from theme songs but also from the narratives and dialogues that have entered into popular memory and conversation: from *Father Knows Best* to *Peter Gunn*, from *The Twilight Zone* to *Candid Camera* (to take only one moment of television's history, and one generation of the rock audience). Similarly, the cinema has contributed its own musical and rhetorical "riffs" to the soundscape of our collective memory: from *The Sound of Music* to *The Graduate*, from *Space Odyssey* to *Jaws*. The fact that rock has a special place in that memory says something about the relations between different media, the ratio between different senses, within rock culture (a point to which I will return later).

Second, rock has always been more than just a soundtrack, more than just "the noise." It has involved images, and the memory of a song is always partly visual as well. For rock has—at least until the 1980s—always carried a great deal of shared visual baggage, which was linked, not only to particular songs, but to the contours of one's taste as well. When you heard rock, you saw it as well, whether live, or in films, or on television, or on record sleeves. And when you listened, you were also seeing the performers and other fans. You were seeing styles of clothing, make-up and hairstyles, images of the sexual body and the body dancing. You were seeing, as well as hearing, fantasies and social experiences, attitudes and emotions. It is precisely because of the complex entanglements surrounding rock music that it has played such a powerful role in the lives of its fans (or perhaps it is the other way round).

The image of the soundtrack fails just because it carries the suggestion of independence; it assumes that the music can be separated from its anchor in other media and forms, that it stands as a commodity in its own right, capable of being isolated, identified and bounded. Rock has always had its own relations to the larger visual media economy, but the way in which it has been inserted into this economy is different for different rock cultures across time and taste. At different moments, for different audiences, the importance of images, the particular forms they take, and the ways they are related to the music, have varied, not only across genres and generations, but also across structures of historical and social difference.

[. . .]

I want to turn my attention to the changing relationship between sound and vision in rock cinema. Although interpreters of rock have always acknowledged the importance of filmic models like James Dean, they have rarely considered the continuing history of the relations between rock and film. In fact, I want to argue here that the contemporary youth-oriented film market is a crucial condition of possibility of music video. It is no coincidence that MTV premiered in 1981, following an enormous explosion of youth films which exhibited an originality and appeal untapped by earlier films.

The relations between film and rock have a long and complex history. In the 1980s, that connection has become crucial in economic terms; film has become an important source of origination, distribution and profit. In 1984, all five of the best-selling pop singles.came from movies. There were eight platinum soundtrack albums (including *Purple Rain, Eddie and the Cruisers, Flashdance, Footloose* and *Saturday Night Fever*). *Saturday Night Fever*, released originally in 1977, had set the stage: it was not only the first film of the decade to focus on the life of contemporary youth, it also demonstrated the mutual benefits of the close relationship between film and soundtracks. *War Games* (1983) was the first film to use rock video to promote itself. This relationship, perfected in such films as *Flashdance* and *Footloose*, has become the norm and it has radically changed not only the system by which films are exploited and promoted, but also the shape of the pop charts. And it has continued, even expanded through the decade, culminating in the phenomenal success of *Dirty Dancing*, which has sold well over 8 million albums, and has become one of the most popular videos of all time. Even films that have little to do with youth and rock culture find it necessary to take their sound-track seriously: *Ghostbusters* created a hit theme-song, *Batman's* soundtrack was written and performed by Prince, and even a film like *Wall Street* uses rock songs as background and narrative commentary.

But the relationship between rock music and youth films goes much deeper. By 1977, 57 per cent of all cinema tickets sold were purchased by those under 25. That figure has continued to grow. Of course, there are many reasons for the importance of cinema to youth audiences in the 1980s and 1990s, and their tastes are not confined to movies which directly represent youth culture. The teenage audience, for example, is the largest segment of the audience for contemporary horror films, and many of the decade's blockbusters (e.g., Spielberg's films, Stallone's films, *Batman*, etc.) depended upon heavy viewing by the under-25 market. Still, I think it is not coincidental that the 1980s have seen a veritable explosion of films directed towards youth which focus on the everyday lives of their audience.

Rock culture and youth movies

Contemporary youth films, and their impact on rock culture, can be more clearly understood if we begin by briefly considering the youth films that were part of the emergence of rock culture. The so-called golden age of rock and "teen films"—from the 1950s through the mid-1960s—was characterized by a small number of genres. First, and perhaps most importantly, there were films which functioned mainly to present images of rock performers and performances. The second-largest category involved films about the threat of teenage culture—juvenile delinquency, motorcycles and hot rods, or vice. The notion that films could and should represent the everyday lives of rock's fans seems to have had a minor place in the spectrum of "teenpics." Of course, there were films about "mainstream" fans, but these often seemed less concerned with the actual experiences of youth than with specific activities (like the beach movies) or with narrative demands set outside the teen audience (e.g., *Gidget*, the films of Pat Boone, Frankie Avalon, etc.). Perhaps the great exception—and certainly the most powerful 1950s teen film—*Rebel Without a Cause*—was able to represent the feelings of its audience by thrusting its alienated hero into the middle of a delinquent subculture. The films produced in the decade between 1967 and 1977 were concerned mostly with the counter-culture: hence, they often focused on the social and historical impact of the events of the decade, including the music (e.g., *Wild in the Streets*, *Privilege*, *Performance*). There were important exceptions to this inflection of the focus on youth and music: *Mean Streets* and *The Graduate* used the music to explore feelings of those not typically included in representations of youth and rock culture. Films such as *Bless the Beast and the Children* and *Joshua Then and Now* spoke more directly to the feelings and experiences of youth, however awkwardly.

The explosion of contemporary youth films provides one of the conditions of possibility for the emergence of music video. This involved not merely linking images with music but gradually shifting the location of the central representations and languages of youth culture. That is, even before MTV premiered in 1981, the cinema was already redefining the media economy of rock, with the ratio shifting from the primacy of musical (sound) images to that of visual images at the intersection of youth and rock cultures. It is not coincidental that the years 1978–80 provided the initial signs of the explosion of youth films, although many of the best movies from this period were not exactly box-office smashes (e.g., *Over the Edge*, *The Wanderers*). If the 1970s ignored youth culture, except retrospectively in its representa-tions of the counterculture (*American Graffiti* in 1973 was a crucial exception, a foreshadowing of at least one trend yet to come), the three years between 1978 and 1980 provided a time for experimenting with all sorts of ways of attracting and representing the youth audience. There were an enormous number of performance films (e.g., *The Last Waltz*, *The Kids are Alright*, *Rust Never Sleeps*, *No Nukes*, *The Secret Policeman's Ball*, *Shell Shock Rock*, *The Decline of Western Civilization*) as well as films about rock (*Heavy Metal*, *The Idolmaker*, *Roadie*, *Can't Stop the Music*) and films about the history of rock, presaging the nostalgia revival (and the fascination with a certain kind of history) of the 1980s (*American Hot Wax*, *The Buddy Holly Story*, *The Blues Brothers*, *Grease*). And there were the first signs of an avant-garde underground (e.g., *Jubilee*, *Union City*).

But most importantly, there were a large number of films about fairly ordinary youth, set in the contemporary context. Here one has to mention the more successful films—*Fame*, *Flashdance*, *Animal House*, *Quadrophenia* (although technically set in the 1960s, it was treated as contemporary rather than historical). Perhaps even more important were a series of films which remained fairly marginal in terms of their box-office receipts. Some of them deserved their failure (*Times Square*, *Breaking Glass*, *I Wanna Hold Your Hand*, *Foxes*) while others were signs of the future of youth-oriented films: *Rock and Roll High School*, *The Wanderers*, Walter Hill's *The Warriors*, and *Over the Edge* (written by Tim Hunter). *The Wanderers*, while apparently nostalgic, explored the anxieties and friendships of urban adolescents. *The Warriors*, like *Rock and Roll High School*, used an almost surreal extremism to redirect attention from the signs of delinquency to the question of everyday survival. And finally, *Over the Edge*, certainly one of the greatest youth films of all time, explored the relations between postwar suburban living, and the alienation, boredom and frustration of middle-class youth. Perhaps more than any other film, it made clear the structural hostility between postwar youth and the parent–education alliance.

Each of these genres continued and multiplied in the 1980s: contemporary performance films (*Stop Making Sense*): films about rock 'n' roll culture (*Sid and Nancy*, *Twist and Shout*, *Spinal Tap*, *Krush Groove*, *Purple Rain*, *Breakin'*, *Beat Street*); nostalgia films (*The Big Chill*, *Diner*, *The Return of the Secaucus' Seven*, *Dirty Dancing*, *Eddie and the Cruisers*, *Stand by Me*, *Breathless*, *Peggy Sue Got Married*). One of the most interesting developments has been the explosion of avant-garde films (some of which achieved reasonable commercial success), including *Smithereens*, *Brazil*, *Uforia*, *Liquid Sky*, *Blue Velvet*, *Repo Man*, *Brother from Another Planet*, *The Adventures of Buckaroo Bonzai*, *Down by Law*, *Stranger than Paradise*, *Robocop*, *Beetlejuice*, *Dead End Drive In*. (If Jack Nicholson was the icon of the 1970s in this genre, Dennis Hopper became the icon of the 1980s.)

Cinema and the representation of youth's alienation

But by far the most obvious explosion has involved films about youth's everyday lives, what have been called "tits and zits" movies, although relatively few have been smash hits (*Back to the Future* is one of the exception). In fact, in order to talk about them, we have to make some internal differentiations. We might separate out those which represent an older fraction of youth (although whether their audience reflected this difference is doubtful): *St Elmo's Fire*, *After Hours*, *Something Wild*, *Bright Lights Big City*, *She's Having a Baby* and, to some extent, *Desperately Seeking Susan* and *Less than Zero*. What is left are what are frequently referred to as "high school" movies, and there have been lots of them. There are literally hundreds of them besides those that I will refer to here; they are often shown on network and cable television. Some of the more successful ones were sombre and often touching recreations of the alienation of youth: *River's Edge*, *The Outsiders*, *Rumblefish*. But most located these feelings in a serio-comic context. A lot of them focused on one person's efforts to achieve some goal: *Girls Just Want to Have Fun*, *Top Gun*, *The Iron Eagle*, *Quicksilver*. In some, it is a question of survival, salvation and the battle between good and evil: *The Legend of Billie Jean*, *Footloose*, *Back to the Future*, *The Last Starfighter*, *Streets of Fire*, *Revenge of the Nerds*, *Porky's*, *Hiding Out*, *Heathers*, *The Karate Kid*. And in the largest group, the films focus on the needs and trials of contemporary life: *Fast Times at Ridgemont High*, *Risky Business*, *Pretty in Pink*, *Ferris Bueller's Day Off*, *Sixteen Candles*, *Valley Girl*, *Class of 1984*, *Meatballs*, *Wild Thing*, *Satisfaction*, *Seven Minutes in Heaven*.

In my experience, I have found that each generation of high-school students during the past decade has adopted a small number of these films as "their own," as expressions of their own experiences. In each instance, a fair number of the students will have seen the films multiple times, and often they have a powerful identification, not with a single character but with the ambience of the film itself. Many of these films follow the genre conventions of other narratives: the hero seeking a particular goal, the hero fighting for justice, the hero attempting (sometimes unknowingly) to save another, the romance which cuts across incompatible cultures (usually defined by style which is sometimes, but not always, correlated with class). But in each instance, the terms of the narrative are translated into the everyday terms and concerns of youth.

I will, in the following discussion, focus on a few of these films. Some of the most successful examples of this genre do not follow typical narrative conventions; rather, they explore the everyday life of high-school students. In at least two of them—*Fast Times at Ridgemont High* and

The Breakfast Club—we are given a map of the different clichés of youth's identity. While the former is unable to break those stereotypes because its narrative focus remains defined by the desire for romance and the demands of the genre of romance, both *The Breakfast Club* and *Ferris Bueller's Day Off* (both produced by John Hughes, the master of 1980s youth films) are about the characters' struggles to transcend such identities and find salvation in a common understanding of themselves as youth and of their alienation. (Hughes' films convey a powerful and very real sense of urgency, one that often strikes me as the visual equivalent of the music of Phil Spector). In these two films, romance is made subservient to the larger questions of youth's sense of identity, belongingness and purpose. If *Fast Times* dwells on the different styles of "cool," *The Breakfast Club* is about breaking through those styles to uncover a shared affective relation to the world. Despite the imposed romantic ending, the film has already made it clear that these five kids—a delinquent, a jock, a preppie, a brain and a weirdo—want, above all, to escape their own imprisonment within these identities. But they cannot, or rather, in the end, they will not.

The Breakfast Club is a film about youth's sense of identity—their acceptance of their own responsibility, not only for their actions, but for their imprisonment. Each one conforms, knows it, hates it, struggles for a moment to escape it and reveal themselves, and then knowingly accepts their own conformity. They each suffer, in the school, and at home. Each in their own way is a small simulacrum of James Dean, a rebel without a cause and, in the 1980s, without a prayer. In the end, *The Breakfast Club* is a tragic statement of youth's continued desire to avoid becoming their parents—parents who beat them, ignore them, pressure them—to avoid growing up because when you do, "your heart dies." It is tragic because their ability to communicate with each other, to form a community of suffering and anger, is voluntarily rejected. They are all content to leave such moments of salvation and empower-ment behind, to assume that they are unavoidably temporary and, even worse, tainted. That sense of alienation and empowerment is encapsulated at the beginning of the film, in Hughes' choice of the epigram (which is shattered like glass at the end of the opening credits) from David Bowie: "And these children/that you spit on/as they try to change their world/are immune to your consultations./They're quite aware of what they're going through." It is this sense of awareness that lends an element of tragedy and empowerment to many of these contemporary films and that places them as both an ally and a competitor of rock.

Ferris Bueller's Day Off is both strikingly similar and frighteningly different: it too is "a day in the life," and it too is framed by the oppressiveness of school. The family, however, remains more problematic, not the oppressor but the site of struggle (with a jealous sister) and manipulation (the film opens with Ferris giving the audience advice about how to manipulate parents). Unlike other films in the genre (with the exception of Walter Hill's), this one constantly breaks the naturalistic conventions of Hollywood realism. Moreover, it is a kind of adolescent version of Indiana Jones: Ferris constantly avoids being discovered only through the most impossible and fortuitous circumstances. Ferris himself is a kind of cool, popular, computer nerd. On the surface he appears to be not a troublemaker, but a rather superficial seeker of pleasure: the fact that he doesn't have a car constantly seems more important to him than issues or beliefs—and he constantly espouses a sort of conservative individual-ism: "A person should not believe in isms, he should just believe in himself." But this attitude, and Ferris's apparent commitment to fun, belies a number of deeper feelings. Ferris is condemned—and he accepts it as inevitable and even right—to a life which he seems not to welcome. As he repeatedly says, "Life moves pretty fast. If you don't stop and look around once in a while, you can miss it" (echoing Risky Business's "Sometimes you've just got to say, 'What the fuck'"). Like the characters in The Breakfast Club, Ferris seems to accept his imprisonment, and can only seek out temporary escapes, moments when the reality of life is manifested because of his own power, through his own actions. But even more importantly, it becomes clear in the end that this film belongs to the subgenre of "salvation plots," for it is at least suggested that the entire day (during which Ferris, his girlfriend and Cameron, his hypochondriac best friend, avoid school and attempt to have the most fun they can) has been staged for Cameron's benefit. It turns out that all of Cameron's problems are due to his oppressive family situation. Until he can assert his own right to exist against the "sick" relationships into which his parents have placed him, he will be condemned to unhappiness, to reliving his own inadequacy. In the end, the film is triumphant when Cameron realizes that he must "take a stand" against his parents: "Right or wrong, I'm gonna defend it!" and assert his own right to exist. What follows—the absurdist race home—is anti-climactic, as the film itself acknowledges.

The entire genre of contemporary youth movies is often dismissed by critics, if not ignored. But these films are a key, not only to understanding the emergence and impact of music video, but also to understanding the changing place of "youth" in contemporary social and political relations. For while these films do hark back to earlier genres of teenpics, they are significantly different. And they refuse to privilege the earlier films or to treat them nostalgically. Rather, they are merely one among many self-conscious references to the media environment in which youth has been constructed, deconstructed and reconstructed. In the last analysis, the contemporary films bear little resemblance to the teenpics of the 1950s and early 1960s. For if the films themselves are self-consciously intertextual, their characters are often equally self-conscious, at least of their own ambiguous sense of, or contradictory search for, identity. In part, this reproduces in narrative form the fact of the multiple and competing definitions of youth available in the contemporary cultural environment: youth is alternating seen as something to be protected, victimized, celebrated, escaped and even sanctified.

If youth as a powerful ideological sign is something whose meaning is being struggled over in popular culture, then the signs of youth themselves have to be continuously reconstituted. In all of these films, there is an effort to define youth in some experiential terms which can transcend different styles, classes, desires and activities. That is, the boundaries of youth can no longer be taken for granted, traced out visually on the age or activities of individuals. Consequently, in these films, it not only seems irrelevant what it is that has to be accomplished (whether becoming the best bike-messenger, or saving one's best friend, or getting to dance on television), it often seems quite difficult to judge the age of the characters when they are not presented in high school. The Brat Pack, who have starred in many of them, are curiously capable of representing youth across a broad span of age groups, from high school to post-college. Youth is represented in terms of the experiential and affective consequences of inhabiting a certain place in the social order, of living everyday life according to someone's else's maps. But youth is rarely presented as intrinsically subordinated or as isolated from the dominant culture. Youth's subordination is always active, never taken for granted or pushed into the background. Moreover, that subordination brings with it the very real sense that youth is a position of power and desire, that youth can empower itself, in its everyday life, to survive and transcend its social position. The contradictions and possibilities of contemporary youth's position seem to push every other consideration into the background;

the films are often naively racist, sexist and homophobic, not in their everyday practices, but in the structural background within which they place themselves. In addition, the films are often puritanical, despite their superficial advocacy of the rock 'n' roll lifestyle. Drugs, nudity and, to a lesser extent, concrete sexuality are virtually absent. (The most blatant exceptions are either treated more as comedies than youth movies—e.g., *Porky's*—or are rather dismal failures—e.g., A *Night in the Life of Jimmy Reardon*.) While this may be, in part, a reflection of the conservatism that contemporary youth must work out its own sense of frustration and alienation. For what is at stake transcends any single element of lifestyle or everyday life: lifestyle is not merely a question of pleasure or fun, and neither pleasure nor fun is ever sought simply for its own sake.

These films celebrate the extraordinary moments within the ordinary everyday life of youth. Or perhaps they are about the power to transform the ordinary into the extraordinary and the extraordinary into the ordinary. The narratively ordinary youth who define the major characters are always, somehow, represented as extraordinary. If the 1950s constructed youth as either carefree and innocent or inarticulate, contemporary films provide models of youth who are always exceptionally articulate and knowledgeable, who have a real need to talk and to prove their abilities, despite the fact that they can never trust talk or such vain efforts at self-justification. These films are about a certain kind of loneliness and uncertainty and the possibilities of identity and belonging. Individualism has become a sentence; condemned to seek their salvation, locked into the patterns (styles, tastes) of their own conformity. In the end, these films resemble their avant-garde cousins, not in formal or aesthetic terms, but in narrative and contextual terms. They represent the historically specific situatedness of contemporary youth, the doubly articulated alienation of history and youth; they are powerful affective statements uttered from particular places in our society, the places occupied by youth.

The last observation I want to make about these films is quite obvious: they all have a rock soundtrack. Sometimes rock defines the object of desire, the symbol of salvation and transcendence, but if one reads across the different films, there is no necessary or intrinsic work assigned to the varied objects which serve this narrative function. And even when rock appears to be privileged (e.g., *Flashdance*), the real victory does not take place in the music but in the struggle to claim the music. The music, which may define the site of struggle, is at best the reward for a victory achieved elsewhere. More often, however, rock is incorporated into the narrative as part of the everyday lives of the characters (as is MTV in the later films). While it may be used (as in *The Breakfast Club*) as the empowering occasion for transgression, it may also be the soundtrack for other transgressive activities. In fact, more than anything else, rock is the soundtrack of the narrative representation of youth. Otherwise it has little privilege of its own.

Unlike the teenpics of earlier decades, in which either fun or resistance defined the taken-for-granted subtext, contemporary youth movies construct a dialectic between a certain sort of alienation and a struggle for empowerment. In so far as they are successful—and I have argued that they are—they compete with rock culture and even threaten to displace it as the voice of youth in the 1980s and 1990s. If rock seeks to empower its audiences by juxtaposing the transcending possibilities of everyday life against the social conditions of contemporary existence (so that everyday life is the site of the transcendence of history), these films rather cynically locate the very need for transcendence within the tortured boundaries of everyday life. If rock heroes exist ambiguously as people we relate to and people we aspire to, the star characters of these films refuse the responsibility of defining their audience's aspirations.

I am making what I suppose will be a rather unpopular claim: that these films construct a different relationship between rock and youth. For they speak about generations which have increasingly seen themselves visually represented, and that audience is broader than the high-school or college-age youth who populate their universes. Unlike the counterculture films of the 1960s and 1970s, these films refuse to accept any single definition of youth as the "proper" locus and identity. And unlike the teenpics of the 1950s and 1960s, these films claim to speak *for* youth. The visual representation has—or at least struggles to—displaced the privileged place of rock, even as it may represent it. Rock is offered, not as the measure of the authenticity of youth, nor even as the soundtrack of youth's lives, but as the soundtrack of youth's media representations, commercial representations of youth's own struggles for salvation and identity. Here visual narratives displace or at least challenge rock music, for the soundtrack of such narratives cannot also be the soundtrack of our lives (at least within the terms of rock's own ideology).

Authenticity and the limits of rock 'n' roll

I want to talk about the possible end of the formation of rock culture. I do not mean to suggest that the music of the 1980s is somehow intrinsically worse. Nor do I mean to suggest that there are objective musical criteria for rock which, for some reason, contemporary producers are unable to fulfil. In fact, I think the rock music of the 1980s is at least as good as any other period in postwar popular culture. Nor do I mean to argue that rock must necessarily politicize its fans—a task which contemporary rock seems decidedly unable to accomplish. I am not talking about rock as a musical form, or as a tool for political consciousness, but as a cultural formation. And as a cultural formation, rock involves much more than just music. It is ultimately dependent on the relationships which exist between the music, other cultural practices, the historical context, and the fans. It is for this reason that it is so difficult to define rock in musical terms, for what music counts as rock, at a particular time and place, for a particular group of fans, depends upon the way in which music is made to (or is able to) function within the everyday lives of its fans.

Objectively, rock is a postwar musical culture, produced by a reconfigured music industry, for an audience, self-consciously defined (by the industry, the audience and other social institutions) by a system of generational and social differences. On this model, rock is music made explicitly for youth, although it remains unclear whether youth is defined by the ever-repeating appearance of younger generations or by the historical appearance of a specific generation of youth. In either case, the socio-cultural field divided by youth's difference is always also divided by structures of class, race and gender. Out of this diversity, a variety of rock cultures are constructed. And often, one of these cultures is taken as the central, dominant or "proper" form of rock. But any attempt to define rock once and for all simply normalizes one group's articulation of it.

As a cultural formation, rock had a beginning and, it is reasonable to assume, it may have an end. It emerged at a specific historical moment, into and as a response to a specific historical context. There were identifiable conditions of possibility which enabled the rock culture to take shape and to occupy such an important place, not only in the cultural lives of its fans but increasingly in the cultural life of the society. I shall only address two of these conditions here.[1] First, the "baby boom" created a very real population explosion, creating a youth generation which had enormous consequences for postwar society. Not only did the baby boom present economic possibilities, it also posed very real social problems. And by its very presence, it was implicated in the growing ideological contradictions of America's sense of its own youthfulness. Consequently, rock functioned as a statement of, and response to, the particular forms of alienation determined by the contradictory structures of empower-ment and subordination into which the baby boom was placed. Second, the appearance of certain rather apocalyptic events, experiences and statements (from the boredom of the suburbs to the terror of the atomic bomb) increasingly presented the world as meaningless, history as irrational and the future as impossible. Whether these were merely the latest example of "fin de siècle" rhetoric is irrelevant for, in the postwar context, they had very real effects. They produced a crisis of sorts in youth's ability to connect the meanings and values which they inherited—the languages they had to speak and in which they had to live their lives—to the historically defined affective or volitional possibilities of survival and empowerment. Increasingly, gaps seemed to appear between the ideological possibilities of controlling one's life and the affective impossibility of intervening into the future. Everyday life seemed to be increasingly marked by places where youth was unable to anchor its maps of what the world means in its maps of what can and should matter. Rock, then, articulated the intersection of this historical experience of "postmodernity" with that of the alienation of youth.

If we want to understand the power of music around which the various rock cultures were constructed, we have to locate the music within this historical context. The power of rock depended upon its ability to be articulated into this context at specific locations, with a very specific mode of functioning. Rock opened up the possibility of investing in the present without the necessity of a future which transcends it. Or perhaps more accurately, it offered salvation without transcendence. It defined those places where ideological and affective maps could be stitched together. By offering itself as something that mattered, as a site of investment in the face of the impossibility of any rational justification for investing, rock culture continuously constructed and reconstructed new mattering maps which empowered fans in new ways. It articulated the need for investing in something (something has to matter) to the rationality of disinvestment. Rock then has to be seen as a tactical response to the changing context and place of youth in contemporary society. It offered a celebration of affective investment based on the historical impossibility of ideological investment.

Thus, rock refers to an affective investment in, and empowerment by, the cultural forms, images and practices which circulate with the music for different groups of fans, each defining its own taste culture (or apparatus). Rock is defined, for particular audiences at different times and places differently, by the affective alliances of sounds, images, practices and experiences within which fans find certain forms of empowerment. Rock culture can only be described as the historically changing, overlapping systems of competing and sympathetic apparatuses, or by its mode of functioning in everyday life.

What defines rock's difference—what made it an acceptable, even an important investment—is simply the fact that it matters.[2] It offers a kind of salvation which depends, in the last instance, on our obsession with it. It constructs a circular relation between the music and the fan: the fact that it matters makes it different; it gives rock an excess which can never be experienced or understood by those outside of the rock culture. And this excess in turn justifies the fan's investment in it. Rock refers, in this sense, to the excess which is granted to the music by virtue of our obsession with it. By virtue of the fact that it matters, rock is granted the excess which justifies its place. Thus it is not so much that rock's real difference matters, but rather the fact that it matters that defines its difference. Rock is empowering because it makes mattering matter again.

Consequently, the musical content and lyrical ideology of rock are always secondary to, or at least dependent upon, the fan's assumption of rock's excess, an excess produced by the ways rock is placed in the fan's everyday life. The "place" of rock defines possible mattering maps which specify the different forms, sites and intensities of what can matter. It positions not only the elements of rock culture but other aspects of everyday life. It can determine how other things matter. Thus, for example, within rock's mattering maps, entertainment matters, but in a very different way. Or, to use a different sort of example, the fact that rock is usually located outside of the ideological institutions of the family and school (which are responsible for disciplining youth) does not guarantee rock's inherent opposition to these institutions. How rock occupies its place, how it is "charged," cannot be separated from how it "charges" or invigorates the fan's life. For rock works by offering the fan places where he or she can locate some sense of their own identity and power, where they can invest and empower themselves in specific ways. It is the investment in and of rock which determines other necessary and possible investments. It is in this sense that rock is enabling or empowering.

The question, then, of rock's death is a question about its changing conditions of possibility, and about its changing place—as a measure of the possibility of our investment in it. It is not merely a question of whether rock still matters, for lots of things matter in many different ways. The question is, does it matter that it matters? While I think that the historical conditions which enabled rock have changed significantly, I will focus on the question of rock's place, which is to say, on the functioning of rock's excess. But if this excess is not objectively contained in the music, how are we to measure its presence and its effects?

If the question of rock's excess escapes any normative definition of rock culture, it is nevertheless identifiable within the discourses and experiences constructed in and around the relationship between the rock fan and the music. Rock is, in part, always described by systems of tastes, and these systems are themselves organized around a particular ideology of excess, an ideology which distinguishes certain kinds of musical/cultural practices and certain kinds of fans (although the two dimensions do not always correspond). This ideology not only draws an absolute distinction between rock and "mere" entertainment, it says that it is that difference that enables rock to matter. This ideological difference has taken many forms, which are not necessarily the same: the centre versus the margin, the mainstream versus the periphery, commercial versus independent, resistant versus co-opted. Moreover, the same distinction can be applied in very different ways to describe the same musics. In different rock apparatuses, the difference can be explained in different ways; for example, the line can be justified aesthetically or ideologically, or in terms of the social position of the audiences, or by the economics of its production, or through the measure of its popularity, or the statement of its politics. In all of these cases, the line serves, for the fan, to distribute rock apparatuses "properly": on the one side, entertainment; on the other, something more— an excess by virtue of which even mere fun can become a significant social statement. The excess links the social position and experience of musicians and fans with rock's ability to redefine the lines of social identity and difference. That is, the excess marks the rock fan's difference. Rock fans have always constructed a difference between authentic and co-opted rock. And it is this which is often interpreted as rock's inextricable tie to resistance, refusal, alienation, marginality, etc.

Additionally, this ideology has determined the structure of the various histories of rock, whether they are produced by fans or critics. At every moment in its history, rock fans have always identified some music which, along with their associated cultural apparatuses and audiences, are dismissed, not merely as bad or inferior rock but somehow as not really rock at all. Critics and fans have always argued that at certain moments, the dominant productions of rock had become "establishment culture," that it has become dominated by economic interest, that it has lost its political edge, etc. Such histories read rock's ability to matter off the taste of the audience: i.e., that music can't possibly matter to anyone. The result is that the history of rock is always seen as a cyclical movement between high (authentic) and low (co-opted) points, although different fans will disagree over which moments constitute the high and the low points. Moreover, fans or critics who find themselves living in what they construct as a low point almost inevitably begin to predict the imminent "death" of rock. It is less important, for my purposes, where the cycles are located than it is that such cycles are a constitutive part of the ideology of rock's excess. Concerns that rock has died or is dying are often the expression of the continuing power of this ideology.

Rock's excess is articulated as an ideology of authenticity.[3] But here we must be careful, for sometimes critics use the term to identify a single—and perhaps the dominant—form which authenticity takes in rock culture. But there are many forms of rock authenticity: one need only compare the various contemporary performers who might qualify as authentic rockers: Springsteen, U2, REM, Tracey Chapman, Sting, Prince, Public Enemy, Talking Heads, The Pet Shop Boys. Part of the problem is that authenticity refers to two separable dimensions: first, how and of what the music speaks (the problem of communication); second, to and for whom the music speaks (the problem of community). Nevertheless, I think it is possible to isolate three versions of this ideological distinction. The first, and most common, is usually linked to hard rock and folk rock. It assumes that authentic rock depends on its ability to articulate private but common desires, feelings and experiences into a shared public language. The consumption of rock constructs or expresses a "community." This romantic ideology displaces sexuality and makes desire matter by fantasizing a community predicated on images of urban mobility, delinquency and artistry. The second, often linked with dance and black music, locates authenticity in the construction of a rhythmic and sexual body. Often identifying sexual mobility and romance, it constructs a fantasy of the tortured individual struggling to transcend the conditions of their inadequacy. The third, often linked with the self-consciousness of art (and manifested in art rock), is built on the explicit recognition and acknowledgement that the difference that rock constructs (and which in turn is assigned back to rock) is always constructed through the creativity and skill of the artist. Despite its rejection of the more common romantic version of authenticity, aesthetic authenticity still produces real and significant differences for its fans. This form of authenticity has—in so-called postmodern pop—increasingly become a self-conscious parody of the ideology of authenticity, by making the artificiality of its construction less a matter of aesthetics and more a matter of image-marketing. The result is that style is celebrated over authenticity, or rather that authenticity is seen as just another style. But this transformation already required the changing media economy which privileges the self-reflexivity of sight over the (assumed) authenticity of sound.

My claim that the formation of rock culture may be ending is not meant as another statement of the difference, intrinsic to rock culture, between authentic rock and co-opted rock. I am not claiming that contemporary rock is co-opted, for that would merely relocate my argument within rock culture itself. I am claiming instead that the ideology of authenticity is increasingly irrelevant to contemporary taste, that the difference no longer makes a difference, that the history of rock is no longer convincingly constructed on the traditional cyclical map. And consequently, the way in which rock matters, its place in the fan's everyday life, is changing. I do not mean to assert that fans do not distinguish, within their own tastes, between authentic and co-opted rock, but rather that they do not invest the difference with any power of its own. While the music may still matter to them, it matters in a different way.[4] Thus, I am not claiming that whatever comes after rock culture will not have its own values and empowering possibilities, but merely that the differences between the contemporary situation and rock culture are significant enough to warrant our taking note of them. If the ideology of authenticity is becoming irrelevant, then the differences do not matter and we can, in very noticeable ways, become rather blasé about the configurations of rock taste. In fact, as many critics have pointed out recently, there is a very real "crisis of taste" in rock culture, where, even for the fan, no single version of rock taste seems any truer than any other. This is manifested, not only in the increasing tolerance of rock fans, and in the increasing number of cross-genre musics, but also in the fact that it is impossible today to define any model of rock taste or culture which could serve as a definition of the centre, of the proper form of rock culture.

Rock's media economy and the end of authenticity

[. . .]

The new cultural formations of youth films and music video increasingly foreground the visual. It is not, however, a matter of attention but of priorities. One need not pay attention to the video screen; one's attention can still be determined by the song which calls one to the television. But increasingly, the visual images compete with the sounds as markers which tie the music to the experience and desires of the audience. And in this way, it becomes irrelevant, for example, that performers are lip-syncing their own songs, or that the performance is highly mediated through the technologies of visual and sonorial editing. In fact, the ability to manipulate the presentation becomes the very measure of affective power (e.g., The Pet Shop Boys).

The second result of the new media economy is that the newly emergent cultural formations have displaced the desire for authenticity into something else. But what is it that these new formations—in which the visual image displaces or at least competes with the privileging of the aural image—offer in its place? They have not given up the demand for a transcendence of and within everyday life, for the possibility of salvation. But they have instituted a new affective logic or, more accurately, they have increasingly foregrounded an element of the rock culture which had previously existed only in contradiction with the ideology of authenticity: namely a logic of authentic inauthenticity. It operated in the circular relationship of excess that located rock at the centre of the fan's mattering map: it is merely the fact that the music matters that makes it different (authentic) and it is this difference which justifies the fact that it matters. But the sonorial text of rock could never explicitly and reflexively code this logic. Increasingly, the media economy of the new cultural formations defines a tone which is determined by this logic.

All images, all realities, are affectively equal—equally serious, equally deserving and undeserving of being allowed to matter, of being made into the markers of one's own illusory authenticity, for all authenticity can only be illusory. The only possible claim to authenticity is derived from the knowledge and admission of your inauthenticity. If we think about the link between ideology and false consciousness, it depends upon a set of specific conditions: people are acting in certain ways which imply a certain condition of the world, but they do not actually realize this implication, nor agree with its conclusion. That is, people are doing something (e.g., acting as if there were a universal ideal measure of value—capital) but they don't know that they are doing it. The logic of authentic inauthenticity is the obverse of ideology: people know what they are doing but they do it anyway, even if they claim not to believe in the values implied by what they are consciously doing: "I believe in the truth though I lie a lot" (The Human League).

Authentic inauthenticity says that authenticity is itself a construction, an image, which is no better and no worse than any other.[5] Authenticity is, in fact, no more authentic than any other self-consciously created identity, and it has no more to do with subjective realities or objective relationships than the choice that anyone makes, at any moment, to present themselves according to the dictates of some cultural cliché. This logic foregrounds an ironic nihilism which refuses to valorize any single image, identity, action or value as somehow intrinsically better than any other. But it goes even further, refusing to accept that there is any basis on which one can justify investing oneself into any such term—even an imaginary excess. There is no reason which would make one's decisions about what matters rational. It is not that nothing matters but that, in the end, it doesn't really matter what matters. Of course, something has to matter. You have to care about some things and not others; you have to make certain choices and not others. You have to construct particular images for yourself and adopt certain identities but, according to the logic of authentic inauthenticity, you must do so reflexively (not necessarily self-consciously, one can just as easily take it for granted) knowing that there is no way to justify the choice. The only authenticity is to know and even admit that you are not being authentic, to fake it without faking the fact that you are faking it.

In terms of the visual representation of rock culture within these new formations, it becomes increasingly important for performers and directors to incorporate signs of their ironic cynicism. Within the emerging languages of these formations, authenticity is no better than and no worse than the most ironically constructed images of inauthenticity. The notion of authenticity is constantly reduced to a signifier of the performer's place within the rock culture: that is, it increasingly serves to mark the generic investments of the performer, to affirm their commitment to particular apparatuses within the rock culture. Or else it serves to reinscribe problematically the codes of performance (e.g., direct-address) which have become little more than the signs of a decreasingly powerful appeal to authenticity.

If this description of the changing media economy and of the emergent cultural logic of the new media formations is correct, it does suggest that the dominant contexts within which popular music operates in the contemporary world can no longer be described as, or in the terms of, rock culture. Nostalgia for the rock culture is an inappropriate response. We cannot assume that all popular culture, or even all popular music, or even all youth-oriented popular music, works in precisely the same ways, on the same grounds, with the same effects. History is constantly being reconstructed, often by our own practices, and often behind our backs. The very specific relationships and effects of the rock culture gave it an enormous power for a short time (and for many fans, it still has some of that power). But that very specificity also condemns it to a finite flexibility. The musical practices which have been at the centre of rock culture are increasingly being appropriated by, rearticulated into, new cultural formations. As the relations to and contexts of the music change, the forms and places of its power change as well. We cannot simply dismiss these new formations; we must look instead at how they are working, and how they can be made to work.

Notes

I would like to thank Andrew Goodwin for his valuable comments on an earlier draft.

1 Two other conditions of possibility are worth mentioning at least. First, the rapid growth of media culture and its extension throughout society and into everyday life depended on changing technological, economic and institutional relations (including a very specific organization of the music industry). Second, rock emerged into a rather unique social and political climate: the moment of the postwar consensus built around the corporatist or social democratic state. This consensus, which rearticulated the American ambivalence towards both progressivism and conservativism, resulted in the unique postwar form of "liberalism." On the one hand, a commitment to extending economic prosperity and civil liberties to all citizens was justified by an imposed sense of unity (the "end of ideology"). On the other hand, a paranoia directed externally to the threats of communism, totalitarianism and mass culture justified a strongly regressive and often repressive political and cultural ideology. The result was a very real ambivalence about emerging cultural forms, practices and values. This political context defined the parameters of the politics of rock culture, often enabling it to assume the liberal consensus and thus to reproduce many of the dominant forms of racism and sexism.
2 I do not mean to deny that textual gestures—music and lyrics—do not play a significant role in determining fans' tastes and the ways in which they are able to use specific musics. But this, it seems to me, does not account for the particularly powerful investment that fans make in their tastes.
3 The desire for authenticity has a long history, and in its most recent appearances is certainly tied to the rise of the middle class. Moreover, the image of authenticity in rock culture derives from a particular, historical imagination of black culture, and of the relationship between the blues and its black performers and fans.
4 For a different interpretation of these processes, see Goodwin (1988).
5 It is interesting to compare the various forms in which women performers have, in the past decade, regained visibility in the various rock apparatuses: e.g., the apparent but marketed authenticity of the Indigo Girls, the obvious inauthenticity of Madonna, the authenticity conferred via the college rock scene to Throwing Muses, etc. I also want to point to MTV as a very obvious site of this logic; it is not surprising, therefore, to find that MTV is increasingly going beyond music video to offer itself as a visual youth culture alternative to other channels.

References

Britton, Andrew (1986) "Blissing out: the politics of Reaganite entertainment", *Movie*, 31/32, 1–42.

Cagin, Seth and Phillip Dray (1984) *Hollywood Films of the Seventies: Sex, Drugs, Violence, Rock 'n' Roll and Politics*, New York: Harper & Row.

Clark, Al (ed.) (1980–3) *The Rock Yearbooks*, 1981–1984, London: Virgin.

Dellar, Fred (1981) NME *Guide to Rock Cinema*, Middlesex: Hamlyn.

Doherty, Thomas (1988) *Teenagers and Teenpics: The Juvenilization of American Movies in the 1950s*, Boston: Unwin Hyman.

Ehrenstein, David and Bill Reed (1982) *Rock on Film*, New York: Delilah.

Freud, Sigmund (1966) *Standard Edition of the Complete Psychological Works*, vol. 19, London: Hogarth.

Gaines, Jane (1991) *Contested Culture: The Image, the Voice and the Law*, Chapel Hill: University of North Carolina.

Goodwin, Andrew (1988) "Sample and hold: pop music in the digital age of reproduction", *Critical Quarterly*, 30 (3), 34–49.

Grossberg, L. (1988) "You still have to 'fight for your right to party': music television as billboard of postmodern difference", *Popular Music*, 7, 315–32.

Guattari, Felix (1984) *Molecular Revolution: Psychiatry and Politics* (trans. Rosemary Sheed), New York: Penguin.

Hoberman, J. (1985) "Ten years that shook the world", *American Film*, June, 34–59.

Lacan, Jacques (1978) *The Four Fundamental Concepts of Psycho-analysis* (trans. Alan Sheridan), New York: W. W. Norton.

Miller, Jim (ed.) (1980) *The Rolling Stone Illustrated History of Rock & Roll*, New York: Random House/Rolling Stone Press.

Robbins, Ira A. (ed.) (1985) *The Rolling Stone Review 1985*, New York: Rolling Stone Press and Charles Scribner's Sons.

7

The Silences of the Palace and the Anxiety of Musical Creation

ANASTASIA VALASSOPOULOS

> Music and songs are a very important part of Arab culture in general . . . in the Arab culture, they're tools to express yourself. An Arab man doesn't say "I love you," but in a song he can.
>
> Moufida Tlatli[1]

> Isn't the society that broadcasts the love songs the same society that puts the noose around everyone that falls in love?
>
> Nawal El Saadawi[2]

> Singing is a remedy for maladies,
> it can cure a suffering heart
>
> Umm Kulthum, "Ghanni li Shwayya Shwayya"[3]

According to Mark Sinker, Moufida Tlatli's 1992 film *The Silences of the Palace* is "stuffed with music."[4] The movie is concerned with the lives of female servants who keep house and entertain the last of the pro-colonial beys (princes) in 1950s Tunisia, and the use of music and singing is integral to the film. Poor, with nowhere to go and given limited access to the outside world as well as burdened with a mentality ruled by fear, these women are exploited, both financially and sexually, which finally forces Alia, the protagonist, to choose another life for herself, initially through her voice when she pursues her career as a singer and finally through the decision to continue her pregnancy. Though this particular ending has been thoroughly examined in other works,[5] I here would like to retrace the steps that allow Alia to use her singing as a vehicle for empowerment rather than view the act of keeping her child as that which offers the only positive potential. More particularly I want to show that the choices Tlatli makes as to *what* Alia will sing and *where* she will sing are choices difficult to discern, in terms of their significance, for the non-Arab viewer. Through taking a closer look at whom Alia decides to imitate, what songs she sings and how she uses the realm of entertainment to her own end, I will argue that the film is not simply indeterminately "stuffed with music" but that in fact the selection of music reveals a certain deliberateness. Also, the choice to place certain music in certain scenes marks a political move that opens up Alia's singing to new possibilities. I will then attempt to elucidate the implications of channelling all of these heavily weighted associations into film, a medium that, I will argue, pursues the signification attributed to oral culture in the Arab world, as well as to discuss briefly how it may be using music to do this. A slight digression here will reveal the importance of oral popular culture in the Middle East and its complicated relationship with literature. This might in turn inform the place of cinema as an antecedent to popular music and broadcasting.

Walter Armbrust in his work *Mass Culture and Modernism in Egypt* presents a significant insight into the consumer's absorption of popular culture. He claims that "the names of entertainers can be mentioned in almost any context to make a point [and] popular culture has been linguistically important in Egypt because it has historically been a qualitatively different vehicle for establishing national identity than official discourse", thus becoming in a sense close to the people's spoken language.[6] Likewise, in their study *The Ambiguous Compromise: Language, Literature and National Identity in Algeria and Morocco*, Kaye and Zoubir conclude

> that literature seeks domain over language and fails to achieve it is particularly clear in the African case of Algeria and Morocco. None of the many books [produced in the Maghreb] has truly seized the imagination of the people in the way that the songs of Oum Kalthoum or Feyrouz do. Unfortunately, neither impeccable political correct-ness nor linguistic virtuosity is a guaranteed *laissez-passer* into a people's in-rooted aesthetic sense. The issue of aesthetics in African literature is avoided and evaded in such correct approaches. Yet pleasure and beauty are the only guarantees of popular appreciation. It is doubtful if print culture will ever make that difficult crossing in any African culture.[7]

Further on in their work, they cite the well-known Maghrebi author Laâbi who humbly admits that

> his voice does not *give voice to others* in the same way as those of Oum Kalthoum and Feyrouz. The reference to these singers in his writing, and its own speech-like qualities, reveal a level of awareness of the vitality of organic culture as it has survived colonialism. The voice of Oum Kalthoum speaks immediately to a sense of *shared appreciation of beauty* which is as old as the tribe.[8]

What is being suggested in the above comments is that literature, inevitably restricted to those with the ability and inclination to read, was overtaken in significance by popular music as it required less technical expertise to listen than to read. By the 1950s (the era in which *The Silences of the Palace* is set), with 72 percent of Lower Egypt and 68 percent of Upper Egypt considered as rural areas and with minimal literacy, radio was effectively established as the most popular information mediator. "Group listening to radio was great in Egypt . . . especially among the lower classes" and "listening increased [because] merchants or owners of coffee shops would have a set to attract customers."[9] Tunisia had been broadcasting radio since 1935 though, after World War II, all "private stations where requisitioned by La Radiodiffusion Francaise (RTF) . . . the bey's decree in 1948 strengthened RTF's direct control of the station by establishing for the first time, state monopoly of broadcasting in Tunisia. This control was later confirmed by 1953."[10] Tunisian radio was therefore strictly controlled by the colonial administrators yet was still very popular. This is obvious in *The Silences of the Palace* where Alia huddles up to a radio and listens, utterly transfixed to the sounds emanating from it. Also, in the servants' quarters the radio seems to be tuned in frequently.

It is important to my argument, and we need to keep in mind, that the "imagin|in|g" of "pleasure" and "beauty" in Arab popular culture is frequently located in a singing voice, and more importantly, in a woman's voice that *gives voice to others*. Music emerges as irreplaceable in the conceptualization of Arab culture and in particular functions as a beacon of authenticity and splendour. This was and is made possible through advanced broadcasting methods and media technology. In particular, the music of the celebrated singer Umm Kulthum[11] (1904–1975) stands out as *the* example of this splendour for reasons that I shall elucidate below. Umm Kulthum has, over the years, become synonymous with the crucial and material existence in Arab culture of the notion of the "authentic" (*asil* in Arabic). The now unquestioned cultural certainty of Umm Kulthum as a repository of this *asil* makes it necessary for us to trace this possibility. To return for a moment to *The Silences of the Palace*, it is Umm Kulthum whom Alia imitates, and Umm Kulthum's renowned and well-known songs that she sings in public and in private. To understand the importance of this, we need to journey a little further into the myth that is Umm Kulthum—"Legendary Songstress of the Arabs."[12] Concurrently, Kulthum's involvement with Arab politics and her intimate connections with the then Egyptian president Nasser's plans for a pan-Arab nation free from colonial influence render her even more consequential in Tlatli's film. I will argue that Kulthum's fame was such that it would have been impossible not to be aware of her songs and music and, by extension, her involvement in public life. Ultimately I want to reveal that Alia, through choosing to sing Umm Kulthum songs, aligns herself with this powerful image, thus lending her performance a legitimacy that allows her to move up from her position of servitude to that of singer and artist. The complicated connections that are not immediately available to the non-Arab viewer, when deciphered, offer a varied interpretation of the use of music in this particular film with singing/acting as a metaphor for the much desired liberation from colonial/patriarchal forces.

Umm Kulthum's life and work have been documented in Virginia Danielson's ground-breaking work *The Voice of Egypt: Umm Kulthum, Arabic Song and Egyptian Society in the Twentieth Century*. Called a possible "hidden feminist" of the Middle East, I want to show that Umm Kulthum managed to empower herself by posing/performing as the maternal figure that could speak of the forbidden-to-her "love, nation or religion" (the "umm" in her name is Arabic for mother).

Though renowned for daring to sing risky songs, Umm Kulthum's demure physical appearance as well as her public connections aided in her accomplishments. Her songs, in embracing such vast topics as mentioned above, allowed her to move between repertories, advancing each one when necessary. Privately, Umm Kulthum remained visually (and virtually) "asexual" and so in a sense redirected all her created emotions *back to the audience* (embodying these erotic emotions materially by way of hair/dress and mannerisms would have jeopardized her role as receptacle of *asil*). Umm Kulthum was able to create these emotions in any given performance in order that she could break the rules *within* her singing. How she successfully orchestrated this shall be explored briefly below. Although I do not wish to diminish the importance of the fact that Alia in Tlatli's film has a very beautiful voice for which she is complimented, I do want to emphasize that embedded in this is a *recognition* of whom she is trying to emulate. I believe that her voice is measured against that of Umm Kulthum. Towards the end of the film Alia admits that she had always felt her songs were stillborn. I shall return to this later as it is after a courageous indiscretion on her part, an indiscretion that breaks with the rules adhered to even by Umm Kulthum, that she becomes a dangerous and unwanted figure. First, a little elaboration on Umm Kulthum.

Tarab is the Arabic emotive word used to describe the enchantment of one by a piece of music, usually evoked by the voice of the singer who is rendering the particular piece of music. To evoke this sense of oneness with the song and so by definition with the performer and the performance, various techniques were in use in the repertory of Umm Kulthum. Danielson explains *tarab* as "the pleasure of listening to a wonderful singer all night; the excellence of the singer who could enchant her audience till dawn . . . the marvellous strength of the voice that could sing until daybreak."[13] To achieve this, certain techniques associated with musical rendition had to be adhered to in order to centralize the *voice* of the singer; *tarab* was no simple feat:

> provided a song was interesting to the listeners, the virtuosity of the piece itself . . . would have virtually precluded one potential for audience rowdiness . . . singing along. The emotional impact of the monologue text and its theatrical aim emphasized the solo singer's role as the center of attention. A by-product of the through-composed structure, virtuosic display and the absence of chorus was to rivet *respectful and appreciative attention to the singer.*[14]

As shown above, *tarab* was connected to the singer in the first instance, it was what the singer *generated*. When Alia performs Umm Kulthum songs, there is a respect given to her from the audience made up of the *beys* and their guests for whom she is called to sing. Though Ela Shohat in her article "Gender and Nation on Middle Eastern/North African Film and Video" claims that "This invitation comes partly because of her singing talent but no less because of the sexual advances she begins to experience as soon as one of the masters notices that the child has turned into a young woman"[15] the invitation in question comes from the *bey* that we assume to be Alia's mother's lover. As there is no hint of incest, I am inclined to read this invitation as one where the *bey* can share the beauty of Alia's voice with others. In order to highlight this, he accompanies her singing on his lute.

Tarab, in turn, was an element incorporated into all of Umm Kulthum's vast repertory, in the love songs as well as the religious and nationalist renditions. Thus, by extension, she was able to occupy the position of a *dignified* singer of passionate lyrics, a title no woman singer had been able to hold successfully. Clever oscillation between these styles ensured that Umm Kulthum was known and remembered for an array of singing styles: namely, that she could sing religious songs as well as nationalist songs convincingly, and most importantly that she could consequently sing about love and passion as though they were discussed freely and without inhibition. This notion is evocative and ensured Kulthum's growing popularity. In the 1950s she sang "nationalist songs for the new republic," thus making her political alignment more solid. Though other singers where involved in similar projects, in the case of Umm Kulthum, these nationalist songs "constituted almost |50 percent| of her repertory |between 1952–1960|"[16] which puts us squarely at the time of Tunisian independence from the French colonial administration in 1956. Umm Kulthum's choice suggested political alignments and highlights her participation in the new emerging nationalism of Nasser's state. Although Danielson argues that Umm Kulthum did not directly involve herself in politics, Hammadi ben Hammed in his work *Oum Kalthoum* does make a case for her role as ambassador for Nasser's plan of a pan-Arab state. Though it is difficult to disprove either, I would be inclined to argue that though Umm Kulthum may not have been intensely political in the activist sense, she did become close friends with Nasser, and this personal affiliation led her to be intensely identified with Egypt's cause, affirming some type of nationalist alliance. She "became willing to speak on issues she considered to be important to every citizen, to remind Egyptians of their national heritage through her expressed opinions as her well as her musical style."[17] Umm Kulthum undoubtedly retained a strong patriotic inclination and nowhere is this more evident than in her songs of and to the new president himself. However, an overtly political stance would have jeopardized her career and objectives. Umm Kulthum sang ambiguous lyrics that can be read on several different levels in order to avoid direct association with particular political movements. An example here of a song to Nasser, "Gamal, Emblem of Patriotism" (1954), emphasizes the love and respect for a brave man rather than a particularly violent political stance:

> Gamal, emblem of patriotism
> you are the leader of our republic
> the most beautiful of our Egyptian celebrations
> Repeat after me,
> The most beautiful of Egyptian celebrations
> was your rise to the leadership of the Republic.
>
> For your dedication to the nation
> we have kept a place for you in our heart
> and the heart protects its loved one
> and is not lured away by loftier affections,
> strong are the promises that the heart makes
> Repeat, repeat after me!
>
> You have freed the Nile from its usurpers
> that are restless and desperate
> In Egypt, today, you have lit a guiding light
> In its shine all countries converge
> You have united the Arab world!
> Repeat, repeat after me![18]

Such revolutionary renditions were popular with the people and secured an audience that could be certain of her affiliations to the new regime and its anti-colonial objectives ("You have freed the Nile from its usurpers"). Her close ties with the political regime also ensured a type of unacknowledged propaganda. Affirmation of a new political power and exultation over its leader left no doubt of Umm Kulthum's nationalist commitment.

Ultimately, the significance of Umm Kulthum in respect to a modern, Arab or non-Arab audience is that she attained recognition at a time of intense political and social upheaval in a country that was still fighting for colonial liberation while trying to maintain a hold on internal concerns, including a reappraisal of religion and traditional Arab values (revivalism). A female singer, valued as it were from outside the dominant discourse, encased within her well-protected domain of entertainment, takes all these factors and moulds the inherent components of a song to make it her own. Umm Kulthum sang a wide range of religious songs that aided the creation of a platform from which to sing nationalist songs and ultimately love songs. Her grandeur was that she sang of religion, her home land, her imaginary love, and in doing so convinced everyone that she was part of all that constituted Islamic and Arabic thought, that she could create *tarab* though she embodied *asil*. In short, Umm Kulthum was a formidable figure. Her fame spread throughout the Arab world and, as *The Silences of the Palace* portrays, no one was left untouched.

Finally we come back to Alia. At significant moments in the film, Alia aligns herself with the dominant figure of Umm Kulthum, and by extension with a particular type of music. As a child, she discovers her love of music, especially the lute. Music pervades the servants' quarters and accompanies all the events of their lives. Significantly, though, as Romney points out:

> Upstairs, where the princes live, is |also| the realm of silence |for the servants|. Downstairs, the servant women sing, drum and squabble. But for Alia, finding a musical voice will be perilous—it will make her an object of predatory lust and her mother's jealousy, and lead to the scandal that causes her name to be silenced. |Alia disappears at the end with a revolutionary.|[19]

Music accompanies every step of the lives of these women. Death, birth, Alia's sickness, where she refuses to speak after she witnesses the rape of her mother by one of the *beys* (but out of which she recovers when her mother and a close friend use all their savings to buy her a lute), the revolution, celebrations; there is not an event to which music does not contribute. On the first occasion mentioned above at which Alia is invited to sing, she recites her favourite Umm Kulthum song, one that she has been practising, "Lesa Faker." This is a well-known love song:

> Do you think that my heart will still give you trust?
> Or one word will bring back what used to be?
> Or do you think that one look will reconnect
> The longing/yearning with the affection?
> Do you still remember?
> That was in the past
> Do you still remember?
> That was in the past
> Do you think that my heart will still give you trust?
> Ah! Or do you think that one word will bring back what used to be?
> Or do you think that one look will recreate the tenderness and passion?
> In my heart, all my days were spent in tears . . . that was my life
> How often you took my love for granted!
> So each time my tears ran they wiped off my hope in you and my patience
> In my heart, all my days were spent in tears . . . that was my life
> Words! words! are all that are left now
> My love has vanished with my wounds.[20]

I feel that Alia's choice ensures a level of respect not attributed to her mother, who is often called upon to belly-dance and who is gazed at by male and female viewers alike. The music rendered by Alia, through its association, allows her to be an artist, a performer of difficult, enchanting songs. In the most significant scene of the film, Alia's moment of triumph, she is asked to sing at the *bey*'s daughter's wedding. Her rendition of an Umm Kulthum song is accomplished and everyone is transfixed. However, Alia uses the subtly achieved concentration to surprise the audience. As they listen to her singing and are caught up in her musical achievement, Alia suddenly stops and begins to sing a revolutionary song that is popular among the Tunisian militant groups and that she has heard on the radio. Guests leave the banquet room as their position is symbolically threatened. To adapt Umm Kulthum is to place Alia among the great singers of the Arab world. Alia does not choose to emulate any other singer but Umm Kulthum and when she leaves the palace and sings at weddings for a living she sings Umm Kulthum songs, in this way aligning herself with Umm Kulthum's achievements. Though Alia's voice is prostituted at cheap weddings where everyone talks and no one listens (in stark contrast to her singing at the *bey*'s palace), Alia remains true to the talent that has led her away from her entrapment.

Several significant issues arise from these plot developments. In a sense, knowledge of Umm Kulthum precludes the associations I mention as they are already present in the consciousness of the audience. When viewing Alia sing, the audience in the film and the audience of the film make the connection with Umm Kulthum and credit her with the respect she is due. By taking on the Umm Kulthum tradition, she strengthens her previously powerless position, and gives herself access to a world that she was excluded from, where she will be able to perform her later ultimate transgression.

Alia uses the opportunity offered to her at the wedding to sing Tunisia's song for independence. As the *bey*'s children's tutor, who is simultaneously an underground revolutionary hiding from the French authorities, lurks in the shadows and watches her sing, Alia breaks into the revolutionary anthem that speaks of freedom and the necessity of breaking away from oppression. Though this has also been read as a plea for Alia's freedom, I do not want to diminish the empowerment achieved through singing itself. Unlike Umm Kulthum, Alia cannot afford subtlety and has to reveal her political leanings. In a sense, this action foresees her downfall. As she herself claims towards the end of the film, "my songs were stillborn." Alia risks herself in her transgression and destroys any hope of achieving success as a singer. Ironically, her openness and bravery do not coincide with Umm Kulthum's manipulation of repertory. Alia bluntly moves from one type of song to another, simultaneously leaving Umm Kulthum's repertory and entering the dialectic that separates her from the aristocratic princes. Were she to have sung a song with abstract political overtones, we could have imagined a different future for Alia, one in which her songs are alive. The notion of "stillborn" evokes the image of life that is cut off without warning, a situation where you may be led to expect life but instead come face to face with death: still/born, born but still, alive but dead at once. The act of giving birth is synonymous with allowing life to reveal itself yet in stillbirth this process is brutally halted. It is interesting that Alia uses this phrase because it suggests to me that Alia's songs, while in her mind, are alive and represent the fulfilment of her creative urge. Once sung, though, once let out into the open, they meet with an audience which does not care, which views her songs as crude entertainment. Though Alia continues to perform Umm Kulthum songs (interestingly, the song Alia recites most, "Lesa Faker," was not performed until 1963; I wonder if Tlatli uses this song because of its popularity *now*, rather than in the 1956 of the film?), she no longer retains the aura of her previous performances. I believe this to be a strategic move on Tlatli's part, as though to signal to us that Alia cannot survive as a performer because she has not learned to conceal her political leanings. Alia's honesty, courage and naivety regrettably result in her failure as an entertainer. Nevertheless, it does point out the difficulty of performance for a woman in the Arab world, and, more than that, it offers us insight into the complications surrounding women's role in popular culture.

I consider issues of recognizability to be integral to this film. Almost all of the songs are well known and appeal to an Arab audience which is attuned to what the songs mean and to whom they are originally attributed. Music then seems to be introduced into the film in order to suggest several meanings to the audience that it assumes they are aware of. What I find most interesting are the different meanings derived from this music by an Arab audience rather than a non-Arab one. While invariably read as a liberating activity by a non-Arab audience, I tend to want to read Alia's singing as the *difficult* route to freedom. Mark Sinker in his review of *The Silences of the Palace* writes that "|Alia| hopes to make her escape route |through music|."[21] Though this may be correct, Alia chooses an impossible route as the ideal reveals itself to be too unreachable. This sense of music is not liberating. In fact, it imprisons Alia and she becomes a parody of the legendary singer as the audiences she performs to talk throughout her performance, an unheard-of occurrence at Umm Kulthum's concerts where persons only applauded and exhibited emotion at her signal and were otherwise totally silent. Alia's failure as a singer can be attributed to her high aspirations and to the impossibility of fulfilling those aspirations within a culture that makes it very difficult to retain respectability within the entertainment industry. Though Umm Kulthum came from a poor peasant family, she had received training in Koranic recitation and had excellent knowledge of official classical Arabic. As Alia herself tells her partner at the beginning of the film (the film is relayed in a series of flashbacks), she has once more been harassed at the wedding celebration where she is singing. It was always in defiance of the popular "cheap" image of public female entertainers that Umm Kulthum herself had risen to fame. Umm Kulthum is said to have exhibited a "dignified demeanour |and| raised the level of respect for female singers generally."[22]

The film makes obvious the chasm between the world of professional music created to be thought of as an independent art form versus the uncomplicated use of music in ritual and everyday life. For example, the songs that are sung while the servants cook the meals, wash the cotton, inaugurate the young Alia, and so on are all integrated into daily activity. The dichotomy is further revealed when we learn that one of the *bey*'s daughters, Sara, is learning to play the lute. Alia is allowed to sit in on the lessons but is forbidden by Sara's mother to handle the instrument. Alia begs to borrow it one day but at her own risk. We also learn that Bey Sidi Ali, whom we presume to be her father, finds expression through playing the lute, too. Though Alia and the servants have access to the radio and their own repertoire of popular ritualistic songs, it is the *beys* who have *access* to sophisticated instruments and who can *distinguish* Alia's excellent rendering of Umm Kulthum's songs. Though Umm Kulthum was extremely popular among people of all classes ("On Thursday evenings, employees and labourers rush|ed| back home from work so as not to miss the transmission of Umm Kulthum's concert"[23]), she was also credited with bringing culture to the masses. In a sense, Alia does not have access to the structure that could support her ambition (namely educational opportunities). Egypt in the 1950s under Nasser was interested in promoting the arts. According to Nieuwkerk, there began with Nasser's rule a "post-revolutionary Arab nationalism and Islamic socialism, a re-appraisal of Arabic culture; folk art, folk music and folk dance, all of which glorified traditional Arabic culture,"[24] while Tunisia was still under colonial rule until 1956. Could this be the reason for Alia's failure?

In a sense we have traced Umm Kulthum's career ahistorically but the 1950s were certainly most significant ones in terms of political involvement. By 1956, the year of Tunisia's independence, is it still too early for the repetition of history? Is Alia a testimony to the uniqueness and non-repeatability of another Umm Kulthum? In other words, can Alia's experience with music function in the film as a metaphor for the difficulty of class movement and equality in the real time of the film, the 1960s? Tunisia is free of colonial rule yet Alia's partner will not marry her and continues to expect her to have abortions. She continues to prostitute her voice in an act of nostalgia to her unfulfilled dream. The death, at the end, of the last *bey*, Sidi Ali, brings with it the realization that her songs are now "stillborn" and that she must fulfil her dream through a live birth, one based in actuality and possibility. On entering her old home located in the grounds of the palace, Alia finds the old lute that has not accompanied her in post-revolutionary Tunisia. Alia gives up her desire to sing in public, possibly realizing that the move into music as an "art form" is one too difficult to achieve. It is worth mentioning here that Umm Kulthum was forbidden to marry the one love of her life, an aristocrat in the pre-Nasser era. She never had children and never spoke of the private details of her life. In many ways she was a constructed public figure; stillborn.

Tlatli's film utilizes music in the many different ways that I have attempted to elucidate. On the one hand, as other critics have pointed out, the music is a form of expression that the servants enjoy. However, the film also imposes another understanding of music, one that seeks to separate "low culture" from "high culture" as well as the people who belong to each respective category. Though Alia is empowered through her clever use of Umm Kulthum's songs, the difference between herself and the aristocrats who oppress her is highlighted when she enters the realm of "high culture" through imitation. Here symbolic use of well-known popular songs pitted against sophisticated musical compositions also serves to highlight to the audience the rigid class structures that are not easily soluble or indeed penetrable. Though appreciated for the beauty of her voice (realized through another's lyrics), this beauty is no longer audible once Alia sings the popular revolutionary song. I believe that the inclusion of these subtleties can only be realized in film due to the excessive importance of oral culture in the Middle East. That these complexities in the film have gone unnoticed reveals that there is a vast field of popular culture in the Arab world that has yet to be examined by English-speaking scholars. Certainties in one field, that of music, pass into film and bring with them a range of interpretive possibilities that allow us to read *The Silences of the Palace* from a different perspective, one involving class, creative possibilities and artistic life.

Notes

1 http://www.film.com/film-review/1995/9421/109/default-review.html.

2 Saadawi, Nawal El, "The Truth Sometimes Shocks", Index on Censorship, 11:3 (1992), 18–20.

3 Umm Kulthum, 1944, M.B. Ettounisi, lyrics, and Z. Ahmed, music.

4 Sinker, Mark, "*The Silences of the Palace*", Sight and Sound, 5:3 (1995), 53.

5 Cowie, Elizabeth, "A Tunisian Search for Independence", Women: A Cultural Review, 6:1 (1995), 124–128 and Naaman, Dorit, "Woman/Nation: A Postcolonial Look at Female Subjectivity", Quarterly Review of Film and Video, 17:4, (200), pp. 333–343.

6 Armbrust, Walter, Mass Culture and Modernism in Egypt (Cambridge: Cambridge University Press, 1996).

7 Kaye, Jaqueline and Abdelhamid Zoubir, The Ambiguous Compromise: Language, Literature and National Identity in Algeria and Morocco (London: Routledge, 1990), p. 133.

8 Ibid., p. 53, my emphasis.

9 Kamalinpour, R. Yahra and Hamid Mowlana, (eds) *Mass Media in the Middle East: A Comprehensive Handbook* (Connecticut: Greenwood Press, 1994), pp. 60–74 (p. 65).

10 Ibid., pp. 278–279.

11 I have decided to spell Umm Kulthum's name in this way. Variations are many including Oum Kalthoum, Umm Kalthoum, etc.

12 This is a phrase used by Habeeb Salloum in his article of the same name, "Umm Kalthum—Legendary Songstress of the Arabs", at http://almashriq.hiof.no/egypt/700/780/umkoulthoum/biography.html.

13 Danielson, Virginia-Louise, *The Voice of Egypt: Umm Kulthum, Arabic Song, and Egyptian Society in the Twentieth Century* (Chicago: University of Chicago Press, 1997), p. 137.

14 Danielson, Virginia-Louise, "Shaping Tradition in Arabic Song: The Career and Repertory of Umm Kulthum" (Ph.D. diss. University of Illinois, 1991), p. 157.

15 I am citing from the on-line version of this article at http://social.chass.ncsu.edu/jouvert/vlil/shohat.htm.

16 Danielson, Virginia-Louise, "Shaping Tradition in Arabic Song: The Career and Repertory of Umm Kulthum", p. 199.

17 Ibid.

18 Translation my own from the French in Hammed, Hammadi ben, *Oum Kalthoum* (Paris: Alif Les Editions Méditerranée, 1997), pp. 136–137.

19 Romney, Jonathan, "Women on the Verge of Rebellion", *New Statesman and Society*, 8:343 (1995), 33–35 (p. 33).

20 Translation provided from the site http://www.shira.net/lyrics.htm#Arabic. This song may be heard on http://www.aramusic.com/ramz/2044304.ram.

21 Sinker, Mark, "*The Silences of the Palace*", p. 53.

22 Danielson, Virginia, "Artists and Interpreneurs: Female Singers in Cairo during the 1920's" in *Women in Middle Eastern History: Shifting Boundaries in Sex and Gender*, ed. Keddie, Nikki R. and Beth Baron (New York: Vail-Ballou Press, 1991), pp. 292–309 (p. 304).

23 *Le Monde*, 12 November 1967. People (it was usually men who attended the shows) who could not afford to attend the live performance would catch the radio broadcast the following day.

24 Nieuwkerk, Karen Van, *A Trade Like Any Other: Female Singers and Dancers in Egypt* (Austin: University of Texas Press, 1995), pp. 44–45.

Must you Remember This?

8

Orchestrating the "standard" pop song in *Sleepless in Seattle*

IAN GARWOOD

Different formats: transforming the pop song into film music

[. . .]

While the bona fide film musical may have fallen out of favour, the songs associated with its golden era have remained a consistent presence in contemporary Hollywood, particularly in the romantic comedy genre. This chapter will discuss the use of the "standard" pop song in modern screen romances, with specific reference to *Sleepless in Seattle* (Nora Ephron, 1993), a hugely successful comedy featuring such musical staples as "Somewhere Over the Rainbow," "Stand By Your Man" and "As Time Goes By."

One strand of my analysis will explore the shaping of pop music into a kind of film music (as underscore), paying attention to its deployment in two familiar roles: as a key to understanding what a *character* may be feeling at a particular moment; and as a type of "guide," suggesting what the *viewer* should be feeling in relation to a particular moment. The other strand of my enquiry concerns the particular cultural assumptions that have influenced the use of the standard song in contemporary comedies: the perception that older songs engage more transparently and expressively with the idea of romance than more modern, and cynical, cultural forms. This assumption goes some way to explaining the recurring association of standard songs with romantic scenarios in contemporary cinema.

The standard song in romantic comedy

The inclusion of old songs in contemporary screen romance has generally been appraised according to the music's ability to indicate the general emotional sincerity of the films in which they appear. Steve Neale counts the standard song amongst the "heavily conventional" signs of old-fashioned romance that make credible these films' preoccupation with a belief in "true love": "In all these films poetic speech and the signs of traditional romance do their work: 'true'—and by implication, lasting—love is finally established."[1] Frank Krutnik, discussing the presence of Frank Sinatra, Ray Charles and Bing Crosby on the soundtrack of *When Harry Met Sally* (Rob Reiner, 1989), claims that the songs summon "a nostalgic vision of romantic certainty to guide the stumbling but inescapable progress of Harry and Sally towards coupledom."[2]

In both Neale's and Krutnik's characterizations, the songs are seen to possess a sense of confidence in their own romantic sentiments. As such, the music acts as a type of counsel for the characters whose romantic adventures it soundtracks: the happy resolution of these intrigues relies on the leads gaining the sense of self-belief that has been discernible all along in the songs that have accompanied their faltering progress.

This observation puts some distance between the song and the action it accompanies, thereby suggesting a different relationship between music and narrative to that ascribed to the traditional score. Claudia Gorbman comes to this summary of film music's conventional roles: "[Film music] bonds: shot to shot, narrative event to meaning, spectator to narrative, spectator to audience . . . Overall, the two overarching roles of background music may be characterized as semiotic (as *ancrage*) and psychological (as suture or bonding)."[3] The standard pop song in modern romantic comedy, as provisionally described, would seem to neglect the first two stages of bonding identified by Gorbman. It may connect spectator to narrative, as a vocal assertion of a belief in old-fashioned romance: a belief that needs to be cultivated in the audience for the eventual commitment of its characters to such an ideal to appear plausible. It may also bond spectator to audience: the success of the song's encouragement of a sense of belief in romance can only be achieved by a shared awareness amongst viewers of how the standard song is capable of denoting non-cynical (that is, non-modern) modes of romance. In this process, however, the song neglects to bond shot with shot, or narrative event with meaning. Under this conception, a song's "fit" with the specific narrative moment it accompanies becomes unimportant.

[. . .]

The effect of a pop song's "autonomy"

The composed score relies on the particular moment it accompanies in a film for its existence, but this is not so obviously the case with the pop song. The presence of a human voice and the awareness, particularly acute when the track is well known, that the music's origins may lay outside a narrative moment can encourage the view that the song possesses more autonomy from the image. However, this quality of "distance" can still be exploited for a specific narrative effect. A brief sequence contrasting Sam and his son Jonah's bedtime preparations with Annie and her current fiance Walter's, soundtracked by Dr John performing "Makin' Whoopee," illustrates how this looser bond between diegetic action and nondiegetic music can cast the singer in the role of detached commentator.

The scene consists of just three shots, which are accompanied by an abridged version of the song, Dr John's rolling piano intro segueing immediately into a brief verse. The music begins in the bathroom, a frontal two-shot of Sam asking for the towel and then rubbing his son's face with it roughly, but in fun, before marching him off screen. The singing only commences after a cut to the bedroom of Annie and Walter, who are framed in a similar two-shot, with their backs turned to each other. Annie passes a bottle of water, some tissues and a small medicine bottle to the hyperallergic Walter, who uses them to fill up and wipe clean his bedside vaporizer. Over this activity, Dr John sings:

Another bride, another groom
Another funny honeymoon
Another season, another reason
for making . . .

whereupon there follows a cut to later that night, Annie lying in bed unable to sleep, while Walter snores contentedly. The final word of the verse, "whoopee," plays over the shot, the song ending abruptly as it is superseded by Carly Simon's version of "In The Wee Small Hours."

Visually, this sequence compares the different levels of physicality displayed in the two relationships on show. Sam's and Jonah's rough-and-tumble sharing of the towel, germs and all, contrasts strongly with Annie's passing of the tissues for Walter as he prepares to ward off any impurities in the air. It has been a staple element of the romantic comedy to bestow upon its "wrong partners" a particular eccentricity which is symptomatic of their unsuitability.[4] In a film that sets such store in the power of touch (the "magic" that passes through Annie and Sam when they finally hold hands), Walter's lack of robustness is a fatal flaw. This sequence reaffirms his physical fragility by measuring it against Sam's and Jonah's assured tactility.

This comparison can be noted without paying attention to the soundtrack. Yet, by using "Makin' Whoopee" instead of scored music, the sequence also begins to suggest the desirability of Annie sharing in the healthily physical relationship displayed by Sam and Jonah. The song is preceded by Jonah asking his dad whether he will have sex when he starts dating again, and if so whether the woman will scratch up his back (he has seen this happen on cable television). Introduced after Jonah's precocious questioning, but before Sam attacks him with the towel, the song's entrance is neatly caught between the two activities upon which the term "makin' whoopee" puns. While the phrase on its own may refer generally to boisterous fun, of the type enjoyed by Sam and Jonah, within the song it clearly stands for sex. So that the contact between father and son is not granted unwholesome connotations, the lyrics which set the phrase within this context are not heard until the scene transfers to Annie and Walter. Here, though, the song moves from attunement with the image (even if the viewer does not recognize the melody, the barrelling piano is appropriate to the scene's unruliness), to ironic distance. Dr John's throaty rasp emphasizes the raucous undertow of the lyrics (whereas the clean swing of Frank Sinatra's version, for example, pays attention to its bouncing rhymes), making the bedroom scene accompanying it a particularly disappointing anticlimax. Isolating the final word "whoopee" (an exclamation of joy) over the close up of Annie's glum face makes resoundingly clear the discrepancy between the expectations of the soundtrack (and Annie), and the visual images with which it is associated.

"Makin' Whoopee" is able to achieve a distance from diegetic space that permits irony, because its origins are autonomous from any specific narrative moment. The audience's familiarity with the song is certainly a factor in why this process can be enacted so fluently, but the innovation of its delivery within the film is equally important. In general, the songs in *Sleepless in Seattle* are not represented by their most popularized versions. Of all the musical numbers in *Sleepless in Seattle*, "Makin' Whoopee," edited down to a short, self-contained excerpt, is the one that has been most clearly doctored to attain a specific narrative affect. That this organization of song and diegetic space results in a deliberate estrangement between the two indicates that the standard song does not simply provide an emotional landscape against which the onscreen romance can appear credible. Instead, "Makin'

Whoopee" works to the opposite affect, dissociating itself from the only romance the film has to offer at this time.

The different values of different types of pop

Two other songs are used ironically in *Sleepless in Seattle*, and these instances call into question another assumption about the use of older pop songs in romantic comedy: that the virtues of the "old-fashioned" visions of romance held by the songs have to be accepted as credible and relevant. The possibility of particular types of music being mocked through their filmic representation is exploited in *Sleepless in Seattle*. The sentiments of its two country and western songs, "Back In The Saddle Again" and "Stand By Your Man," are held up for ridicule by the way they are positioned within the narrative.

Interestingly, they are also the two most evidently classic versions to be used on the soundtrack. The musical numbers in *Sleepless in Seattle* are generally marked by an effort to renew them, to allay their canonical status with a freshness of arrangement that gives them a distinctive narrative resonance: Dr John's version of "Makin' Whoopee," for example, is chosen for the physicality of his voice. "Stand By Your Man," in contrast, is Tammy Wynette's definitive rendition, while the antiquated nature of Gene Autry's "Back in the Saddle Again" is marked by an accompanying crackle of static (like a dusty old record), and the primitive mono recording which reduces his voice to a flat nasal twang.

The two sequences in which the songs appear pair together as examples of the falseness of the romantic visions that maintain distance between Sam and Annie. Both reveal the characters' self-deception by highlighting their strained efforts to display confidence. In the first, "Back In The Saddle Again" soundtracks Sam's awkward attempts to set up his first date since the death of his wife. In the second, "Stand By Your Man" accompanies a montage sequence in which Annie receives a Valentine's Day card from Walter, informs her best friend that she has finally put all thoughts of Sam from her mind, and eventually arrives at Walter's hotel room in New York.

The irony within these sequences is of a different order to that contained in the "Makin' Whoopee" scene. The latter speaks from a position of authority within the sequence: it imposes a vital, physical urging upon diegetic action bereft of this quality, suggesting in the process that a clearly unfulfilled Annie would benefit from joining Sam and Jonah, whose playing around has been presented as in keeping with the song's tone. The ironic affect is created, therefore, by a divergence between song and image. "Stand By Your Man" and "Back In The Saddle Again," in contrast, are integrated into sequences whose textual strategies as a whole betray a distance from those used in the rest of the narrative.

As Sam phones up his potential date, as much as anything to prove to his son that he still understands the rules of engagement, the camera cuts restlessly around his fidgeting figure, switching between angles directly on the 180-degree line, and moving rapidly between midshots and close-ups. This uncomfortable framing amplifies the nervousness Sam demonstrates in his phone manner, underlining the impression that, at this moment, he does not quite know where he stands. While the lyrics of "Back In The Saddle Again" may seem more sure of themselves, detailing the manly activities of a Wild West cowboy ("toting my old 44"), the presentation of the song robs it of its potential to ridicule Sam's lack of wherewithal (as was the case with "Makin' Whoopee" in relation to Walter). The thinness of the song's primitive recording makes the voicing of its own certainties as unconvincing as Sam's attempts to take the initiative in setting up his date. This aural deficiency is felt by the viewer not only because of their expectations of high-quality sound reproduction in modern cinema, but also on account of the otherwise pristine versions of songs that occur throughout *Sleepless in Seattle*. Consequently, the song's vision of masculine behaviour, to which Sam is unable to do justice, is coded in any case as being antiquatedly irrelevant. Sam's approach to courtship and the sentiments of the song are shown to be as outdated as each other.

The framing of Annie's involvement in the "Stand By Your Man" sequence is as discernibly inelegant as the nervous cutting around Sam on the phone. As Tammy Wynette's song strikes up, there is a zoom from a tacky plastic loveheart in the window of a wedding store; as it fades out under Annie and Walter's conversation, there is a further zoom away from another kitschy symbol of romance: a globe encircled with a chain of lovehearts hanging from the ceiling of another shop. In between, Annie has made an all too self-conscious show of her determination to follow the advice of the song and stick with her fiancé, declaiming his name to the air as she hugs a card from him, telling her friend how much he means to her, and, as the song reaches its refrain, throwing her arms around him. Her attempts at intimate embrace, however, are considerably hindered by the number of bags hanging from her body, as well as her partner's natural clumsiness.

The two country and western songs in *Sleepless in Seattle* make a mockery of their own sentiments at the same time as they soundtrack scenes in which the two main characters make a mockery of themselves. Tammy Wynette's impassioned plea for women to remain faithful through thick and thin becomes the musical voice of the kitsch mise-en-scene, overemphatic proclamations and uncomfortable body language that indicate Annie's self-deception. Gene Autry's anachronistic vision of self-assured masculinity offers an appropriately unsuitable backing for Sam's misguided attempts to set up a date with the wrong woman. The lack of belief the film holds in the relationships on display at these points is conveyed by the way both music and image are presented as drained of emotional authenticity.

Narrowing the "gap" between song and narrative events

It may be the case that it is more common to create irony, of whatever type, by using an "imported" pop song, rather than through the specially composed score. However, there are at least two provisos to this observation. Firstly, as the use of the country and western songs in *Sleepless in Seattle* demonstrates, music and image may both be equally complicit in constructing an ironic effect. It is not necessarily the case that a sequence must maintain a quality of "distance" between the song and visual action in order to create irony, even if this is the strategy adopted in the "Makin' Whoopee" scene. Secondly, pop songs are routinely used in a manner which minimizes any sense of detachment between soundtrack and image. In other words, the song is often, like the composed score, asked to express through music the "true" feelings of the characters it soundtracks.

The clearest examples in *Sleepless in Seattle* of this type of use can be found in two more songs which, like the country and western numbers, can be regarded as a pair. Nat King Cole's "Stardust" and Carly Simon's "In The Wee Small Hours Of The Morning" accompany matching scenes of lonely reverie, in which the characters think of, and suffer ghostly interventions from, the two people that are weighing on their mind. On New Year's Eve, Sam walks around his house restlessly, finding no joy in the fireworks that shoot into the sky above him. Settling onto his sofa, the ghost of his wife enters the frame and talks to him. Similarly, after the "Makin' Whoopee" sequence, Annie is unable to sleep, "In The Wee Small Hours" beginning, like "Stardust," as she walks down the stairs. She is confronted by the source of her unease in the kitchen, where the radio replays Sam's phone-in conversation, his disembodied voice bringing Annie to tears once more. In both cases the song provides a suitable setting for the characters' sleepless pondering: "Stardust" describes someone losing themself in memories, like Sam; "In The Wee Small Hours Of The Morning" articulates that feeling of nagging worry which is keeping Annie awake. Unlike the other musical sequences I have analyzed, in these two instances the songs are attuned to the "real" emotions of the characters, that is to say the feelings they reveal when they are alone.

Romantic comedies as "incomplete" musicals

The closing of the "gap" between the song and other narrative events can be viewed in this manner, as a strategy which transforms the song into a more conventional type of scored music. However, the insistent integration of older songs into the narrative of *Sleepless in Seattle* allows for another possibility: the potential for this type of modern romantic comedy to be viewed as a kind of musical, albeit one whose attachment to the ideals of the bona fide musical remains incomplete.

[. . .]

An example of this incomplete attachment presents itself in *Sleepless in Seattle*, in the passage soundtracked by Joe Cocker's version of "Bye, Bye Blackbird." Of all the song sequences in the film, this is the one most choreographed as a dance. Announced within the film as the simple lullaby with which Jonah's mother used to send her son to sleep, the version used here is rapturous and expansive rather than homespun and intimate. The image engineers its pace to the rhythm of the song, and also responds to its sense of expansion, so that the sequence opens out the introspection the memory of the song has engendered in Sam to include the thoughts of Annie, the woman who holds the key to his escape from an entrapment in his past.

The song's quality of expansion stems from the gradual introduction of different instrumentation to bolster its rhythmic base. Beginning from a loose arrangement of drums and piano, a clipped guitar figure tightens the rhythm after its first refrain. After the second chorus, the song goes into its release, the piano lending it urgency by reforming its previous melodic, bluesy feel into insistently stabbing chords. The return to the verse from the release is accompanied by short piano phrases that undulate unpredictably, rather than stab insistently.

These rhythmic variations find expression in the image. On the introduction of the guitar, the sequence makes its first expansive cut, away from the close shots between Sam and Jonah in Seattle, as father tells son about his mother, to a long shot of Annie being dropped off in the street in Baltimore. The movement into the release is accompanied by another cut from Sam to Annie, the camera panning in step with Annie as she walks up from a deserted street onto the pavement. This step actually entails a small, but deliberate, kick of her right leg, which falls in time with the first stabbing piano chord. The sweep of the camera movement, compared with the static positions which characterize all the preceding shots in the sequence, adds to the sense of momentum being gathered. Finally, after the release Annie flexes her legs up and down while seated on a bench, her movement choreographed in time with the first melodic piano phrase of the new verse.

The graphic matches with the rhythmic base of the song are consolidated by a corresponding attempt to expand the image in accordance with the song's increasingly epic scale. As strings rise on the soundtrack, the gospel backing vocals become more prevalent, and Cocker's vocals become increasingly tortured, the action opens out from the initial close-ups of Sam and Jonah: to the long shot of Annie; an even more distanced view of Sam coming out to his porch; the introduction of movement with Annie's step up onto the pavement; the longest shot yet of Sam as he sits down on his bench overlooking the river; and then a closer shot of Annie also sitting down on a bench overlooking water, as the sequence reverts back to a series of close-ups, this time between Sam and Annie.

Expansion, as Richard Dyer has suggested, is fundamental to the creation of a utopian space in the song and dance sequences of musicals.[5] The numbers work as moments of escape into a mode of emotional expression that cannot be enacted in the non-singing sections of the narrative. Yet, the expansion in the "Bye, Bye Blackbird" sequence does not unlock its featured characters from their vague feelings of loneliness and isolation. Their expressions and body language as they look over the water consistently denote undefined unease, rather than being transformed into fuller expression through the utopian release of the song.

The sequence does, nevertheless, create a type of magical space. It provides a point of connection between two characters who assume they are alone. An emphasis is placed on the similarities between their feelings of isolation, the geographical distances between them being reduced to nothing during the process of reaching out and drawing together enacted by the song. In contrast to the number in the musical, however, this utopian moment (finding togetherness in the most unpromising of scenarios) is only felt by the viewer. The diegetic characters remain unaware and unmoved by it. The song enters as if to provide a suitable soundtrack for the emotions of Sam and Jonah, voicing their shared desire to hold on to the memory of their wife and mother. However the yearning, aspirational qualities of Joe Cocker's performance exceeds this narrative function, the sequence continuing to be organized around its affective charge rather than the visible emotions of Sam or Annie.

The "excessive" emotional range of the pop song

The ability of a nondiegetic song to exceed the emotional range displayed by diegetic characters finds its most extreme enactment in the first musical number after the title sequence. As Sam's emotional intervention on the radio phone-in show draws to its close, Annie, who has been listening in the car, pulls up to Walter's house, the lights from their Christmas trees visible on the left of the frame. Obviously moved by what she has heard (she has been crying, and her face is now sombre), the gloominess of her mood and the literal darkness of the side of the frame she occupies clash sharply with the festive glow of the lights. Similarly, a cut to Sam putting the phone down thoughtfully shows the reflection of Christmas lights in a glass panel to his side. The two shots are accompanied by a nondiegetic version of "Somewhere Over The Rainbow," sung by Ray Charles. Unidentifiable at first, as it emerges just before its chorus amongst the mêlée of sound created by Annie's car and the voice of the radio presenter, Charles breaks into the famous refrain just as Sam puts down the phone.

Claudia Gorbman has suggested that Ray Charles "speaks for" Sam in this sequence.[6] Yet, the song, both lyrically and in the way it is performed, does not correspond to the emotions the mise-en-scene suggests Sam is feeling at this time. Nor does Gorbman's observation take into account the initial emergence of the music over an image of Annie. Like "Bye, Bye Blackbird," Ray Charles's version of "Somewhere Over The Rainbow" is sung in the style of aspirational soul. The lyric's celebrated yearning for transportation to a magical place, as yet out of sight, is rendered faithfully by the longing contained in Charles's singing. There is no such aspiration registered in the deportment of Annie and Sam. The two shots of them reveal only sobriety: Annie may be lost in thought as she wonders why Sam's story has affected her so strongly; Sam is equally perplexed as he mulls over the strangeness of having been forced to reveal his feelings about his wife on air. Neither, though, could be judged to be looking forward to a scenario in which these nagging thoughts could be banished.

The sequence, however, continues to seek suitable visual imagery to express the sentiments contained in the song. After Charles has sung, "I know somewhere over the rainbow," there is a cut to a boat crossing the frame in front of Sam's house. Over this image we hear the number's final lyric: "the bluebirds fly, birds fly over the rainbow, why man oh why can't I?" The boat, beautifully lit up and passing serenely from left to right, is clearly intended as a representation of the "pot of gold" beyond the rainbow for which the singer yearns. A harmonious relationship with lights is integral to Sam and Annie's eventual coupling, but at this stage in the narrative they are estranged from light: blurred in the background in the shot of Annie; and distorted by its reflection next to Sam. Furthermore, there is no suggestion at this stage that they are asserting an active desire for that light to be brought into focus for them.

The song as voiceover

Standard songs in modern romantic comedies often do serve to set romantic standards (presenting a "nostalgic vision of romantic certainty"[7] for the viewer). This is not all they do, however, as their variety of uses in *Sleepless in Seattle* demonstrates. Yet, no matter how detailed the choreography of a song to a particular narrative moment may be, its specificity as a certain type of musical form, different from both the composed score and the song-and-dance number, is a crucial factor. The fact that these songs are not composed for a specific narrative moment (unlike the score), and do not emanate from the bodies of diegetic characters (unlike the number in the musical), can result in instances like the "Somewhere Over The Rainbow" sequence, where the song's own urgency of aspiration is registered in the mise-en-scene.

In this case, that urgency is provided by Ray Charles's vocals. *Sleepless in Seattle* offers examples of the particular role songs with words can play in narrative films. The ironic representation of Annie and Walter's relationship as they prepare for bed, for instance, is enacted through the mismatch between onscreen action and Dr John's earthy delivery of the lyrics of "Makin' Whoopee": the same effect could not have been achieved without the presence of a "commentating" voice on the soundtrack.

This suggests that words sung "offscreen" can act as a special instance of a common narrational device: the voiceover. Film sound theorist Michel Chion identifies the power of the voiceover (which he refers to as "textual speech") in the following manner: "Textual speech has the power to make visible the images it evokes through sound—that is, to change the setting, to call up a thing, moment, place, or characters at will."[8] The image of the lit boat during "Somewhere Over The Rainbow" is conjured up by Charles's "voiceover." However, there is no "pressure" on the film automatically to match the singer's words with an appropriate image. When a film character intones a voiceover, any significant divergences between offscreen commentary and onscreen action raise the possibility of the narrator's unreliability. The nondiegetic song is saved from this burden of responsibility, partly because the words sung are only one amongst a number of musical elements that could find articulation in the image, but also due to the quality of distance inherent in its use: a quality which necessitates an effort of attachment to be made between a song and particular narrative elements. A narrative film that consistently immersed itself in the details of the songs playing on the soundtrack, to the expense of its "story," would be as remarkable (and unlikely) as a film with a voiceover narration that bore no relation at all to the events being depicted on screen.

In the single shot of the boat, however, the "Somewhere Over The Rainbow" sequence does offer a glimpse of what such a film might look like. *Sleepless in Seattle*'s claims to classicism lie in part in its narrow focus on the romantic lives of its lovers: this film displays a "refreshingly old-fashioned" interest in the feelings of two human beings. Yet, by displaying faith in the equally emotionally "interested" voice of Ray Charles singing "Somewhere Over The Rainbow," this exemplary "human" comedy yields an interesting paradox: the presence of its human beings on screen is made momentarily impossible.

Notes

1 Steve Neale, "The big romance or something wild?: romantic comedy today", *Screen*, vol. 33, no. 3 (1992), pp. 284–99, p. 296.

2 Frank Krutnik, "Love lies: romantic fabrication in contemporary romantic comedy", in Peter William Evans and Celestino Deleyto (eds), *Terms of Endearment: Hollywood Romantic Comedy of the 1980s and 1990s* (Edinburgh: Edinburgh University Press, 1998), pp. 15–36, p. 25. Krutnik argues that "true love" for the film's characters in the new romance involves embracing the romantic ideal as a necessary fiction—notions of emotional sincerity are thus bound with a character's acceptance of their own self-deception. *Sleepless in Seattle* appears to me, however, to be an attempt to reassert the ideal of the "truly" sincere.

3 Claudia Gorbman, *Unheard Melodies: Narrative Film Music* (London: British Film Institute, 1987), p. 55.

4 Neale, "The big romance or something wild?", pp. 289–90.

5 Richard Dyer, in a keynote lecture given to a conference on music in film held at Southampton University in May 1996.

6 Claudia Gorbman, in a keynote lecture given to a conference on music in film held at Southampton University in May 1996.

7 Frank Krutnik, "Love lies", p. 25. It should be noted that Krutnik also discusses different roles played by the standard song in romantic comedies.

8 Michel Chion (translated by Claudia Gorbman), *Audio-Vision: Sound on Screen* (New York: Columbia University Press, 1994), p. 172.

PART THREE

THE FORMAL POLITICS OF MUSIC ON FILM

This third section focuses on the potential difficulties of joining musical and filmic modes of expression. Evidently, the pressure to create a harmonious formal whole is sometimes scuppered when radically different codes of artistic practice collide. And, although most books on movie music train their attentions on moments when music and image create an effortless rapport, there is much to be learned from the instances when the two seem to be talking over each other or arguing. What does any supposition that states that a soundtrack, say, "doesn't work" reveal about the ideological positions of tradition and taste? What does it mean for a soundtrack not to further the themes of the image, or for a narrative to be incapable of backing up a musical idea? Such problems lead us back to an understanding that these media cannot always be effortlessly aligned and that this often tells us a great deal about the enunciative and political limitations of film and music.

Gabbard interrogates the disjunction between music and the moving image through an examination of how African American jazz musicians have been drawn into the, by and large, racially exclusive spectacle of cinema. His concern is the fact that concepts of "race" in America (and beyond) are unevenly laid out within different cultural spheres. Music-making from various parts of the African diaspora has enormous global clout (although this does not mean it escapes racism), while the history of Hollywood production has kept African Americans in a much more marginal position, to say the least. In working through how (African American) jazz has been incorporated into the film industry, Gabbard reveals how integral such cultural spaces have been in creating the harsh regulations of social categories such as "race."

By investigating the relationship between existing "classical" music and animation (from both the Warner Brothers and the Disney stables), Brophy's chapter assesses how this alliance might support, or possibly subvert, certain class assumptions which are regularly projected on to the art forms in question. Brophy celebrates the ingenuity and ultimately the musicality of animation (as well as stressing how "animated" music also is), showing how formal ideas skip between the two different media. In *Fantasia* (1940) he spots a reverence towards the music, a desire for a synaesthetic smoothness and an integrity towards its aims. Whether the film achieves this or not is a moot point and one which tells us a great deal about the social standing of both art music and animation. In contrast, Warner Brothers cartoons like *The Rabbit of Seville* (1950) and *What's Opera, Doc?* (1959) are just as musical in their formation, but much less worshipful in their feelings about highbrow culture. Their lyricism is dextrous, but also bawdy and raucous.

Ultimately, both sets of cartoons provide highly attuned commentary on the cultural weightiness of such music, although each example has its own sense of how seriously to take this gravitas.

My own effort again attempts to penetrate how the image might try to emulate a musical presence—this time through the style known as "the MTV aesthetic." While critics have been known to find this mode of presentation a tasteless affront to certain visual norms and logics, I am keener to fathom what it might also offer certain sections of its audience and I do so by referring to various commercial strategies present in eighties and nineties youth culture.

Although the subjects of these chapters are diverse, they all raise intriguing questions about the ruptures—rather than the amicability—which can happen when music and film are placed side by side. This section of the anthology aims to open out film music scholarship so that it might also encourage the potential to enjoy (or at least seriously analyse, rather than dismiss) moments of incompatibility. These chapters begin not by noting the concordance of the film and music interplay, but by proving that their vastly differing histories and biases can cause as much mutual irreconcilability as they can happy alliances. Evidently, these clashes are messy scuffles to some and abstract beauty to others. Yet what is most important here is our dedication to sorting out what these reactions mean in terms of the fluctuating politics embedded in the film and music experience.

9

Whose Jazz, Whose Cinema?

KRIN GABBARD

Most jazz films aren't really about jazz. But then, most jazz isn't really about jazz, at least not in terms of how it is actually consumed. Jazz is usually about race, sexuality, and spectacle. Since the 1980s, perhaps even since the 1950s, it has also been about art. The carefully cultivated atmosphere in nightclubs, the photographs on album covers, the insider patter of jazz disc jockeys, the colored lights that play on musicians in concert halls, the studied aloofness of the performers—what Walter Benjamin (1969) would call the 'aura" of jazz—are difficult if not impossible to separate from the music. In fact, it may be more accurate to think about jazz as *inseparable* from its aura and from displays of race, sexuality, and art. But doing so would mean setting aside some forty years of jazz criticism that have characterized the music as an autonomous art form which, like all autonomous art forms, can be pursued outside its historical and cultural moment.[1] I would suggest that the myth of jazz's autonomy has served its purpose and that new myths ought to be proposed. The old myths—as well as the new ones—ought to he seen as products of particular cultural moments and ideologies.

[. . .]

Although much jazz criticism has been devoted to unraveling the old mythology and to taking political stances both acknowledged and unacknowledged, the unravelers have created their own myths. As almost everyone knows by now, the classical Hollywood cinema has regularly trivialized the lives of blacks, women, and ethnic minorities, often to the point of caricature. As Roland Barthes (1972) has argued, the film industry is one of the many institutions that create mythology by transforming *history into nature*, by presenting culturally determined situations as the inevitable product of natural law. According to 1950s Hollywood, for example, blacks may play jazz more "naturally," but it is in the "nature" of white musicians to surpass them by learning to play a music that people really want to hear. My goal is not simply to condemn Hollywood mythology but to examine its transformations more closely in hopes of learning something about jazz, the movies, and the American obsessions to which they answer.

In a sense, I will be writing the "other history" of jazz, the history that jazz criticism has been scrupulously devoted to correcting. I would strenuously agree that correcting this history is an admirable pursuit since it is shot through with bigotry, sexism, cynical manipulation, and popular misconception. This other view of jazz has been created by the movies but also by those novelists, photographers, and journalists who have looked to jazz for Otherness as well as for reassurance that they themselves belong to the healthy, normal Same. As David Meltzer (1993) argues, even those white writers who support jazz have engaged in "permissible racism" by idealizing a black other as spontaneous, transgressive, and ecstatically free of bourgeois restraints. By concentrating on jazz myths and their development, however, a writing of the other history can also reveal a great deal about the dialogic relationship between jazz criticism and popular representations of the music. The other history has even provided a meta-language for critics who are devoted to writing the more official histories. Thanks to Dorothy Baker's 1938 novel, *Young Man with a Horn*, the esteemed critic Gary Giddins can indicate the depth of his disappointment with a late recording of Miles Davis by writing, "Worst of all, |Davis| recorded a narcissistic sop to the airwaves with a title, 'The Man with a Horn,' that is scarifyingly close to Dorothy Baker's daydreams about trumpet players" (Giddins 1985, 80). Such statements suggest that a critical look at the old daydreams may be in order.

The myth of jazz purity

The daydreams, after all, often speak to very real needs. Almost from its beginnings jazz has provoked daydreams and associations. Like all music in the twentieth century, jazz has been heavily dependent on the technologies that make it available to the vast majority of its listeners. Jazz has always been heard primarily through mechanical reproduction, beginning with the national craze set off by the first records of the Original Dixieland Jazz Band in 1917. A condition of the music's existence on record, and later on radio, was the missing bodies of the musicians, who could be dreamed of in forms as romantic as anything in Dorothy Baker's novel. The myth of the music's autonomy is dependent upon forgetting what the technology lacks and also upon overlooking what it actually has. John Corbett has compared the conventional study of music to a massive act of denial: students listening to a work of Beethoven with a record, a turntable, and a set of headphones are asked to understand the music as if the technology staring them in the face did not exist: "This is disavowal, as in the Land of Oz: 'Pay no attention to that man behind the curtain'" (Corbett 1994, 36).

|. . .|

For many fans, whatever is gained by the reintegration of sound and image is lost in the subordination of jazz to narrative and the attendant ideologies of the American cinema. As both psychoanalytic and structuralist film theorists have pointed out, musical numbers bring the film's story to an abrupt halt (Mulvey 1975; Altman 1989). Since narrative is indisputably what most audiences crave, then a film about jazz or a film with jazz cannot dwell on the music for too long. The music gets shoved aside to make way for the action, or worse, the music continues, barely audible in the background while the actors talk. Still worse, performances by some of the most revered jazz artists are the least likely to appear on film. For many years black artists were simply left out or confined to short performance scenes that could be excised by nervous exhibitors.

Even when blacks were not entirely excluded, they faced the same reality as all jazz artists. On the one hand, those performers who play to the crowd—"Clap your hands! We love you!

You're a beautiful audience!"—seldom win the respect of the true believers, who prefer that performers devote their energies exclusively to the music. The devout fan who insists upon the music's autonomous value can choose to ignore the stage shenanigans of a Louis Armstrong or a Dizzy Gillespie and simply collect their records. The shenanigans might even be tolerated as a sop to the less sophisticated members of the audience, an interlude between the moments of improvisatory art. On the other hand, such interludes are what matter most to filmmakers. Consider Charlie Parker. At least in terms of what is known to exist, Parker was filmed for fewer than ten minutes during his fourteen years as a recording artists. Bebop was almost entirely ignored by Hollywood during Parker's life, so we can scarcely expect to see him popping up in movies. But when Clint Eastwood made Bird (1988), the first fiction film explicitly about Parker's life, the key moments were not the performance scenes but the spectacles that surrounded them. The most legendary of the visualizable moments in the Parker legend is the flying cymbal with which Jo Jones allegedly put an end to a young Parker's solo during a Kansas City jam session. In Bird, the cymbal flies repeatedly as Parker recalls the humiliation. At the end it becomes an omen of death.

Director Eastwood and writer Joel Oliansky invented an even more striking spectacle when they filmed their version of Parker's extraordinary "Lover Man" recording session of 1946. Gulping wine to stave off the effects of heroin withdrawal, Parker (Forest Whitaker) staggers his way through the tortuously beautiful performance. Told by the engineer that the recording is "very nice," Parker throws his saxophone through the glass of the recording booth. There is nothing in the Parker biographies to suggest that he threw anything during this particular session. Bird, however, protects itself against the charge that it has relegated music to spectacle by staging a climactic scene toward the end in which Parker walks in on a performance of Buster Franklin, a fictional alto saxophonist who had mocked the youthful Parker at the legendary Kansas City jam session. In the middle of the film, after Franklin has been driven to despair by hearing the mature Parker at a club date with Dizzy Gillsepie, he unceremoniously drops his horn into a river. Now wearing a zebra-striped tuxedo and playing what a member of his entourage calls "rock and roll," Franklin works his rhinestone-encrusted horn into an elaborately choreographed stage show while a large crowd cheers him on. Parker is of course appalled, chastising Franklin for only knowing how to play in B-flat and for never playing "more than one note at a time." But the real charge against Franklin is that he has subordinated his music to mere display. Much the same can be said of Bird.

Display in jazz is much more important than devotees like to admit. Especially for male jazz artists, the music provides a unique opportunity for sex and gender display. Part of what has made jazz so intriguing is the number of alternatives it has offered to conventional notions of masculinity and male sexuality. For me, struggling through adolescence in Middle America with no real interest in sports, jazz offered appealingly unconventional paradigms of masculinity that did not necessarily involve the brute simplicity of high school athletics. I found role models in artists such as Miles Davis, Art Farmer, and Bill Evans, all of whom could express elegance, vulnerability, and romance alongside the more conventional desiderata for young men such as power, technical mastery, and cool strutting. With varying degrees of consciousness, most jazz artists cultivate these qualities in their performance demeanor even if only within purely musical gestures. And, of course, the articulation of maleness and sexuality takes different forms as the age, social class, and historical moments of the artists change. Much the same can be said for the differences in performance practice among female artists, who have experienced even greater changes in sex and gender role-playing over the past several decades.[2] The current ideology of jazz writing tends to repress the artist's display, but this will undoubtedly change as poststructuralist discourses of the body make their way into jazz studies.

Policing Definitions: *The King of Jazz* and *The Jazz Singer*

I am excruciatingly aware of the problems raised by the term jazz. Many artists with permanent places in the jazz canon have rejected the term. Duke Ellington, Max Roach, and Anthony Braxton are only three of the most prominent. Before the modern era, jazz probably had a sexual reference, perhaps even evolving from an African word for sexual intercourse (Major 1994, 255). Early in the twentieth century it became associated with a specific music produced primarily by blacks in New Orleans. In the 1920s, after "hot" music had caught on with a national audience, the word came to mean nightlife and good times. The casual racism of the twenties simply repressed the African American component of the music. After all, the first jazz records that caused such a stir in 1917 were recorded entirely by white musicians. In 1926, Henry Osgood could write a book about jazz without mentioning a single black artist. One year later, the film of *The Jazz Singer* at least acknowledged black participation in jazz, but a white man in blackface was still "the jazz singer." The first talkie was not the first film, however, that attracted audiences with the term jazz while neglecting to include black actors and musicians. In his essay in *The New Grove Dictionary of Jazz*, Ernie Smith (1988) lists several movies with titles such as *The Jazz Bandits* (1920) and *Children of Jazz* (1923) in which the only goal of the consistently white characters seems to be "the pursuit of pleasure" (376).

Nevertheless, I am reluctant, on the one hand, to jettison the word jazz or, on the other, to redefine it in the more contemporary fashion that centers canonical geniuses but excludes some black premodernists and many white imitators. I will use the term broadly throughout this study if only to preserve the meanings that jazz has carried for filmmakers and audiences during this century. Jazz is the music that large groups of people have called jazz at particular moments in history. This broader sense of the term also acknowledges the extensive influence that jazz has had throughout cinema history, especially in terms of narrative conventions that were established early on. The 1927 *Jazz Singer* was a founding moment for a basic American myth of generational revolt and successful assimilation by second-generation immigrants. The myth was forged in the lopsided interracial romance of the Jazz Age (lopsided because the desire went mostly one way), but it was still alive sixty years later in *La Bamba*, the biopic about the Mexican-American rock star Ritchie Valens who found success with a large Anglo-American audience but never completely abandoned his own culture. In *La Bamba*, Ritchie even has Donna, a wholesome blonde trophy of his crossover success, at the same time that his musical desire takes him in another direction, toward African American male performers.

As the case of *La Bamba* makes clear, rock and roll long ago replaced jazz as the music of circumscribed rebellion and social change. In the 1920s, Bix Beiderbecke scandalized his bourgeois midwestern parents by playing music associated with the brothels of New Orleans. By the 1950s, however, the records of Bix Beiderbecke were unceremoniously trashed by young men in black leather jackets in *Blackboard Jungle* (1955). Although audiences were supposed to feel sympathy for the balding, bespectacled high school teacher (Richard Kiley) whose records were being smashed, the film itself became a recruiting poster for a new urban youth culture. "Rock Around the Clock" had been a minor hit for a little-known band called Bill Haley and the Comets, but when *Blackboard Jungle*'s director Richard Brooks chose the tune—perhaps ironically—to play behind the opening credits of his film, the record became a million-copy seller (Doherty 1988, 76). Kiley's character, who preferred Beiderbecke and Stan Kenton, seemed out of touch, stuffy, and elitist. A defiant youth culture built around the rockabilly sounds of Bill Haley was much more attractive for a significant portion of the audience.

Although the early meaning of jazz is forgotten in *La Bamba* and reversed in *Blackboard Jungle*, current notions of the music ought not to obstruct an understanding of how the music functioned during the first decades of the American cinema. Our current sense of jazz as art is less than fifty years old, and even younger in its institutionalized forms such as the new repertory orchestras and the jazz division at Lincoln Center. I believe that these contemporary understandings of jazz ought not to be read into interpretations of cultural artifacts from an earlier moment.

A revealing, though not entirely innocent example of how many Americans once perceived jazz is offered by the 1930 vehicle for Paul Whiteman, *The King of Jazz*. A more elaborate, more thorough denial of the African American role in jazz is difficult to imagine. Not surprisingly, the repression of blackness leaves its mark all over the film: there are constant allusions to African Americans, and much of the film explicitly evokes minstrelsy, the film's grand predecessor in the ambivalent appropriation of blackness by whites. Directed and "devised" by John Murray Anderson, the film is a gaudy, two-color Technicolor translation to the screen of the kind of Broadway revues staged by impresarios such as George White and Florenz Ziegfeld in the 1920s and 1930s. In embracing the change from stage to cinema, however, *The King of Jazz* makes use of all the possibilities of the newer medium, including double exposure, matting, and animation. Early in the film, for example, Whiteman arrives with a portable bandstand about the size of a doll house. He opens a small box and watches while tiny men use a ladder to climb out and assemble on the bandstand.

Perhaps the most memorable scene in *The King of Jazz* takes place immediately after the opening credits. Charles Irwin, the dapper announcer with a British accent, comes forth to tell us how Whiteman was crowned King of Jazz. The ensuing two-minute cartoon, created by Walter Lantz before Woody Woodpecker made him famous, has much of the pop surrealism that also flourished in the cartoons of Max and Dave Fleischer. The animated Whiteman first appears dancing with a musket in what the announcer has called "darkest Africa" even though the mise-en-scène has the colorful look of a comic book (Grant 1989). When he fires his gun at a lion pursuing him, the lion strips off his skin and allows the bullet to play on his ribs like mallets on a xylophone. When Whiteman fires a second round, the lion smiles broadly and the lead bounces along his teeth as if they were piano keys. After the lion has prepared to eat Whiteman by removing his teeth and stropping them on his elongated tongue, the bandleader soothes the savage beast by playing music on his violin. The lion falls to its knees and cries out, "Mammy!" A few caricatured African natives are briefly seen stepping to the music, but Whiteman mostly encounters animals in this cartoon Africa, including a rabbit, a monkey, an elephant, and a snake with a derby hat. Although the sequence begins by suggesting that Whiteman is in Africa to hunt for something, perhaps musical inspiration, the cartoon ultimately portrays Whiteman as bringing music to Africa.

The rest of *The King of Jazz* consists of musical numbers and short blackout sketches without a narrative thread to link them. An early number takes place in a stylized Louis XVI palace in which a white woman with blonde hair and white clothes sings of the joys of marriage. In dead seriousness, she watches as a procession of white women, also in elaborate white gowns and white feathered headdresses, descend a staircase. To extend the references to the court of Marie Antoinette, several children appear with ornate shepherd staffs. The orchestra plays a minuet by Mozart and "Long, Long Ago."

Later, in still another surfeit of whiteness, members of Whiteman's band coax a performance out of the white "prop man," whose name is Jeff White. They call him "Old Black Joe" in spite of his color and his name. As Henry Jenkins (1992) has written, *The King of Jazz* draws heavily upon a "vaudeville aesthetic" that combines a variety of genres without any narrative thread (132–36). But the Jeff White episode also shows how vaudeville faithfully maintained the traditions of nineteenth-century minstrelsy. The non-narrative flow of musical numbers interrupted with comic sketches and short blackouts is firmly rooted in the minstrel tradition. So is a stage setting in which several musicians sit in a semicircle behind a single performer who delivers a "stump speech" full of images reaching back "to long-prohibited pleasure in nonlogical modes of thinking and speaking" (Lott 1993, 143). Very much the clever fool who was central to minstrelsy, the prop man in *The King of Jazz* narrates a stream-of-consciousness story that includes a boxing match between a tuna and a bass in a fish store. Like the endmen in the semicircle of minstrel performers, members of the band call out derisive remarks and produce vulgar sounds on their instruments.

In a sequence in still another theatrical style, Whiteman's vocal trio, The Rhythm Boys (Bing Crosby, Harry Barris, and Al Rinker), appear as black silhouettes against a bright background. They sing "Happy as a cow, chewing on a cud, when the darkies beat their feet on the Mississippi mud" before the lights reveal their white faces. One member of the trio protests that the importance of this "super super special special production" demands a loftier song than the one they have been singing. They then perform a song about bluebirds and blackbirds. The exact message of the song is obscure—something about the need for cooperation to produce fair weather—but today, lines such as "The blackbirds said 'We're birds of a different feather,' so the bluebirds and the blackbirds got together" inevitably point to the missing black presence in a film with jazz in its title.

But black people are not completely absent from *The King of Jazz*. African American faces appear twice. About halfway through the film, in a song about lovers in a park, members of the band play their instruments, each dressed in a sailor suit and seated with an affectionate female companion. Whiteman, also in sailor drag, sits in front of the band with his back to the camera. When he turns to face the audience, he has a small, smiling black girl on his lap. He winks at her as she pinches his cheek. Later on, the second black character is indirectly introduced by Whiteman at the beginning of a major production number: "No record of American music would be complete without George Gershwin's *Rhapsody in Blue*, which was written for the Whiteman Orchestra and first played in Aeolian Hall in 1924. The most primitive and the most modern musical elements are combined in this rhapsody, for jazz was born in the African jungle to the beating of the voodoo drum." After Whiteman has offered this introduction, the camera cuts to a coal-black, muscular body with a "voodoo" headdress dancing on a large drum with an animal hide stretched tightly over it. Reminiscent of the *faux* Africanist dancing of Josephine Baker, the black man's movements are accompanied solely by percussion and serve as the prologue to a spectacular, art-deco, all-white performance of Gershwin's well-known fusion of jazz and symphonic music. These two visions of African Americans in *The King of Jazz* show the degree to which blacks were contained in

Hollywood even when they were physically present. The black female is sexualized at the same time she is comfortably infantilized; the black male is stigmatized as primitive and eroticized as all body. Any sexual threat of the black male body is defused by isolating the body on a huge drum, thus rendering it as impotent as a puppet.

But if blacks are present in these two short scenes, they are notably absent from the film's final number. "The Melting Pot of Music" is introduced by an announcer reading aloud the same words that are printed behind him: "America is a melting pot of music wherein the melodies of all nations are fused into one great new rhythm. JAZZ." As a huge, boiling cauldron takes center stage on a set that anticipates the stadium in Leni Riefenstahl's *Triumph of the Will*, large groups in the familiar garb of European nationalities sing and dance to their native music: "Italians" play accordions, "Scotsmen" bagpipes, "Russians" balalaikas; there is an Irish tenor, a Flamenco guitarist, and Frenchmen in Revolutionary garb. After the parade of Europeans, Whiteman stirs the cauldron while circles of colored light magically ascend from the steaming mix. Several images from the preceding processions are then super-imposed over a vortex as the camera looks into the pot to see the different musical traditions melt together. At the grand finale, a group of female "Americans" emerge from the cauldron wearing Rough Rider outfits and performing a dance that is inflected with Jazz Age gestures and the clichés of an Indian war dance. Rows of men in derbies with saxophones sway behind them. Meanwhile, the Whiteman band plays a medley of songs previously featured in the film before breaking into "Stars and Stripes Forever." The "Melting Pot of Music" is especially remarkable in 1930, six years after the Aeolian Hall concert in which Whiteman had presented a similar "history of jazz" that also excluded African Americans. One of Whiteman's admirers wrote that the concert was an "Emancipation Proclamation, in which slavery to European formalism was signed away" (Goldberg 1931, 36). As Michael Rogin (1992b) has observed, Whiteman was also emancipating jazz from black Americans (1065). But if the sin of erasing black people from jazz was ever called to his attention after the 1924 performance, Whiteman clearly was under no pressure to atone for the omission when he made his film in 1930.[3] It should also be pointed out that Jews are not included in the Whiteman melting pot, at least not *as* Jews. In spite of the highly visible role in popular music assumed by performers such as Al Jolson and songwriters such as Irving Berlin, and in spite of the prominent place afforded George Gershwin in *The King of Jazz* itself, the film makes Jews as invisible as blacks.

This refusal to credit African Americans can and should be attributed to simple racism. However, we should accept that jazz held a different meaning for Whiteman's audience in the 1920s than it does for most consumers of the music today. A brief passage in Rogin's essay on *The Jazz Singer* shows the kind of confusion that results when definitions of jazz from different eras are invoked simultaneously. I would first insist that Rogin in "Blackface, White Noise: The Jewish Jazz Singer Finds His Voice" (1992a) undertakes psychoanalytic, struc-turalist, and sociocultural analyses that are a model of how a film ought to be read. In fact, when I first began a book on jazz and film some years ago, I had no intention of including a discussion of *The Jazz Singer*. I believed that the film had nothing to do with jazz in spite of its title. Many writers supported this conviction, including David Meeker, whose *Jazz on Film*, with its thorough listing of all films that feature some kind of jazz performance, has gone through two editions without devoting more than a few lines to *The Jazz Singer*. Most jazz writers, if they have treated the film at all, have done so only with contempt. But Rogin's essay convinced me that the film cannot be overlooked.

I take issue only with a few brief sections toward the end of Rogin's essay. He writes, "The most obvious fact about *The Jazz Singer*, unmentioned in all the critical commentary, is that it contains no jazz" (Rogin 1992a, 447). Rogin first admits that "the 'jazz' of the jazz age, to be sure, was not the music of King Oliver, Louis Armstrong, Jelly Roll Morton, and Fletcher Henderson." He then criticizes the film for what he has just admitted was the received wisdom of its time: "Jazz may have been the jazz age's name for any up-tempo music, but that no more excuses *The Jazz Singer*'s missing sound than blackface compensates for its absence of blacks" (449). Without rejecting any substantial portion of Rogin's argument about the film, I would submit that he is reading a contemporary conception of jazz back into a text from the 1920s. I would also argue that he has posited a questionable model of a "pure" black jazz separate from what he considers racist imitations of the music by whites.

Rogin's insistence that *The Jazz Singer* ought to have embraced a jazz canon that was constructed more than thirty years later is especially surprising considering his accurate characterization of popular attitudes toward jazz at the time of *The Jazz Singer*. He correctly points out that most Americans in the 1920s associated jazz with Whiteman ("The King of Jazz"), Irving Berlin ("Mr. Jazz Himself"), and Sophie Tucker ("The Queen of Jazz"). Rogin also admits that, "almost without exception, popular culture writing in the 1920s treated Negro primitivism as the raw material out of which whites fashioned jazz . . . Jazz was identified with freedom as emotional release rather than as technical prowess. Improvisational skill, instead of being recognized in African-American musicians, was overlooked as central to jazz, and attributed to such performers as Jolson instead" (448). The achievement of many African American artists has in fact been the ability to *improvise* new melodies on old ones, often creating solos of great beauty and complexity, even at breakneck speed. But, to return to the canon of black jazz artists that Rogin cites earlier in his article—Armstrong, Oliver, Henderson, and Morton—only Armstrong was known primarily as an improviser. The other three are now recognized for other achievements. Jelly Roll Morton has been called the "first great composer" in jazz (Schuller 1968. 134); Fletcher Henderson is considered "the pioneer of big band arranging" (McCarthy 1968, 128); and King Oliver is credited with perfecting a "musical whole greater than the sum talents of the individual members" (Williams 1983, 10). I take nothing away from these three artists by saying that their most celebrated achievements were other than and in addition to improvisation. I would add that white players such as Beiderbecke, Frankie Trumbauer, Joe Venuti, and Red Nichols were all accomplished improvisers playing a style of jazz in the 1920s that ought to be understood as something other than white theft of black capital.

[. . .]

Rogin also supports his "no jazz in *The Jazz Singer*" claim by separating *urban* black music from other musical manifestations called jazz. He writes, "African-American jazz was the music of the urban, New Negro, from New Orleans to Chicago to Kansas City, Harlem, and San Francisco. Blackface minstrelsy in the jazz age, by contrast, ventriloquized blacks as rural nostalgia. Domesticating the primitive, in the renderings of Jolson and other songwriters and performers, the plantation supplied the lost-and-longed-for, innocent origins of jazz" (448). First, a long-standing tradition always existed of vocal black blues that was predominantly rural but without which the urban jazz of the New Negro would have been unthinkable: the first jazz instrumentalists were basically playing the blues on trumpets, clarinets, and trombones instead of singing it. These musicians definitely assimilated a great deal of other influences, but the blues, developed outside urban areas, was the single most important element separating early jazz from the white mainstream. More importantly, while Louis Armstrong is the only member of Rogin's pantheon of four who supports the portion of Rogin's jazz paradigm that privileges improvisation, Armstrong also stands as the most striking *refutation* of the portion that privileges the city. Although Armstrong grew up in New Orleans and spent his glory years in Chicago and New York, he also spent a large portion of his career perpetuating the same nostalgia for the mythological plantation that Rogin attributes to Jolson and *The Jazz Singer*. Rather than embracing an urban persona, Armstrong recorded "When It's Sleepy Time Down South" in 1930 and used it as his theme song right up until his death in 1971. He was even filmed singing the song in a 1943 "soundie" wearing the stereotypical garb of a slave. "When It's Sleepy Time Down South" is straight out of the minstrel tradition with "mammies falling on their knees and darkies crooning soft . . . |I|n general |the song| celebrates the dear old Southland from which blacks were then fleeing by the tens of thousands into the ghettos of the cold cities of the North . . . |Armstrong| went on singing about the joys of this mythical South for two generations, not even substituting another word for 'darkies' until he was pressed to do so by the civil rights movement years later" (Collier 1983, 245). Armstrong built much of his popularity on songs like "Sleepy Time Down South," "Shine," "Snowball," and "Shoe Shine Boy": he was content to please audiences even if he could be accused of embodying the black stereotypes that populated the minds of many of his white spectators. However, Armstrong was a complex, even enigmatic man who was also capable of vehemently denouncing white racism.

If, as Rogin asserts, "*The Jazz Singer* emasculated revolutionary, black modern music," then so did numerous black artists who played the music, including those mentioned by Rogin. Not only Armstrong performed and recorded music associated with minstrelsy: in the 1920s, Fletcher Henderson recorded "Old Black Joe Blues," "Darktown Has a Gay White Way" and "Cotton Picker's Ball," and in 1927, the same year as *The Jazz Singer*, King Oliver recorded a song called "Aunt Jemima." While this repertoire probably was forced on black entertainers by white impresarios, it is the only body of work through which we can come to know these black entertainers. There is no such thing as a pure, uncorrupted, uncommercialized black music that is somehow knowable without the apparatus of the culture industry. As any good deconstructionist can tell you, the "original" and the "copy" are not so easily distinguished.[4] Nor are the black urban original and the white nostalgic imitation so strictly delineated. What is more easily identified—and what Rogin justly emphasizes in his writings—is the gross power imbalance between black artists and the predominantly white industry that exploited them. An early history of jazz must include some black/white interactions if only because jazz could never have developed without a background of military marches, Tin Pan Alley songs, polite dance music, and other aspects of a predominantly white culture. Although *The Jazz Singer* ought not to win praise for eliminating blacks from its presentation of "jazz," the film should not be held responsible for using the term in the same way that most whites would have understood it in the 1920s.

The history of jazz that Rogin implicitly accepts—and that was until the 1990s almost uniformly reified in the jazz histories—was developed primarily by critics such as Martin Williams, Marshall Stearns, and Barry Ulanov, all of whom learned formalist principles of literary criticism in university English departments. These critics applied their lessons to jazz, forging a romantic, Leavisite narrative built around a handful of genius composers and soloists who passed along a great tradition isolation from cultural forces. In the terms of this idealized history, early jazz gives us Jelly Roll Morton, "the first great composer" and one of the music's "first theorists" (Williams 1983, 46), rather than the "sloppy" music of the legendary but unrecorded Buddy Bolden (Baraka 1963, 145). Or compare the canonizing language lavished on Morton with the account of jazz in turn-of-the-century New Orleans reported in the autobiography of the black bassist Pops Foster: "I only saw Buddy Bolden's band play once at Johnson's Park. That's where the rough people went. I knew all the guys in the band and later on played with them. Buddy played very good for the style of stuff he was doing. He played nothing but blues and all that stink music, and he played it very loud" (Foster 1971, 16).

The Jazz Singer's substitution of Jolson's plantation songs for more authentic jazz would seem to be consistent with the film's substitution of blackface for real African American performers. But what happens in a film when African Americans are in fact present along with whites in blackface? Is the result any less offensive than when blacks are entirely absent as in The Jazz Singer? Alongside The King of Jazz, I would offer a second test case, Rhapsody in Blue, Irving Rapper's 1945 biopic in which Robert Alda plays George Gershwin. An important scene in the film stages a recreation of a composition that Gershwin wrote for George White's Scandals of 1922. Before the piece has been accepted for the show, White tells Gershwin that his blackface number will not be well received by audiences: "Harlem . . . dame shoots a guy . . . that's not for The Scandals." Gershwin, however, believes that the number must be a part of the show. Paul Whiteman, playing himself in the film, reluctantly expresses admiration for the number and agrees to conduct the pit orchestra. The film asks us to side with the daring Gershwin for having the courage to put a sequence on stage in which white actors in blackface perform his short operetta Blue Monday. The action takes place in a dicty Harlem nightclub populated by strutting, overdressed patrons. At the climax of the story a jealous woman stabs her man after he receives a letter she suspects is from another woman. The letter turns out to be from the man's sister, who has written to say that their mother is dying. As he expires, the wounded man sings, "I'm going to see my mother, mother mine. God, how I miss my mother . . ." The film first asks the audience to accept the stereotypical view that blacks are violent, uncontrollably passionate, and mother-fixated. But during the climax of the operetta, these images are validated by a reaction shot of two real African Americans. One appears to be an usher, the other a maid, both of them presumably at the back of the theater— the camera does not establish their precise whereabouts. What is clear is that the black man is spellbound and the woman is quietly shedding tears. Earlier the camera had cut to the well-dressed white audience responding uncomfortably to the display of passion in a Harlem nightclub. The shot of the black couple asserts that the operetta is an accurate representation of their lives, something that the affluent white patrons cannot understand. As Rogin has argued, The Jazz Singer capitalizes on "the surplus symbolic value of blacks" (417); this scene from Rhapsody in Blue doubly exploits African Americans, first as represented in blackface and then, allegedly, as the real thing.

The Jazz Singer is not unique in using the highly problematic term "jazz" to describe the songs of a white man in blackface at a time when, rightly or wrongly, most Americans understood jazz in this way. One does not have to look far, however, to find much more egregious exploitations of blacks in Hollywood's long history of making African Americans stand for, as Rogin puts it, "something other than themselves."

Notes

1 For the most sophisticated critiques of the trope of jazz as autonomous art, see Tomlinson (1991) and DeVeaux (1991). Also see my introduction and the essays in the anthology *Jazz among the Discourses* (Gabbard 1995).

2 See, for example, the analysis by Steven B. Elworth (1995) of the sexual persona projected by drummer Cindy Blackman (74).

3 The denial of blackness in *King of Jazz* must have been even more ironic when it was shown in some theaters on the same bill which *Black and Tan* (1929), Dudley Murphy's black-cast film that featured Duke Ellington and his orchestra.

4 The false binarism—original/copy—is an essential part of Jacques Derrida's project. See his "Plato's Pharmacy" (1981). In addition, see Andrew Ross's discussion of the tendency to associate a discourse of race with a discourse of commercialization: "it is often assumed that the two are necessarily aligned; that commercialized music = whitened music, that the black performance of uncommercialized and therefore undiluted black music constitutes the only truly genuine form of protest or resistance against the white culture industry and its controlling interests, and that black music which submits to that industry automatically loses its autonomous power. To subscribe to this equation is to imagine a very mechanical process indeed, whereby a music, which is authentically black, constitutes an initial raw material which is then appropriated and reduced in cultural force and meaning by contact with a white industry. Accordingly, music is never 'made,' and only ever exploited, in this process of industrialization" (Ross 1989, 69–70).

References

Altman, R. (1989) *The American Film Musical*. Bloomington: Indiana University Press

Baraka, A. (1963) *Blues People: Negro Music in White America*. New York: Morrow

Barthes, R. (trans. Lavers, A.) (1972) *Mythologies*. New York: Hill and Wang

Benjamin, W. (trans. Zohn, H.) (1969) "The Work of Art in the Age of Mechanical Reproduction" in *Illuminations*. New York: Schocken, pp. 217–52

Collier, J. (1983) *Louis Armstrong: An American Genius*. New York: Oxford University Press

Corbett, J. (1994) *Extended Play: Sounding off from John Cage to Dr Funkenstein*. Durham, NC: Duke University Press

Derrida, J. (trans. Johnson, B.) (1981) "Plato's Pharmacy" in *Disseminations* Chicago: Chicago University Press

DeVeaux, S. (1991) "Constructing the Jazz Tradition: Jazz Historiography" in *Black American Literature Forum* 25/3, pp. 525–60

Doherty, T. (1988) *Teenagers and Teenpics: The Juvenilization of American Movies in the 1950s*. Boston: Unwin Hyman

Elworth, S. (1995) "Jazz in Crisis, 1948–1958: Ideology and Representation" in Gabbard, K. (ed.) *Jazz among the Discourses*. Durham, NC: Duke University Press, pp. 57–75

Foster, P. (1971) *The Autobiography of a New Orleans Jazzman*. Berkeley: University of California Press

Gabbard, K. (ed.) (1995) *Jazz among the Discourses*. Durham, NC: Duke University Press

Giddins, G. (1985) "Miles's Wiles" in *Rhythm-a-ning: Jazz Tradition and Innovation in the '80s*. New York: Oxford University Press, pp. 78–85

Goldberg, I. (1931) *George Gershwin*. New York: Simon and Schuster

Grant, B. (1989) "'Jungle Nights in Harlem': Jazz, Ideology and the Animated Cartoon" in *University of Hartford Studies in Literature* 21: 3, pp. 3–12

Jenkins, H. (1992) *What Made Pistachio Nuts? Early Sound Cinema and the Vaudeville Aesthetic*. New York: Columbia University Press

Lott, E. (1993) *Love and Theft: Blackface Minstrelsy and the American Working Class*. New York: Oxford University Press

McCarthy, A. (1968) "Fletcher Henderson" in McCarthy, A., Morgan, A., Oliver, P., and Harrison, M. (eds) *Jazz on Record: A Critical Guide to the First 50 Years*. London: Hanover Books, pp. 128–30

Major, C. (ed.) (1994) *Juba to Jive: A Dictionary of African-American Slang*. New York: Viking

Meltzer, D. (ed.) (1993) *Reading Jazz*. San Francisco: Mercury House

Mulvey, L. (1975) "Visual Pleasure and Narrative Cinema" in *Screen* 16:3, pp. 6–18

Rogin, A. (1992a) "Black Face, White Noise: The Jewish Jazz Singer Finds His Voice" in *Critical Inquiry* 18:4, pp. 417–53

Rogin, A. (1992b) "Making America Home: Racial Masquerade and Ethnic Assimilation in the Transition to Talking Pictures" in *The Journal of American History* 79:3, pp. 1050–77

Ross, A. (1989) *No Respect: Intellectuals and Popular Culture*. New York: Routledge

Schuller, G. (1968) *Early Jazz: Its Roots and Musical Development*. New York: Oxford University Press

Smith, E. (1988) "Films" in Kernfeld, B. (ed.) *New Grove Dictionary of Jazz*. London: Macmillan

Tomlinson, G. (1991) "Cultural Dialogues and Jazz: A White Historian Signifies" in *Black Music Research Journal* 11/2, pp. 229–64

Williams, R. (1983) *Keywords: A Vocabulary of Culture and Society*. New York: Oxford University Press

The Animation of Sound

10

PHILIP BROPHY

[. . .]

Fantasia (1940) is the poetic peak of Disney animation. This is not just because it capitalizes on the preceding twelve years of experimentation at the Disney studio but also because its narrative deals with precomposed musical texts. As such, *Fantasia* is not just an homage to a body of baroque, classical, romantic and early 20th-century compositions, but also an honouring of the organic life of music to which the trickery of animated imagery could only aspire.

[. . .]

[The] A *World Is Born* [. . .] section of *Fantasia*[1] speeds up the mobilization and condenses the flow, streamlining the whole symphonic process. This streamlining is clearly evident in the temporal spans and phases which tangentially connect the Stravinsky musical text with the Disney animation text, setting into motion an incredible networking of morphological and molecular microcosms and macrocosms. The main seeding here is between:

(1) Stravinsky's *Rite of Spring—Scenes of Pagan Russia in Two Parts* (1912): a musical narration (originally for ballet) of a Slavonic tribal ritual which celebrates planetary life cycles (determined by the passage of the four seasons) and centring on Spring as the key period of creation of life on the planet.
(2) Disney's A *World is Born—A Narrative Interpretation* (1940): an animated narration of a populist scientific view of the planet's own life cycle (determined by its passage through states of existence) and centring on the life/death cycles determined by the changing nature of the planet.

Here Disney exploits one of the quintessential marvels of music: how its relationship with time is never comparative but always relative. This means that any tempo musical unit (span, phase, development, passage, movement, etc.) in a musical composition will only generate a sense of temporality by its relation to other preceding/following tempo musical units. (The voiceover narration alludes to such relationships through its description of stars: "All stars are neither large nor small, except in relation to their neighbours.") Whereas the literalness of the adaptation of Dukas' *The Sorcerer's Apprentice* is the result of the primarily chronological/linear deployment of the narrative, the expansiveness of the *A World is Born* adaptation is the result of a temporal/lateral deployment of the narrative, where time is not only a sequence of events but also a state of transition. For this reason *A World is Born* concentrates on morphological development (of the physical animation of animal, vegetable and mineral matter) to highlight the existence of life as a state of transition (as the voiceover states: "life seems to develop for ever"). The Stravinsky score is equally focused on the "state of transition" but from a different direction. While *Rite of Spring* uses the inherent symbolism of the ritual (which symbolizes the effects of nature) to resymbolize the intensities of creative forces, acts and events, Disney reverses the symbolic line so that the Stravinsky text (its manifest dynamics over its symbolic contents) is used to symbolize the creation of "our world."[2] *A World is Born* is the most complex section of *Fantasia*, mainly because of its primary ordering of four textual levels which intensify the symphonic process and experience: the music score, the graphic images, the dynamic movement of the images and the voiceover narration. In fact it is probably the voiceover (by Deems Taylor, recognized then as one of the most popular populists of "long hair music") which is the prime force in energizing the corporate text, delivering a literal content which transforms the cartoon into a dizzy hyper-reflexive commentary on the whole "illusion of life."

This is because the spoken words have the strange effect of simultaneously describing the states of both the musical composition and its geographical analogy. *Rite of Spring* commences with that distinctive swirling flute motif whose slight dissonance[3] suggests a delicate feeling of continual swirling movement for the reason that the form of the motif is never fixed but always reshaping itself. The voiceover text recognizes that no actual or extant form is present here and thus suggests that this motif is a virtual presence, the potential for the creation of life: "One bubble of froth in ten million miles of ocean." Once again we have Disney's accent on the fluid, on how the "form" of liquids is never anything more than the potential and the means for gaining form. The voiceover refers to pre-planetary space as a dimension with "no up or down no forward or back," which is just about as perfect a summation of Stravinsky's angle on 20th-century tonality as you can get! This concept of continually reshaping a form in a formless dimension is an important feature of the Stravinsky work as a whole in that, due to its harmonic construction, nothing ever stays still—a precept echoed later in the voiceover: "Life seems to develop for ever."[4]

The second section of *A World is Born* is marked simultaneously as the advent of form and the event of rhythm. With the earth covered by volcanoes, the voiceover refers to "the giant furnace of creation melting and pouring and forging a new world." With this occurrence of mass and weight (the start of the earth's solidity) comes the gravity of tonality (the feeling of being comfortably located in the musical text) and the strict marking of time in the heavy, thumping one-note burst of the orchestra. Through synchronism, the earth is turned into a single instrument: a weird wind instrument whose surface is covered with holes (the volcanoes) through which bursts of creative energy are pushed, giving us the orchestral bursts. In comparison to "man mastering nature" in the Silly Symphonies, we have nature performing "by itself" unleashing an untamed violence to which Stravinsky's score alludes in its use of a pagan ritual to propel its atonality (noting that the two parts of *Rite of Spring* are entitled "Adoration of the Earth" and "The Sacrifice"). The key pagan figure here, of course, is the violence of rhythm and its links with barbaric behaviour and celebration, not to mention its suggestion of reproductive and procreative activity. The earth at this stage is implicitly still involved in such acts: "a glowing ball, still hot with the fires of its beginnings."

If the volcano section and its coupling with those distinctive orchestral bursts is the phallic thrust of creation (tagged in Stravinsky's original ballet score as the "Ritual of Abduction"), the Disney text follows this with the combined visual and musical suggestion of the erotics of orgasm with the overflowing volcanoes that generate cascades and torrents of white-hot liquid lava: a river of life which contains the molecular material "for me and you." Replaying the erotics of both Mickey's seductive dream and nightmare reality in *The Sorcerer's Apprentice*, the movement of lava is essentially one of liquid. Its heat factor is of little consequence, as the visual dynamics of its movement always convey an intensity similar to any liquid movement. Hence, the lava flow is cooled by winds which are depicted with similar liquefied dynamics: clouds rise, swirl, sweep and disperse with an intensity similar to both the lava and Mickey's water. As mentioned before, Disney uses liquefication (as state and process) as a prime means for visually symbolizing the organic flow of music. *A World is Born* indicates this most vividly in its correlation of dramatic states and musical intensities with various states of water: white hot and boiling, gushing and immense, nebulous and gaseous, swirling and evaporating, raging and torrential, etc. That particular dynamic flow of the Disney sound animation is here cited again as the state of transition focused on is qualified by the peaks and troughs of material transformations, where music outlays and traverses its "plane of the present."

These material transformations (of lava into steam into cloud into water, of the instability of the planet's evolving form) fully accommodate the temporal transitions of the music and do so by an inherent effect of the animation process: time-lapse photography. This effect is ever so popular today (*Koyaanisqatsi* is virtually *Fantasia* revisited, but that is another story), where clouds roll over the landscape at an unreal rate. While the effect is presented today mostly as a dislocated arty gesture, its formal origins are fairly complex. Firstly, such an effect symbolizes nature and its elemental forces marking their presence, making us more forcibly subject to their action and movement (a symbolic device used in countless mystical film scenarios, where the skies roll by just prior to some momentous event). Secondly, the mythological heritage of this figure is based on the ritualization of events when nature did go through such turbulent changes as to make its presence felt forcibly: earthquakes, monsoons, tidal waves, eclipses, equinoxes, etc. Subsequently, this effect of clouds moving fast, of vapours swirling around, etc., evokes a feeling of imminence: of the suspense of something on the verge of happening, of the erotics of eventfulness. Following this line, there is something appropriate about Disney employing such an effect that: (a) textually captures such a lineage; (b) fully exploits the technological essence of the animation process creating the artificial movement of time; and (c) highlights some of his major underlying drives to depict the movement of liquid, to state movement as liquid, and to qualify movement as force.

Following all these ethereal and material impregnations comes the gestation period of the planet ("a warm ocean covers the earth") wherein cells divide and connect to give us an array of morphological developments (each development in essence a particular harmonic development of a figure in the Stravinsky score). Each phase here is marked by an ominous low-frequency orchestral waver, combined with the wonderfully literal voiceover: "Now, a million years roll over the earth like a rumble under the water." As corny as it sounds, the image of black swelling up and obliterating the screen in sync with the deep orchestral murmur conveys only too well the unstoppable force of time itself (in much the same way that water filling the screen conveys Mickey's lack of control over nature). All these transitions and transformations lead up to an actual eclipse which in turn marks the next major development of the earth's form: the earthquake that erases the surface existence of life, which at that point had reached its zenith (dinosaurs, etc.). This is the first instance in the scenario of architectural blocks and shapes marking their presence, as huge mountains pierce and rupture the earth's surface to the distorted alarm calls of blasting horns. The life cycle of material forces thus starts up again, giving us an escalating sense of dynamic transmogrification as "time and time again, whole continents fell in the fury of waves"—sonic waves, musical waves, material waves—waves being the most suitable approximation of structural division to constitute the dynamic text.

A *World is Born* eventually ends on a disquieting note as the opening swirling flute motif lays itself to rest: "All that you have seen was but the brief twinkle of a star in the immensity of time." (Note: the original score does not repeat this motif at the end; this cyclical closure is only in the Disney "Narrative Interpretation.") Deems Taylor's voice even starts to quake slightly as he speaks of this time before as "a world larger than our own" a phrase which is now readable as a reflection on how the mimetic is eternally snared by the contingencies of representation, of creating worlds on the screen which essentially affirm the magnitude of other worlds, physical or symbolic. Be this effect one of awe, dread, terror or delight (or a confusion among them), the dynamic flow of these cartoons' textuality is giddy, dizzy, vertiginous, disorienting, unsettling an exacting conglomeration of all the schisms which aid in our identification between states, between zones, between phases. Whereas Disneyland and Walt Disney World manipulate scale and perspective to transform the real into a controlled environment which works upon and confounds our perceptual mechanisms, the Disney animated shorts and features manipulate sound/image relationships to mobilize narrative construction and our place within the text. This is the "frightening power" displayed by and in Disney's worlds; worlds "larger than our own."

[. . .]

Anti-symphony and anti-opera

After the war the Disney studio appeared to grow more desperate in its promotion of the harmony of life, for what was a rich dynamic flow in *Fantasia* gradually thickened into the sentimental sludge of the deliberately low-brow *Make Mine Music* (1946), which hams, yams and yucks up popular postwar music styles by enlisting the likes of Dinah Shore, Nelson Eddy, The Andrews Sisters and Benny Goodman. Compared to *Fantasia*, *Make Mine Music*—with its commonfolk/plainspeak/consumerist title—delivers only the most skeletal, sketchy and obvious fusions of music with imagery. This is because each of the individual sections of the film (a) uses the voices of known identities and (b) uses the lyric content of songs to (c) speak from a pop culture level to (d) flatten out any substantial differences between jazz, blues, bebop, romantic, balletic and classical music. There is also a cathartic anti-intellectualism released throughout the film, as if it is exorcizing itself of the well-meaning aspirations of *Fantasia*. Many scenes in *Make Mine Music* are painfully populist: a whale dreams of singing at the Met; cupid silhouettes move as ballerinas; and Prokofiev's decidedly educationalist *Peter* and the Wolf is "modernized" for the postwar child. The intention for the film to "relax" one (in the environmental massage of a growing postwar affluence) is perfectly carried out by the text's basic inability to mobilize the subject, to set in motion any narratological dynamism once the differences of the musical styles have been erased for the universal culture of "entertainment." This is further reflected in the homogeneous form and shape of Make Mine Music, which is in contrast to Fantasia's mixed and fractured sectional narrative. Ultimately, Make Mine Music is what many people falsely accuse Fantasia of being: a rush of pretty pictures set to a wash of lush music. While the latter carries out an intense investigation into musical form, the former essentially uses music as a social tool to absent any cultural clash in musical differences, a strategy recognized as part of the Disney syndrome of fabricating its beautiful world.

Accepting Fantasia and Make Mine Music as the poles of Disney's symphonic territorialization of image/music combination, Warner Bros. produced a set of cartoons which, when compared with those two Disney pictures, could be termed "anti-symphonic/anti-operatic" in that they tear away at the musical, musicological and cultural barricades with which the Disney studio was fortifying its fabricated world. The most relevant cartoons here are Rhapsody Rabbit (1946), Long Haired Hare (1949), Rabbit of Seville (1950), What's Opera, Doc? (1957) and Baton Bunny (1959). The term "anti-symphonic/anti-operatic" does not point to straight parody and satire because that could only be the result of a narrow sociocultural reading of the cartoons in their handling of classical/romantic/operatic scores. (For this reason Corny Concerto (1943), a straight parody of Fantasia with Elmer Fudd recreating Deems Taylor's role, is not included with the above group.) All these cartoons use the musical score as the prime means for constructing their narratives so that the resultant textuality is strongly connected to the musical textuality in terms of flow, movement, mobilization and dynamics. While the visuals (the animated gags, puns, punchlines, jokes, etc.) orient the sarcastic and sacrilegious thrust of these cartoons, the soundtrack as a specifically constructed version, appropriation and condensation of the original scores provides a series of cues for what is developed in other cartoons as a cacophonic approach to sound/image fusion.

Rhapsody Rabbit has the weakest textual flow here because (a) the gags are arbitrarily laid on to the performance of the Liszt rhapsody, and (b) the dramatic shape of the narrative is equally arbitrary through its musical editing and juxtaposition. Basically, the dynamics of this cartoon are controlled by Bugs' performance of the music, with Bugs as the pianist who has to overcome the difficulties of performing the piece (exaggerated by the continual interruptions of a mouse wanting to play along with Bugs). In this sense the humour of the situation is very much derived from Chico Marx's piano performances, where gesture is transformed into ridicule and musical suggestion is blown up into comic display by Bugs' ironically mimicking the "feel" of the music. While this cartoon is an outright satire on the preciousness of concert recitals (Liszt even rings up Bugs during the performance, to which Bugs replies, "What's up, Doc? . . . Franz Liszt? Never hoid of 'im!", while later the mouse cuts in with a boogie-woogie piano roll), the figure of Bugs distancing himself from the music in the act of performing it is epicentral to the other "anti-symphonic/anti-operatic" cartoons and in this instance is realized textually through bringing the music into conflict with its performance. (This notion of distancing and conflict, of course, rarely appears in the Disney symphonic cartoons as they are mostly concerned with "musicalizing" every aspect of their fiction.)

Baton Bunny is virtually the remake of Rhapsody Rabbit but this time with Bugs as "guest conductor" of the "Warner Brothers Symphony Orchestra performing Franz Von Suppé's

Morning, Noon, and Night in Vienna." (All this is detailed in special credit cards at the start of the cartoon.) The first gag is a replay of the first gag in *Rhapsody Rabbit*. Someone coughs as Bugs prepares himself; Bugs shoots offscreen and a body hits the ground in *Rhapsody*; Bugs holds up a sign "THROW THE BUM OUT" followed by the sound of body being thrown out crashing into backstage props in *Baton*. A few gags follow: reading sheet music with glasses upside down/ notes are shown upside down; picking and chalking a baton like a billiard cue. Remarkably, the first thirty seconds are nearly totally silent, a rarity in Warner Bros. cartoons. This silence, though, is an introductory backdrop for the comic atmosphere which picks at the sacrosanct aura of the recital's environment. This whole preparation is also a direct reference to the fairly forced positioning of Leopold Stokowski within the *Fantasia* sequence, where he is presented as a godly director of the proceedings with his huge face occasionally filling the screen, illuminated by the menacing "light" of the musicians beneath him, energies he must control in the name of music. In *Baton Bunny* the conductor figure is depicted in more human terms as Bugs tries to control the forces of the orchestra (rarely shown in this case), of nature (that damned fly that buzzes around him) and even of his own costume (a sign of the ridiculous ritualization of musical appreciation). While Stokowski is a sovereign conductor of musical energy, Bugs is a manic engineer of musical force; where Stokowski calms and controls the sounds of nature, Bugs is enraged and controlled by its noise.

Bugs might be the synchronous "performer" of the music in this cartoon, but perhaps even more so his body is both performer and performance. In contrast to the "being" of Bugs (the perceivable character of Bugs Bunny as a formed identity) mugging the music in *Rhapsody*, Bugs' "being" here remains in control of the score's direction while his body experiences the music in ways which confound his direction of the music. This is a perverse replay of Mickey in *The Sorcerer's Apprentice*, who is able to fuse direction and experience in his dream, which in turn symbolizes the symbiotic functioning of the musical conductor. Bugs symbolizes the inability of the conductor to fuse direction and experience—or at least only to do so under forces, terms and conditions which overcome the creative impulse and execution. Mickey rises to a mystical mountaintop while Bugs writhes on the stage floor, each in response to the music's dramatics. The bulk of *Baton Bunny*'s scenario is a succession of bodily attacks on Bugs by the music: his body virtually explodes into weird contortions to the opening orchestral bursts; his tail and coattails are seduced into swaying by the waltz movement; and his body "reanthropomorphizes" itself into cowboy and Indian figures as he mimes the galloping chase feel of the music. The finale is truly an ending to all possible symphonic control as Bugs chases the buzzing fly into the various sections of the orchestra, diving head first into the instruments to produce a cacophony of bangs, clangs and bum notes—musical noise resulting from his attempts to prevent non-musical sound interrupting the music. While the Disney worlds are seamlessly sealed (like the doors closed once the recital commences), the Warner Bros. musical environment is always encroached upon by outside forces (the traffic outside the concert hall) so that its world is forever sounding crisis.

In the Warner Bros. world, struggles are replaced by battles, fights, wars. Such a clash of opposing forces is generally sited in the soundtrack, especially in terms of how sound effects are worked into the musical score and vice versa, where one is always impinging on the other's territory. In *Baton Bunny* the clash is sited in the body/being dichotomy of Bugs' performance; in *Long Haired Hare* the clash is channelled into a character conflict between the lowbrow Bugs and the highbrow tenor practising his arias in his country abode. What is most interesting is how Bugs' singing generates a musicological discourse which infects the refined lineage of the operatic arias of the tenor. This clash is in effect a metaphor for the "infectious" quality of simple pop/folk melodies and how they are regarded as disease by a musical establishment which takes pride in its sanitary measures. The humour in this cartoon arises precisely when the tenor is infected, when he starts joining in with Bugs, for Bugs' choice of song and his delivery are clearly part of his character while the tenor breaks out of character, generating comic effect through inappropriateness.

The model of cultural clash through character conflict was previously developed in *Back Alley Oproar* (1948), which featured Sylvester as a tom in heat who expresses his desires through an incredible array of Tin Pan Alley hits (remembering that Tin Pan Alley is the industrialization of the "popular song phenomenon" as it arose in the Gay Nineties, following it through to the Depression). The metaphor for the original pop music industry here references the origins of its name, where sheet music barkers would try to sell their wares by, paradoxically enough, banging on trash cans and the like to drown out their opposition: an environment where the desire to seduce was confounded by the desire to sell; a music industry founded on the noise of competition. In one scene of *Back Alley Oproar*, Sylvester even performs a string of songs as a series of "jump cuts" where each phrase or chorus is interrupted by the next, punctuated by Sylvester smashing bottles on his head, lighting firecrackers and blowing whistles. Here we touch on the sublime origins of Warner Bros.' approach and attitude towards popular song, for while Disney was always bent on communicating to the public his classicist preoccupations (from the Silly Symphonies to *Fantasia*), Warner Bros. was originally part of the pop music industry that developed from Tin Pan Alley.[5] A cultural stance is clearly reflected in Warner Bros.' prewar work, a stance derived from and extending entertainment forms from that era, especially in regard to humour (vaudeville), narration (slapstick) and music (burlesque). The higher cultural plane in *Back Alley Oproar* is ridiculed through Elmer Fudd's exasperated attempts to gag Sylvester. Surely one of Warner Bros.' most savagely anti-operatic scenes is where Sylvester straps on huge bovver boots to stomp up and down the stairs outside Elmer's window to a can-can melody, bellowing out "TRA! TRA! TRA!" That famous "quote" of Leon Schlesinger (which just about every Warner animator recalls in interviews) never found a more succinct realization here: "Disney can make the chicken salad. I wanna make the chicken shit!"

The shit really hits the fan in Warner Bros.' two most outwardly anti-operatic cartoons, *Rabbit of Seville* and *What's Opera, Doc? Rabbit of Seville* sites the culture clash this time within the narrative's structural framework. The cartoon starts off, once again, not unlike the start of *Fantasia's* orchestral tune-up, with people filing past a lobby card announcing the Rossini opera. At the sound of distant gunshots the camera is drawn towards small bursts of light on the distant hills. Eventually Bugs rushes in through the stage door and slams it shut. Elmer—literally—has chased Bugs into the cartoon narrative, into a scenario which at once should not have involved them but which could not evolve without them. In repayment of kind, Bugs raises the curtain on Elmer, pushing him into the fictional narrative (the operatic narrative within the cartoon), which was the original province of the cartoon narrative.

A weird narratological balance is struck by the intrusion of the Elmer/Bugs chase (a chase which travels across a whole series of cartoons). This distinction between the two narratives is carried through as the conductor (a Leopold lookalike who glances at his watch when the curtain rises, shrugs his shoulders and starts conducting) maintains the narrative's "original" score. The newly transformed narrative, though, is signified by the synchronous sound effects and replacement libretto sung by Bugs on top of the original score. The cultural clash is thus harmoniously combined, which, of course, only serves to heighten the absurdity of the clash being resolvable in the first place. The gags are thus thematically fractured and abstracted (hinged only on Bugs' crazy interpretation of the score through an overly literal understanding of the role of the barber within the operatic narrative) while being perfectly timed to the musical flow. This heightens the oppositional tack taken in preventing any ideal operatic blending of voice/lyric with orchestra/melody. By the end of the cartoon, both narratives (the cartoon metanarrative and the internal operatic narrative) cave in on each other as the music reaches its dramatic climax: as the music climbs high in pitch, Elmer and Bugs race each other upwards into the wings on their barber chairs; as the orchestration becomes more powerful, Bugs and Elmer confront each other with increasingly larger weaponry; and as the score starts its final series of cadences, Bugs rushes Elmer into a hurried "shotgun" marriage in order to resolve the operatic plot by the time the music has resounded its final climax.

In What's Opera, Doc? we have perhaps the fullest version of a Warner Bros. world in opposition to a Disney world, for in this cartoon—and this is almost never the case with Warner Bros.—a totally homogeneous environment is created, where sound and image actually fuse but in such an overblown and distorted fashion that the end result once again is a world which can barely maintain the energy of its own presence. For a cartoon produced so late—1957—where it was the norm for characters always to present themselves at a remove from their own scenarios, What's Opera, Doc? uniquely starts and finishes within an operatic narrative, unlike the opening to Rabbit of Seville. But there is still a feeling that the opera scenario is already encased within some other narrative which—in a proto-New Novel fashion—is not disclosed. The opera narrative thus resonates with the unrealized potential for Bugs and Elmer somehow, somewhere and at some time to break out of the opera and throw an aside to us—perversely delivered only seconds prior to the closing iris of the cartoon's ending. This is virtually a closed opera, with the right music and the appropriate spacing of the libretto, except that it is performed by Bugs and Elmer. It is almost as if this is actually a serious cartoon—which is precisely what makes it so comical.

The base of the "harmony" between image and music is in Maurice Noble's incredible set designs, which do not simply replicate the gaudy excesses of Wagner's music but stylize even further conventional opera set design already replicating such formal extremes. To this end, Noble provides a set of images whose perspective exaggerations dynamize each frame so much that there can be no normal sequencing nor continuity between frames. This is a very good example of how the Warner Bros. cartoons intensify their formalism too much. The end result in this cartoon is like overapplying Eisenstein's theory of montage, applying it to the point of abstraction. Noble's designs are based on instilling a sense of motion in a still design concept. He designs everything as if it were caught in motion or anticipating a move, a shift, a push, a turn, some sort of dynamic encounter. Combine this with camera movement, character movement and editing and you have a narrative structure that would tongue tie Christian Metz![6] Finally, compare the architectural design in this cartoon with The Sorcerer's Apprentice. In Apprentice the movement is basically dictated by the spread of water: too much water, too much for the eye to follow, so that the retina and cornea collapse into each other's fields of vision. In What's Opera, Doc? that overload of movement is conveyed by the set design (itself pregnant with motion) and compounded by the montage so that flow is turned to rupture.

At this point it might be helpful to summarize the ways in which the Warner Bros. cartoons mentioned above (key examples of tendencies exhibited in a vast number of their cartoons) textually evidence an "anti-symphonic/anti-operatic" sensibility. This musicological antagonism is realized by placing:

(1)   the music score in conflict with its performance,
(2)   the performer's body in conflict with its being,
(3)   a character in conflict with another character,
(4)   a musical style in conflict with another musical style,
(5)   the cartoon narrative in conflict with the music narrative, and
(6)   the music score in conflict with its realization.

[. . .]

Warner Bros. cartoons are truly modern. They are violent, destructive and overpowering, replicating the prime modernist impulse of the 20th century: to destroy representation in the act of representation. In terms of cinema history they sit well alongside all other attacks on figurative form and formal realism (from Sergei Eisenstein and Dziga Vertov to Alain Robbe Grillet and Jean Luc Godard). But more importantly, the Warner Bros. cartoons' cacophonic destruction of sound/image fusion (formal synchronism, acoustical realism, musical accompaniment, dynamic construction, effects generation, etc.) has left us with the material means by which they (as "techno texts") follow through their modernist impulses.

Such is the legacy of the processes of animation and the animatic apparatus: displaced by whatever abstractions we entertain as governing our reality, these cartoons (along with their Disney counterparts) are, unavoidably and alone, material. Their own material, with their own dynamic energy and textual life. In the most straightforward way, they demonstrate the act of filming not as "bringing something to life" but as "film itself coming to life."

Notes

1   The actual credit for this section of *Fantasia* is verbally introduced as *Rite of Spring*; however, this section was released some time after *Fantasia*'s initial release as a discrete short titled *A World is Born*. Deems Taylor's voiceover narration only appears in this short and not in the *Fantasia* version. I shall be discussing the short version, which is the same in every other detail (length, visuals, score). I take this liberty for two reasons. First, *Fantasia* is an anthology, one conceptualized and formed as such only after completion of *The Sorcerer's Apprentice*. Only certain sections of *Fantasia* are relevant to the terms of my analysis and I therefore do not address the film as a whole. Secondly, since the inception of the *Disneyland* TV series in 1954, much of the Disney studio's output has been re-edited and recompiled for television, 35mm European theatrical release and/or 16mm educational distribution. The Disney oeuvre is largely governed by fragmentation and regurgitation.
2   However, Disney's macrocosmic approach implies a desire to encompass the total symbolic potential of the Stravinsky text, thus falling prey to a certain literalness in its depiction of the effects of time (large-scale time potential = the life span of the world). The year cycle of nature's processes in Stravinsky's work is symbolic of the more abstract relationships between time and life as expressible through music and thus already represents a latent intent to encompass "big concepts" prior to Disney's graphic visualization of this symbolic drive.

3 This is in comparison with Arnold Schoenberg's more strident and disciplined approach to 20th-century composition, serialism, which he defined as a means for "the emancipation of dissonance."

4 Compare this notion of "no up or down, no forward or back" with the clearly defined architecture of *The Sorcerer's Apprentice*, where both Mickey and the music are forever going up and down, back and forth. Yet another obtuse connection can be made between *The Sorcerer's Apprentice* and *A World is Born*: at the start of the latter the voiceover ponders, "Could you touch the sky from a mountain top?" That is exactly what Mickey does in his dream in the former. Both these animated shorts (more than the other sections in *Fantasia*) reaffirm the Disney drive to feel the narrative in motion.

5 Warner Bros.' Merrie Melodies (1930–1963) and Looney Toons (1931–1963) were originated by two ex-Disney associates, Rudolph Ising and Hugh Harman, who directed and produced both series independently for Warner Bros. from 1930 to 1933. When they left to head MGM's animation department, Leon Schlesinger produced these series as in-house Warner Bros. cartoons with Friz Freleng as the initial series director. All the other major Warner Bros. cartoon directors developed here. (For a complete listing of all these cartoons with credits and dates, see Jeff Lenburg's *The Encyclopedia of Animated Cartoon Series* (New York: Da Capo Press, 1981) and Jerry Beck and Will Friedwald's *Looney Toons and Merrie Melodies: A Complete Illustrated Guide to The Warner Bros. Cartoons* (New York: Henry Holt and Company, 1989).) Because of Warner Bros.' diversification into music publishing and copyright, the focus of the cartoons under Schlesinger was to push songs and tunes to which they already had the rights. So while there initially was a side reference to the market success of Disney's Silly Symphonies, this angle was replaced by an internal industrial concern. Carl Stalling, one of the major musical directors of Warner Bros.' cartoons, was originally one of Disney's prime musical directors, also acknowledged as having proposed the concept for *The Skeleton Dance* and having launched the Silly Symphonies series. With his shift to Warner Bros. in the early thirties, the Merrie Melodies and Looney Toons cartoons progressed from the straight parody of Disney conventions to the bilateral development of key Disney concerns (percussive synchronism and popular song referencing). Many of the apparent oppositions between Disney and Warner Bros. are actually formed along similar lines of exploration. Furthermore, Stalling was originally an organist for silent cinema (like most early orchestrators and musical directors around this time), so he was well attuned to the role popular music played in the musical accompaniment to film. (This, however, leads us into the most forgotten epoch of film history: the relationship between Tin Pan Alley and silent film accompaniment. The Warner Bros. cartoons are the major surviving examples of such a legacy, considering how much early "All Singing/All Dancing/All Talking" film musicals were competing with Broadway's hold on musicals.)

6 Some comments by Noble in a 1971 interview (Joe Adamson, "Well, For Heaven's Sake! Grown Men!", *Film Comment*, Vol.11, No.1, January/February 1975, p. 19): "I design in motion . . . When you're on a panoramic shot . . . your overall total has to balance out to be an interesting eye experience: your large areas and small areas are exhibited to the eye as the pan goes along, and the spaces and rhythms of this whole thing, this total overall, is a visual composition in motion."

11

Pop, Speed, Teenagers and the "MTV Aesthetic"

KAY DICKINSON

|. . .|

The teen movie whose visual structure is intentionally rearranged to fit the pop soundtrack it bears is a much commented-on, yet rarely intellectually scrutinized presence. While scholarly analyses of various specific movies occasionally touch upon this, there is still much work to be done on the broader cultural significance of certain recurrent stylistic motifs which are encouraged by the assimilation of popular music into contemporary cinema. In these films, visual features such as editing seem infused with a certain pop musicality, namely the "MTV aesthetic": a characteristic which derives from the peculiar stylistic conventions of the music video. What renders these attributes seemingly unorthodox is the submission of editing to the customary tempi of popular music, a presentation of shots which defies the standard broadcast rhythm of around three seconds minimum each. Obviously not all music videos manipulate their footage in line with this convention, obviously not all disruptively pacy editing recalls pop promotional clips (for example, this is obviously not an Eisensteinian's intent), but the term has increasingly become short-hand for this trend in post-production.

While such a relation to time is common to, even sought out, in our reception of music, it is uncomfortably fast for the eye. Chion points out the differences in certain perceptual skills that establish this disjunction:

> the ear analyzes, processes and synthesizes faster than the eye. Take a rapid visual movement—a hand gesture—and compare it to an abrupt sound trajectory of the same duration. That fast visual movement will not form a distinct figure, its trajectory will not enter the memory in a precise picture. In the same length of time the sound trajectory will succeed in out-lining a clear and definite form, individuated, recognizable, distinguishable from others . . . the eye is more spatially adept and the ear more temporally adept.
>
> (Chion, 1994: 10–11)

Yet music video editing need not be this fast in order to imitate the music's tempo, which, after all, is always divisible. This predilection instead compensates, perhaps, for a quality which, although alien to the moving image, is intrinsic to popular music: the repetition of decidedly short phrases (the riff) and a disregard of narrative progression (popular music instead alternates between any arrangement of verse, chorus and middle eight). Considering musical repetition's controlled stasis and its subsequent incompatibility with visual conventions, this recourse to flashing visual imagery is perhaps a strategic one. Within the structure of the music video, speed helps diminish the, at times, deadening visual connotations of repetition.

Although such visible tempi originally expressed a compliance with musical form that was necessary to the thematic restrictions of music video, these characteristics have since seeped into other mainstream audio-visual media, especially those eager to express "youth." The "MTV aesthetic" is now a pervasive stylistic element of television, of adverts, and, in particular, of feature films.

A traditional film studies reading of this type of editing in isolation would refer, no doubt, to its "decentring" qualities, judging them, perhaps, less revolutionary than blasé and postmodern in their motives. E. Ann Kaplan's foundational text on music video, *Rocking around the Clock: Music Television, Postmodernism and Consumer Culture*, offers one such application. However, a closer analysis of the film's structure, one not so blinkered by theories of the *gaze*'s influence on the relationship between the film and the spectator, one more eager to unblock its ears to the subject positionings offered by the soundtrack, may proffer a divergent reading. While understandings of a fragmented subject position from this formal visual quality are, of course, far from invalid, I wish here to dwell upon how the "MTV aesthetic" might paradoxically and in parallel offer a completely different, though no less coherent, sense of self which is primarily constituted through the popular music on the soundtrack and its side-effects. With these issues in mind, I would like to undertake a brief classificatory tour of a film that employs this technique, Baz Luhrmann's 1996 *William Shakespeare's Romeo and Juliet*. I must apologize in advance for failing to fathom the more subtle and specific semantics that are exchanged between this film and the specific songs on its soundtrack—such a vast task is beyond the limitations of this type of analysis.

With each introduction of a new *Romeo and Juliet*, the emphasis must be on provoking a sense of novelty, even of capturing a teen sensibility (West Side Story (1961) acting as the obvious precedent). To a large extent, *William Shakespeare's Romeo and Juliet*'s manipulation of the "MTV aesthetic" achieved the desired effect formally. The film was deemed a resounding hit by teenage audiences, despite the potential of its language to alienate or deter them. The success of the film can be attributed at least partially to its attainment of stylistic contemporaneity which few critics or audience members failed to ascribe to the influence of music video.

The greater proportion of *William Shakespeare's Romeo and Juliet* (indeed almost all but the scenes of love declaration or tragedy) is composed of rapid edits, often constituted from restless moving shots, zooms and swish pans of, at times, less than a second's length. Tempo is sustained through an impatience with the shot/reverse shot typical of film dialogue. Cuts between characters mid-speech which serve little reactive purpose (as is evident in Mercutio and Romeo's pre-ball conversation) are not infrequent. Cinematically unconventional montages built up of shots covering objects from only slightly differing angles are brutally intercut with disjunctive single shots bearing other subject matter. At times, the pace is accelerated by a blatant, even comedic, use of speeded-up footage (examples include the first confrontation and the Capulet household's preparation for the ball). From time to time, the editing flashes from shot to shot as a character stresses individual words; this is residual from music video's visual accentuation of rhythmic tempo and indeed is more prevalent when the music becomes diegetically symbolic.

References to music video style are most overtly and successfully enlisted in the film's interlude scenes, a space where it is not only less likely to clash with the thrust of the narrative, but may even help to ease it forward. The switch from the church to Mercutio and Benvolio's beach scene is engineered through a play on music video form. As the church choir embarks upon a performance of "When Doves Cry," the editing presents the song in video-style disjunctive images (hearts and a dove in slow motion) which enhance both the song's theme and the immediate narrative concerns. With the viewer now in "music video mode," the sliding of the images into beach motifs (complete with swish pans of bikinied women in the backs of cars) is less disorientating, smoothly seguing into this as the location for the next scene.

The music video link is more blatantly enforced by Mercutio's miming to Kym Mazelle's "Young Hearts Run Free" at the ball: a burlesque sequence which is half video, half drag cabaret act. The ball scene also allows for the incorporation of another song, Des'ree's "Kissing You" which she performs diegetically while playing a hired singer.

The ways in which popular music, music video and the aesthetics of the film are constantly pointing at each other here is symptomatic of the specific horizontal integration of the major film, television and music corporations of the 1980s and 1990s. As Sanjek points out:

> the entertainment conglomerates have mitigated the decline in box office receipts by selling the music featured in films as vigorously as (in some cases even more so than) the motion picture itself. Evidence of such cross-media marketing is supported by the fact that, with a single exception, the number one song on the yearly pop chart since 1991 also appeared in a motion picture soundtrack
>
> (Sanjek, "Popular Music and the Synergy of Corporate Culture" in Swiss *et al.*, 1998: 177–178)

[. . .]

With these financial priorities placed centre stage, the "MTV aesthetic" in film might be seen as a more economical means of covering several bases at once when, say, the use of the individual rock star him/herself has always proved a particularly hazardous venture.

[. . .]

In order to fathom what these interwoven commerical interests might be, it is worth returning to *Shakespeare's Romeo and Juliet*: a Twentieth Century–Fox film whose soundtrack was released on Capitol Records. While the two companies are parts of different media empires, the union proves advantageous for both. Twentieth Century–Fox is owned by Rupert Murdoch's News Corporation which has vested interests in all (image-based) aspects of show business as fodder for his various publications (HarperCollins books, the *Sun*, *The Times* and so on). More importantly, the promotion of an MTV style potentially entices the viewer to subscribe to the station via satellite, something which is of obvious benefit to the News Corporation. As controller not only of the Sky network, but also of the satellite encryption technology, Murdoch profits from all satellite viewing regardless of whether he owns the individual television station. In countries where MTV is not received via cable (such as Britain), its signal cannot be descrambled without the News Corporation making money. Of course, Murdoch's control of satellite, terrestrial television (Fox TV, Star TV, which covers most of Asia, and Hindi network UTV) and a film studio entitles him to more rigid control of and profit from the fruits of the latter via the former.

Similarly, the EMI Group, which owns Capitol Records, benefits on many levels from its role in this film. It can sell the soundtrack (Capitol has established a tradition of fine-quality soundtracks which date back to their success with *Oklahoma!* in 1955) and the video in its retail outlets and, less directly, it is in its interests, as producer of stereos and videos, to promote the art forms which these types of equipment play. The corporation also owns VIVA, the major music video channel in Germany and most of Asia (Timbrell and Tweedie, 1998: 504 and 1051). More important for Capitol, as a smaller company within a larger network, is the wider airplay that the film gives several of its artists. Although this film has striven hard to maintain the image that its pop soundtrack was a product of love and integrity with tracks specially chosen by Nellee Hooper for their concordance with the film's themes, the presence of the bands Everclear and Radiohead (both on EMI labels) is telling. Moreover, several of these tracks' videos, effortless and cheap through their deployment of footage from the film, also served as a free advertisement for the film each time they were aired.

Miklos Rozsa (with, as a renowned Hollywood scorer, more than a vested interest) has railed against the intrusive and disruptive influence of such songs' deposition of the type of score which subtly complies with its film's narrative priorities: "all they want is to sell a song, play a cheap tune over and over, and sell records. The high ideal of the *Gesamtkunstwerk* has gone out the window" (uncited quotation from Evans, 1975: 207). Yet surely this "high ideal of the *Gesamtkunstwerk*" has, in fact, returned to film in reverse, with the visual elements, as we have seen, increasingly mirroring popular musical form. Although this may be "the wrong way round," its very diversion from the norm means it may purport to articulate generational difference while simultaneously highlighting a shift in how films may, at present, derive a great deal of their revenue.

[. . .]

Unlike the conventionally established (though distinctly culturally relative) snug moulding of the soundtrack around narrative themes, the essentially closed formal unit of the pop song is far less malleable. Here, perhaps, is buried the root of the revulsion towards the pop soundtrack: that this insistent, even invasive musical presence bearing with it all manner of overt social connotations may belie the fact that narrative or even traditional visual tropes may not feature as highly on film's agenda as they used to. There are more ways for music to interact with the film image than semi-consciously reiterating its visual and narrative themes, ideas that certain strains of film studies often seem reluctant to welcome on board. Moreover, sweeping the pop soundtrack under the carpet does little to silence its impact upon the constructed subjecthoods of targeted teen audiences. It is worth stressing that, to certain audiences, the pop song amidst a film narrative is far from (purely) a disruptive cash-in and may, in fact, be distinctly more pertinent to their identity formulation than the unobtrusive seduction that a classical score often so relentlessly strives for in an idiom alien to their particular language. While pop songs may seem transitory, base or mindless to certain film-goers, to a teenage audience they often play a vital role in both self-definition and micro-cultural stratification.

[. . .]

While an admitted unfamiliarity with soundtrack discourse might exempt the average film theorist from tackling the derivations of the "MTV aesthetic," its leaching into that most cherished element of film—the presentation of the image—surely cannot be so easily side-stepped. Alongside the more commercial manipulations of the "MTV aesthetic," the potency of this *visual* (though musically derived) formal quality in the articulation or, more pessimistically, interpellation of youth identity must not go unsung—as it does, say, in Smith's (1998) consideration of the "MTV aesthetic." While the author offers an engaging investigation into the commercial motives behind the "MTV aesthetic," he neglects to analyse its semantic debris. As my earlier recourse to Chion elaborates, the translation of musical tempi into visual forms unsettles many a viewer. While its sly opportunism (often anathema to the discerning leftist theorist) warrants our guarded attention, so too does the possible whole which might equal more than the sum of these exploitative parts. How might the audio-visual play upon jittery editing embody some form of "resistance" for a youth audience despite, even regardless of its entrenchment in big business? How might their aestheticization of *speed* (especially in terms of visual disruption) pronounce difference in terms of advantage rather than subordination? Here space permits anything but a cursory treatment. However, as will become apparent, a teen understanding of speed shrugs off depth anyway and my treatment, if not conclusive, is at least conducive to its environment. To get bogged down in speed means becoming a traitor to its fundamental aims.

Beneath the narrative specificities of any "MTV aesthetic" film (examples of which would include *Flashdance* (1983), *Top Gun* (1986), *Batman Forever* (1995) and *The Faculty* (1998)) lies a more sturdy foundation—the enduring preference for rapid-fire presentation. As each generation must demarcate its space, the lure of speed is a perennial favourite. Speed has been important to teen identity since at least the "invention of the teenager" and the "MTV aesthetic" is merely a more recent convulsion in this seductive mode of self-definition. If we trace these developments back to the 1950s, then it is worth noting the allure of speed to the beatniks (evident in Kerouac's writing in particular) and the frantic tempi of some of the jazz being played at that time. Since then, speed has played a sizeable role in youth differentiation from adult lumberings: quick-witted youth versus faltering age. A glorification of the moment—the moment of their "prime," a moment which disavows history and the primes of others now grown old.

Similarly, the accelerated pace of the "MTV aesthetic" became a new language for youth from the 1980s onwards, something which distinguished them from a parent culture then very knowledgeable about pop music from their own youth experience, who might even have watched *Top of the Pops* with them, thereby enormously decreasing the rebellious cachet of such music. And Kerouac simply will not do when he might be on the GCSE reading list. For contemporary youth it is speed in b.p.m., in increasingly commodified sports, speed the amphetamine which enables prolonged dancing, fast food, speed in computer games.

Chris Stanley makes the point that contemporary dance "music is 'impossible' to dance to, given its rapidity generated by synthesizers and computers. The music does not ask you to engage with it, but rather to chase it, to lose it or to establish a transcendental relationship with it" (Chris Stanley, "Urban Narratives of Dissent in the Wild Zone" in Redhead, 1997: 51) This, I would like to add, is a selection process in itself, one which allows entry into the guarded area of youth's collective loss. Speed in most of these forms works within a system of relativities in which it assumes superiority. There is also a certain amount of prestige and advantage attributed socially to attaining speed. Speed is elitist. Speed eliminates those who cannot keep up; weeds the weak from the strong in youth fashion terms.

This at times upturned hierarchy feeds back into the reception of music video and its stylistic genealogy, the viewers who are not frustrated by its editing speeds twisting them to their advantage in at least two ways. Firstly, they claim the authority of those able to interpret adeptly otherwise indecipherably fast images. Secondly, there is the potential to proclaim depth (the very quality fast editing denies the moving image) a redundant concept. Robert Pittman, MTV's founding CEO, has laid down the stereotypical perspective on youth viewing and has incorporated it into his station's aesthetic: "You're dealing with a culture of tv babies . . . What kids can't do today is follow things too long. They get bored and distracted, their minds wander. If information is presented to them in tight fragments that don't necessarily follow each other, kids can comprehend that" (Robert Pittman in the *New York Times* 8 May 1983, p. 43 as cited by Denisoff, 1991: 241). The clichéd notion that teenagers have limited attention spans is thus appropriated as a positive quality. In a decidedly teenage fashion, this move disregards the significance of penetration and its entrenched social value. The film theorist, of course, is faced here with a contradiction to the history of moving image development where depth, and especially a Bazinian notion of deep focus, has been equated with both realism and democracy, the freedom to choose what to focus one's eyes upon.

Speed also mocks certain concepts of labour. In the adult workplace there is an increasing trend towards rewarding accomplishment rather than hours put in—speed therefore is of the essence. The nature of menial teenage work, on the other hand, is largely based around clock-watching the sluggishly passing time, trying to expend as little effort as possible within it. In this case, then, the teenage cult of speed somewhat ridicules the adult work ethic, converting speed into a leisure concept with more to do with consumption than production. The speed of the "MTV aesthetic" and the computer game does not allow the eye to *rest*. A reformulation of the work/leisure dichotomy is undergone whereby leisure warrants more attention than labour rather than acting as an anodyne after the gruelling working day.

This restlessness is one of speed's most captivating qualities. Stanley comments:

> The importance of speed and movement—of being nomadic—has been identified in the sense that to move is to be unstable and to deny order and fixity, from which reference in a strategy of control can be exercised. But speed and movement also deny order and fixity in the sense of constantly re-negotiating particular spaces. Ordered spaces can be disrupted and plunged into disorder . . . These are events which seek not to territorialize or colonize particular spaces, but rather temporarily to reconstitute and reconfigure particular spatial forms and then move on.
>
> (Chris Stanley, "Urban Narratives of Dissent in the Wild Zone" in Redhead, 1997: 52)

Deleuze and Guattari emphasize an important point about the nature and necessity of speed:

> There is no structure, any more than there is genesis. There are only relations of movement and rest, speed and slowness between unformed elements, or at least

between elements that are relatively unformed . . . Nothing develops, but things arrive late or early, and form this or that assemblage depending on their compositions of speed.
(Deleuze and Guattari, 1996: 266)

This situation is particularly pertinent to the teenage condition; it realigns instability so that it may be beneficial, blurs the lines to the point of adult indecipherability and, as with the concomitant preference for structural repetition in the "MTV aesthetic," undermines the importance of "getting there" by glorifying the means rather than the end.

The rendition of space into place within moving image art forms is traditionally achieved through a steady narrative and a solidity of spatial rendition which counteracts any discontinuity the editing process may bestow upon it. None of these attributes are common to the "MTV aesthetic," something which may be seen as advantageous by its fans: the denial of space and all its restrictive implications. This is not to say that this is a zone of freedom, but maybe that it is sold as such, as an exclusive realm, yet firmly ensconced in the commercial sphere. The following comment from Virilio is both questionable and compelling in its concordance with teen utopianism: "Territory has lost its significance in favor of the projectile. *In fact, the strategic value of the non-place of speed has definitely supplanted that of place,* and the question of possession of Time has revived that of territorial appropriation" (Virilio, 1986: 133). Although I am not in accordance with Virilio's movement away from the socio-political importance of space, his idea of the obliteration of space may prove fecund. Within the more specific context of the teenage restrictions of space, its denial, the creation of a "non-place of speed," or even an unsurveyed blurred movement between regulated zones, seems advantageous. However, this is all formulated in relation to the controls exerted upon their use of and access to concrete space and herein lies the paradox of these philosophies.

The teenage appropriation of speed dwells close to the treadmill and the supermarket: enhanced speed, after all, requires more fuel, greater consumption. These usages of speed are staged subversion within the domains of capitalism, small-scale assertions of difference expressed through the lure of the commercial. Such strategies are appealing from a position of no real ownership or control, but a heightened knowledge of the market place: these subjects being neither dupes nor revolutionaries.

Thus we see youth not as oppositional in market terms, but as a marketable notion of opposition. As ever, the identities of youth cultures are largely centred on the consumption of various carefully chosen items (the construction of a taste culture) in which speed and pop music are currently still proving enduring. Here it is the use of a visual insinuation of speed, the glaring obviousness of a contemporary pop soundtrack and the subordination of the gaze to the whims of the music industry's promotional strategies which offer, through exploitative means evident to almost all involved, a strangely solid sense of self which differs from what is similarly fixed as "adult" as its defining point of opposition.

That this obstructive incentive to polarize (adult:teen, deep:shallow, slow:fast, classical:pop and so on) should stall in the middle of two-way traffic is telling in its revelation of the conservatism of certain aesthetic value systems—not least that of the teen. Yet surely it is best not to ignore the actual fluidity of the formal developments I have highlighted, especially as they may unbalance a formal hierarchy which privileges the gaze-driven narrative when contemporary cinema may be accenting other qualities. Evidently there is, whether we like it or not, a shift in the emphases of certain films and denigrating them does nothing to further our understanding of how the film industry implicates meaning and subjecthood at present.

Beyond industrial particularities, there has only recently been an echo of these aims in the academic treatment of the "high-concept" film, a category in which one could place *William Shakespeare's Romeo and Juliet's* look and musical sound, if not its language (Lewis (1998) and Neale and Smith (1998) in particular move outwards from economic specificity into examinations of identification). These commercial packages which eschew narrative centrality for a deliberately catchy and depthless surface (where Shakespeare's play fits in here is a moot point) evidently "mean" more than corporate profit. Even on that level, though, the manufacture of a plethora of potentially purchasable fetish goods defies a logic bred of closer readings of filmic circumscription and suture. If these texts are fractured, it may be so we have a diverse range of (commercially exploitable) paths to follow: we can buy more information, a more sustained gaze at the stars and so on. Film studies is still struggling to devise an analytical strategy which can read such "decentring" as neither an ineffectual shortcoming, nor a liberating embrace of postmodern flux. If nothing else, the relentless invocation of rhythm in these movies (editorial and musical) brings to mind the ticking of a clock which may serve to remind us that our concepts of the gaze are growing old and maybe a little too weak to rule supreme. Our most pressing task must be the invention of methodologies for contemplating how these newer types of film help construct different classes of audiences and consumers—surely questions paramount to film studies' agenda anyway.

That this configuration of selfhood, of (inter)textual reference, is increasingly the norm in mainstream cinema (and indeed it has always been present) should surely not lead us exhaustedly to bemoan the passing of a more standard understanding of quality—be that in terms of a steady visual track, seemingly more obliging nondiegetic music or a privilege of narrative over other filmic elements. [. . .] Yet, while the "MTV aesthetic" should not be read as either schizophrenic visual disjointedness or a volley of "meaningless" music, our definition of it in these terms may play straight into "their" hands. After all, perhaps the most potent rallying call and deliberate distancing device used by teens is the phrase "You just don't understand!"

References

Chion, M. (trans. Gorbman, C.) (1994) *Audio-Vision: Sound on Screen*. New York: Columbia

Deleuze, G. and Guattari, F. (trans. Massumi, B.) (1996) *A Thousand Plateaus: Capitalism and Schizophrenia*. London: Athlone Press

Denisoff, R. (1991) *Inside* MTV. New Brunswick and London: Transaction Publishers

Evans, M. (1975) *Soundtrack: The Music of the Movies*. New York: Hopkinson and Blake

Kaplan, E. A. (1987) *Rocking around the Clock: Music Television, Postmodernism and Consumer Culture*. New York and London: Routledge

Lewis, J. (ed.) (1998) *The New American Cinema*. Durham, NC, and London: Duke University Press

Neale, S. and Smith, M. (eds) (1998) *Contemporary Hollywood Cinema*. London and New York: Routledge

Redhead, S. (ed.) (1997) *The Clubcultures Reader: Readings in Popular Cultural Studies*. Oxford: Blackwells

Smith, J. (1998) *The Sounds of Commerce: Marketing Popular Film Music*. New York: Columbia University Press

Swiss, T., Sloop, J. and Herman, A. (eds) (1998) *Mapping the Beat: Popular Music and Contemporary Theory*. Malden and Oxford: Blackwell Publishers

Timbrell, M. and Tweedie, D. (1998) *Directory of Multinationals*, Volumes 1 and 2. London: Waterlow Specialist Information Publishing

Virilio, P. (trans. Pollizzotti, M.) (1986) *Speed and Politics: An Essay on Dromology*. New York: Semiotext(e)

PART FOUR

CROSSING OVER INTO THE NARRATIVE

The volume ends with a group of articles which pick through films where musicians can actually be seen on screen, where they penetrate the narrative either as characters or as actors (and usually as a strange combination of both). As this book's general introduction argues, there is a range of cinematic material laced with stories from the musical world, from fictional accounts, to biopics and documentaries. Likewise, there have been numerous movies which revolve around a musician playing the protagonist.

Here the film/music arrangement takes on a completely new set of dimensions, very few of which have been absorbed into the canons of what is studied in the university environment. If the preceding section exposed how we might gently coax film and music studies into expanding its territory, the remaining three chapters in this book also insinuate that our understanding of "movie music" is due for an augmentation. By reflecting on such factors, this section suggests how we might begin to study the implications not only of what musicians sound like on film, but also what they look like, what they wear, how they talk, how they behave in certain situations, and, perhaps more importantly, why we love or hate them so much for doing so. Here it is well worth contemplating the intricate reasoning behind why we identify (or not) with music stars: persuasive factors might include their biography, assumed mannerisms or grooming as well as (or in preference to) performance ability. If these characteristics are so integral to our consumption of a star's image, surely the means by which they are roped in to films is ripe for analysis.

Plantinga remarks upon how the "mockumentary" *This is Spinal Tap* (1984) satirizes certain codes of masculine behaviour and does so by condensing them into the particularly potent figure of the male rock musician. The chapter points out how many immediate associations the phrase "heavy metal" sets in motion for film as well as music fans. That the movie could be a resounding hit as a comedy implies that its ideas are not rooted purely in musical subcultures, that the ripple effects of music and its definitions of gender are felt far beyond their immediate surroundings. After all, something can only be considered funny widely if its references are broadly understood.

Keightley probes a number of films from the late fifties and early sixties which are either about or star rock 'n' roll musicians. He spots a trend in the majority of these movies: a predilection for protagonists whose integrities are under threat and who are encouraged to make a form of Faustian bargain in order to gain their fame. In penetrating the depiction of celebrity manufacture at this historical moment, Keightley notices that a specific incarnation of "authenticity," one which can hold firm against the corrupt forces of the culture industries, is a recurrent trope. This focus upon authenticity is one also shared with Grossberg's chapter in Part 2 of this book. The fact that both of these writers are perhaps more aligned with popular music studies (where "authenticity" is a central topic of debate) gives us an indication of how much these cross-disciplinary exchanges can inform and enrich academic enquiry.

Walking on the same ground as Keightley, where the distinctions between film character and musician-as-actor/persona are deliberately muddied, is Lewis's chapter. In her investigation of the extra-textual network set in place by Madonna's appearance in *Desperately Seeking Susan* (1985), Lewis draws together many of the debates which are set in motion by the other chapters in this section. Lewis's article, however, is less a study of what a film's plot may say about the social function of music (although there is that element to her work) and more an investigation into the repercussions of cross-marketing between media. She weaves together details about ancillary merchandise and co-ordinated promotional events—from pop videos and records, to Madonna fashions and lookalike competitions—to produce a complicated and compelling argument about star image, consumerism, female identification and feminism. Where this chapter draws in fresh ideas is in its reference to the subject area of cultural studies, particularly its dedication to understanding consumption and fan practice. In refusing to hold up the film text (whatever that might be) as the rightful analytical starting point, theorists such as Lewis have opened our eyes to the extent of the objects which can be considered worthy of our academic attention. And, indeed, it is this tradition which has done much to fight for the place of previously maligned pop music within university curricula.

Like Lewis's essay, the two other chapters refuse to accept that a soundtrack is the limit of music's appearance on film. All three persistently argue that any visual or diegetic musical presence will drag extra baggage with it into cinema from the outside world. These occurrences are as demanding in their need for specific analysis as an interpretation of a score might be and, right now, this is a refreshingly uncolonized area in which to be working.

Gender, Power, and a Cucumber

Satirizing masculinity in *This Is Spinal Tap*

CARL PLANTINGA

As a military term in the nineteenth century, "heavy metal" signified "large guns, carrying balls of a large size" (Walser I); today "heavy metal" refers to a kind of rock music practiced by bands such as Metallica, Black Sabbath, and Motley Crüe. The two meanings are not unrelated, as the satiric *This Is Spinal Tap* (1984) implies. During a concert tour of North America, a member of the fictional band Spinal Tap has trouble clearing an airport security checkpoint. With each pass through the metal detector, bass player Derek Smalls (Harry Shearer) trips the alarm. After several unsuccessful attempts, and having now become the object of many stares, Derek sheepishly reaches into his spandex tights and removes the item that tripped the alarm—an oversized cucumber wrapped in aluminum foil.

This moment succinctly embodies a chief satiric target of *This Is Spinal Tap*—the hyper-masculinity of Spinal Tap and heavy metal culture, taking its most exaggerated form in Derek's phallic cucumber. Spinal Tap's masculinity is expressed through flashy displays of technical virtuosity, a choreography of sexual display and male bonding, the "power chords" of the music itself, and phallic guitars and microphones. The band promotes what one (fictional) reviewer calls a "retarded" sexuality stripped of all romanticism or spirituality. Moreover, it is significant that the security guards at the airport checkpoint are women. Heavy metal's emphasis on male power is sometimes manifested in celebrations of the domination of females, and defines femininity as passive and erotically available. That it is two *women* who force Derek publicly to reveal his pretensions thus doubles the embarrassment.

The promotion of stereotypical gender roles is the province not merely of heavy metal, but of rock music generally. Simon Frith and Angela McRobbie claim that rock music solidifies gender stereotypes, and that hard rock, or what they call "cock rock," is a "male form" (373). "Both in its presentation and in its use," they write, "rock has confirmed traditional definitions of what constitutes masculinity and femininity" (387). The music video has also been scrutinized for its gender implications (Kaplan, Lewis). Lisa Lewis argues that rock videos draw on ideologies of adolescence and masculinity, creating a "male preferred address" which supports "a social system of male privilege" (35). In this regard, heavy metal is not qualitatively different than mainstream rock music; it is simply more extreme.

Heavy metal has diverse critics, ranging from the religious right to Tipper Gore to rock critics on the progressive left. Yet even sympathetic commentators describe heavy metal as a discourse of power and masculinity that defines masculinity in traditional terms as the binary opposite of femininity (Weinstein 102–6; Walser 108–36). The audience for heavy metal, as Deena Weinstein notes, "is more than just male; it is masculinist" (104). Recent developments in heavy metal culture include "lite" or "glam" metal (with bands such as Poison and Bon Jovi), forms which attract more female audiences. At the time of This Is Spinal Tap's 1984 release, however, heavy metal culture was, when not overtly misogynist, unwelcoming to females, excluding women from the rank of equals, and emphasizing male bonding. Yet like Derek's cucumber, heavy metal's image of masculinity is a fabrication and an exaggeration. And like the security guards at the airport, This Is Spinal Tap displays the pretensions of this hypermasculinist discourse for all to see.

[. . .]

Central to heavy metal culture is the concert performance—an expression of power, intensity, energy, freedom, and virtuosity. In a context in which power is construed as essentially male, the heavy metal performer marshals every technique possible to express potency and power—through music, costume, staging, choreography, and displays of skill with voice and instrument. The music features a heavy beat with a deep bass "bottom rhythm," together with power chords and distorted voices, both produced literally by excessive power, as the performers intentionally exceed the capacities of guitar amplifiers and vocal chords.

[. . .]

Much of the visual humor of the film occurs during the tour and performances. Heavy metal, Walser writes, "often stages fantasies of masculine virtuosity and control" (108), in which "spectacular gladiators compete to register and affect ideas of masculinity, sexuality, and gender relations' (111). Spinal Tap's pathetic reality contrasts with these delusions of mastery and grandiosity. Coverage of the tour begins with an optimistic, energetic montage as Spinal Tap arrives in New York, with the requisite shots of the band members moving purposefully through the airport, roadies unloading equipment, excited fans wildly cheering in a packed concert hall, and the band itself in the film's first concert footage. However, the tour soon leads Spinal Tap on a downward spiral of failure and humiliation. And though the concert performances are designed to convey grandeur, power, and virtuosic skill, various mishaps create an opposite sense. One of the film's best visual gags occurs at "Shank Hall" in Milwaukee, where during the performance the band is supposed to emerge, in a choreographed "birth," from three egglike pods.[1] Unfortunately, Derek's pod malfunctions and does not open, and while he tries to retain his composure, a roadie hacks at the pod with a hammer and then burns it with a blowtorch. Finally it opens and the relieved Derek bursts free, but at just the wrong moment—immediately after David (Michael McKean) and Nigel (Christopher Guest) have returned to their pods for the end of the number. What is intended as a skilled display of choreographed movement turns into travesty and farce.

In Chicago, the band checks into the Holiday Inn, where on the familiar company sign we read "Welcome National Company of the Wiz and Spinal Tap," a juxtaposition which belies the grandiose image Spinal Tap strives to create. Promo man Artie Fufkin (Paul Shaeffer) has set up an autograph session at a Chicago record store, but as the band sits glumly, dressed as "metal gods" to receive the adulation of their fans, no customers show up. Cleveland finds the band wandering in mazelike passageways beneath the stage, unable to find its way to the waiting audience. A band that cannot find the stage hardly conveys skill and power. Heavy metal bands often turn to images and themes of the occult or of Satan that supposedly carry implications of mystery and power. The occult theme backfires for Spinal Tap, however. The Stonehenge debacle, during which, after a breakdown in communication, a diminutive 18-inch (rather than 18-foot) Stonehenge sculpture descends from the rafters and is almost trampled by two dancing dwarves, leads to audience peals of laughter and to the departure of manager Ian Faith (Tony Hedra). But more importantly, it serves again to contrast pretensions of grandeur with actuality.

David's partner, Jeanine Pettibone (June Chadwick), takes over as manager, but she is unable to reverse the band's downward trend. In Seattle, their regular gig is canceled so they find themselves playing for the "monthly at-ease weekend" at Lindbergh Air Force Base, where the audience expects easy-listening music. (Black Sabbath—then called "Earth"—once found itself in a similar predicament: a booking mistake found them at a party where the audience expected waltzes; Weinstein 32–33). At the base Lt. Bob Hogstraat allows the band thirty minutes to set up so they can "get it over with." After transmissions from a control tower interfere with the guitars, Nigel decides he has had enough, walks off stage, and quits the band. Near the bottom of Spinal Tap's steady downward trajectory, the band appears at Themeland Amusement Park, where the billboard reads "Puppet Show and Spinal Tap." Jeanine tries to put an optimistic face on events, noting that at least they've got a large dressing room. David sarcastically replies, "Oh, we've got a bigger dressing room than the puppets!" In all of these cases, the satire foregrounds the incongruity between the music and its presentation, which are intended to signify extreme vitality and power, and the pathetic situations in which the band finds itself.

Heavy metal performance celebrates maleness specifically through sexual and virtuosic display. Performance in what Frith and McRobbie call "cock rock" "is an explicit, crude, and often aggressive expression of male sexuality" (374). For example, Van Halen lead singer David Lee Roth sometimes performed while wearing tight leather pants with the cloth around the buttocks cut out. On the cover of the band's first album, *Van Halen* (1978), Roth appears with a naked chest and a microphone jutting from his crotch. His running, jumping, and gymnastic moves on stage all were meant to signify physical prowess and sexual vitality. Such individualistic display is often allowed only to the lead singer and lead guitarist, although the drummer sometimes gets his solo as well.

It is thus fitting that Derek, the bass player, is the quiet man of Spinal Tap, content to allow David and Nigel center stage. With his measured demeanor, thick beard, and meerschaum pipe, he initially seems older and wiser than Nigel and David, carrying an air of dignity and intelligence. All such pretensions disappear when he speaks, however. During one interview he calls Nigel and David the visionaries of the band, rather like English poets Shelley and Byron. (The band regularly equates itself with canonized writers and composers.) If Nigel and David are like fire and ice, Derek says, he stands somewhere in between, like "lukewarm water." Lead singer David St. Hubbins, who says he is named after "the patron saint of quality footwear," is the group's intellectual "force" (such as it is), and the "straight man" of the group. The lead singer of a heavy metal band often "fronts" the group, acting as spokesperson in interviews. So David is more articulate than Derek and Nigel, with fewer comic quirks and eccentricities. He is the only band member who apparently remains separate from the groupies populating the film, and is the only member to have a steady partner. (At the Recording Industry Convention, however, Derek, Nigel, *and* David have prominent herpes sores on their lips.) David's chief function is to serve as leader and stabilizing figure, until his weaknesses allow Jeanine's "female intrusions" into the male enclave and result in the film's chief dramatic conflict.

Through Nigel, Spinal Tap's lead guitarist and the film's lead player, the film most pointedly satirizes the hypermasculine theater of heavy metal performers—especially guitarists. On stage, Nigel's strutting gyrations, facial contortions, and tongue-wagging exaggerate what every wanna-be rocker recognizes as the conventions of heavy metal's "cult of the lead guitarist." The performances of Nigel and the band reduce sexual relations to animal drives and strutting sexual display. While the music keeps time to a throbbing, erotic rhythm, the lyrics to songs such as "Sex Farm" and "Big Bottom" ("I just can't leave her behind") equate sexuality with expressions of aggression and lust. Moreover, the stage show becomes a display of erotic gymnastics. Spandex was introduced to heavy metal around 1980. As Weinstein notes, "Pants made of this material allow greater freedom of movement on stage and better display of the athletic bodies of the performers, thereby promoting an image of vital power" (30). Moreover, for Spinal Tap, the skin-tight Spandex outfits feed their obsession with penis size (also echoed by Derek's airport incident). Nigel imagines that the band's impressive bodies and bulging genitalia cause "terror" in many of their fans. His guitar-playing epitomizes the band's sexual display; his instrument metaphorically becomes a giant phallus, as he holds it against his crotch and swings it toward the crowd, while grimacing and suggestively wagging his tongue. In short, the art this band practices is a none-too-subtle celebration of animal masculinity.

Heavy metal emphasizes the guitar solo as much as any subgenre of rock; nearly every heavy metal song features at least one such solo, and few other instruments are allowed solos. The guitar solo is a primary means through which the heavy metal performer expresses *virtuosity*; it is a forum for the display not only of musical skill and technical wizardry, but of a more diffuse masculine quality. As Walser writes, "Virtuosity—ultimately derived from the Latin root *vir* |man|—has always been concerned with demonstrating and enacting a particular kind of power and freedom that might be called 'potency'" (76). Thus Eddie Van Halen's extended guitar solo on *Van Halen* is called "Eruption," a metaphor for male ejaculation.

In *This Is Spinal Tap*, all displays of what the band considers virtuosity become ironic implications of its lack. Nigel has meager talents at best, as is clear from a dismal guitar solo during which, after the requisite riff of repeated high notes, he grates his tennis shoe and then a violin against the guitar strings, creating a deafening cacophony. During another solo, he is so overcome by the sublimity of his playing that he descends—in orgasmic bliss, it seems—to the stage floor, where a roadie tries to pick him up without disturbing his performance. (The mediocrity of Nigel's playing stands in contrast to the guitar skills of the best *actual* metal guitarists—e.g., Eddie Van Halen, Randy Rhoads—whose obvious technical skill belies the contention that just anyone could play heavy metal guitar.)

Nigel's pretensions and fastidious nature—both privileges of rock stardom—become one of the film's motifs. Spoiled fussiness is apparent at Vandermint Auditorium in North Carolina, where Nigel becomes infuriated at the miniature bread (which confuses him because the meat slices are full-size) and at the fact that some of the Spanish olives are missing their little red pimentos. Later Nigel plays piano and ruminates about his music with |the fictional director of the rockumentary Marti| Di Bergi. As he plinks on the keyboard, Nigel speaks of the key of B-minor, which "makes people weep instantly." "I'm really influenced by

Mozart and Bach," he says, in a transparent attempt to link his virtuosity and musical genius with theirs. The tune he plays, "a Mach piece really," he calls "Lick My Love Pump." The neologism he creates—"Mach"—not only suggests the heavy metal guitarist's emphasis on speed, but also refers to Ringo's joke in A Hard Day's Night (1964), where after a question about whether he's a mod or a rocker, he answers that he's a "mocker."

Another memorable scene has Nigel walking Di Bergi through the room which houses Nigel's collection of electric guitars. One might expect a skilled guitarist, as a requirement of virtuosity, to have expert knowledge of his instrument. Unlike Eddie Van Halen, who constructed some of his guitars himself, Nigel seems to know little about the instruments. At each guitar or piece of equipment, Nigel displays either capriciousness or ignorance. As they stop at the first guitar, Nigel asks Di Bergi to listen to the "sustain." When Di Bergi protests that he doesn't hear anything, Nigel thinks for a moment, then replies, "You would if it were playing." Nigel has difficulty describing a guitar with special equipment allowing him to roam the stage freely, and Di Bergi tells the uninformed collector that it's called a "wireless." An heroic fantasy requires sacred idols, and for Nigel this is his "virginal" guitar, which has never been played. Nigel tells Di Bergi not to touch it, then not to point at it. Di Bergi asks if he can look at it. Loudness contributes to an ethos of power and intensity, and This Is Spinal Tap pokes fun at the mentality that valorizes sheer volume. As Nigel and Di Bergi move on to an amplifier with volume controls that reach "11" rather than "10," Nigel impresses on Di Bergi the importance of being able to play one notch louder. Di Bergi tries to explain that an "11" rather than "10" on the volume control doesn't guarantee a louder amplifier.

Heavy metal's theater of hypermasculinity doesn't simply relate to men; it has implications for women as well. Weinstein notes that "Women are aliens in the heavy metal subculture because of their otherness," and that heavy metal culture is "an enormous male bonding group" (135). Walser describes what he calls the "exscription," or exclusion, of women from heavy metal culture, and its misogyny. Heavy metal, he writes, is "a world of action, excess, transgression . . . , one in which men are the only actors, and in which male bonding among members of the 'hero team' is the only important social relationship" (114–15). Women are also seen as a threat because their attractiveness "threatens to disrupt both male self-control and the collective strength of male bonding (Walser 118). This in part accounts for the misogynistic lyrics of bands such as W.A.S.P., Guns N' Roses, and Motley Crüe, and the prevalence of the *femme fatale* figure in the songs of Dokken and Whitesnake, for example.

Essential to the theme of misogyny and exclusion, as developed in This is Spinal Tap, is the arrival of Jeanine Pettibone. After the Memphis show is canceled, David is heartened because Jeanine has announced that she is coming from England to accompany David and the band. Other than Jeanine and the relatively positive character of Bobbi Fleckman (Fran Drescher), who articulately castigates Ian for the band's sexist album cover, the women who populate This is Spinal Tap are groupies whose main function is to adore the band members and reinforce their masculine identities. Jeanine hearkens to media caricatures of well-known rock 'n' roll wives such as Yoko Ono and Linda McCartney. She represents a threat to Spinal Tap's unity, not only because she is a female who demands power in this boy's club, but because she is secretive, scheming, and utterly humorless. She eventually usurps Ian's role as manager and controls David, and thus the band. The film takes care to emphasize the lifelong friendship of Nigel and David with pictures of their boyhood life in "Squatney," to set up Jeanine, in the eyes of Nigel, as an intruder in this world of "legitimate" male relationships.

Jeanine is controlling and a bit dotty, charting the band's travel plans according to horoscopes. Her hold on David, and through him her influence on the band, is significant. David needs the "direction" she gives, saying that she "sorted out his life for him." On the telephone before she arrives, she tells David she can determine by his voice that he's been eating too much sugar. Jeanine becomes a kind of nuclear threat to the male culture of *This Is Spinal Tap*. She monopolizes and influences David, and associates little with other band members. In the band's bus, David and Jeanine sit in front, and Jeanine refuses David's mumbling requests for permission to join the other band members at the rear. During an interview David says that Jeanine influences the band's music through the criticisms she reveals only to him: "She gives me the brutally frank version and I sort of tart it up for [the rest of the band]." She sometimes whispers into David's ear, and he obediently acts. Despite David's claim that Jeanine and Nigel love each other (though admittedly their "communication is blocked"), their mutual antipathy is obvious in their competition for David's attentions. During a recording session, Nigel loudly criticizes David's playing, saying that Jeanine has been distracting him. The real issue is that Jeanine violates the masculine code of the band, because she usurps the power usually reserved for men.

As Jeanine assumes greater control, both Nigel and Ian become increasingly alienated. During a restaurant meeting, Jeanine suggests that their latest album has been mixed poorly, but her references to "Dobly" (rather than "Dolby") give Nigel cause to make fun of her. She then unveils her ideas for a new production design for the band, featuring masks for the three band leaders that not-too-subtly reveal her sympathies. While Nigel is to wear a Capricorn mask that resembles a devilish goat, and Derek a scorpion-face derived from Scorpio, David's Leo mask would be a handsome lion. Nigel quickly rejects Jeanine's plans, and hastily draws the Stonehenge sketch on a napkin, which becomes the ill-fated idea for their newest prop.

The conflict comes to a head after the Stonehenge concert, when David and Jeanine suggest that Ian share managing duties with Jeanine. Ian sees this as a demotion and an insult, especially since his would-be partner, as he notes, is "a woman." Lugging his cricket bat as a totem of phallic power, and after the requisite round of insults (cruelty is the surest sign of power over others), he quits the band and storms out. Later Nigel walks off the stage mid-concert at the Lindbergh Air Force Base, when his electric guitar picks up control tower transmissions. Of his departed partner, David later says, "We shan't work together again." At their lowest point, the short-handed band plays free-form "jazz" to a jeering audience at Themeland Amusement Park. Having successfully replaced both Ian and Nigel, Jeanine joins the band on stage with a tambourine, her presence breaking the unwritten rule that the heavy metal stage be a site of masculine theater and male bonding.

Neither the band members nor their manager accept women as equals; for them women are either complacent sex kittens or monstrous manipulators. The band's sexism is "retarded," or juvenile, because it is completely unselfconscious. The album cover for their release, *Smell the Glove*, alludes to the ties between heavy metal and sadomasochism, and features a greased, naked woman on all fours, wearing a dog collar and leash, supine before a black glove, pushed to her face. When Bobbi Fleckman denounces the cover to Ian, he tells her she "should have seen the cover they wanted to do. It wasn't a glove, believe me." When the band is told that the album will not be released due to its sexist cover, Nigel naively asks, "What's wrong with being sexy?"

Ian is a well-drawn character, and an important means by which the film satirizes a masculinity that can barely control aggression. Ian percolates with the threat of both verbal and physical violence (he carries the phallic cricket bat with him wherever he goes). Weinstein notes that heavy metal culture is homophobic, tending toward "an attitude of extreme intolerance toward male homosexuality" (106). Although this aspect of heavy metal culture is mostly ignored in *This Is Spinal Tap*, it is apparent in the insults Ian hurls at other adult men, featuring derogatory terms for homosexuals. Sir Dennis Eaton-Hogg (Patrick MacNee) is the over-stuffed president of Polymer Records (the pun on "Polydor" denoting the plastic or ersatz nature of his enterprise). When Sir Dennis cancels plans for the album cover, Ian covers the telephone mouthpiece and mutters, "fucking old poofter." Later Ian abuses a thickly lensed hotel clerk, calling him a "twisted old fruit."[2]

Although *This Is Spinal Tap* satirizes the hypermasculine theater of Spinal Tap and heavy metal, the film transcends mean-spirited ridicule. Thomas Hobbes, one of many thinkers who have mused on the psychology of humor, explained laughter as a sudden rush of self-esteem occurring when we imagine our superiority over the situation or state of others (quoted in Munro 91). At first glance, the humor of *This Is Spinal Tap* would seem to fit this formula, as we guffaw at the naive antics of this untalented band on their descent from stardom. Yet humor is not necessarily grounded in sneering contempt (though it sometimes is), but often stems from a more democratic view in which we all look pretty much alike in our weaknesses, pretenses, and fundamental lovableness. *This Is Spinal Tap* makes its major characters (Nigel, David, and Derek) into likable fools, quite boyish and gentle despite their macho posing and tough lyrics. Though we feel confident they would find some way blithely to rationalize total failure, we nonetheless cheer for what may be their final triumph when, at film's end, they reunite for a road trip to Japan.

The North American tour temporarily sends the band on a downward trend of canceled gigs and interpersonal conflict. This move toward defeat and disintegration, characteristic of ironic narrative structure, culminates at the "End of Tour Party" in Los Angeles. The scene begins with a reverse zoom from two old women lying on lawn chairs by the pool, an image expressing the opposite of energy and power, and suggesting that the band has lost its adolescent male audience. Nigel and Ian have quit the band and are absent, and the small number of guests makes the party seem lonely. One interviewer, in a reference to the Scorsese film, asks David if this is Spinal Tap's "Last Waltz." David feebly philosophizes about what "the end" really means, in an attempt to avoid the implications of the question. Derek and Nigel then engage in a classic example of rationalization. Derek asks, "Who wants to be a 45-year-old rock 'n' roller farting around for people less than half our age, cranking out some mediocre head-banging bullshit? . . . It's beneath us." They begin to talk about future projects—for example, a rock musical based on the life of Jack the Ripper ("You're a naughty one, saucy Jack")—that suggest a continued naive promotion of "retarded sexuality." They conclude that they are "lucky." "People should be envying us," Derek says optimistically. "I envy us."

The film's ironic ending is essential to its project. Backstage, before their planned last show, Nigel returns unexpectedly to "deliver a message" from Ian. "Sex Farm" is on the charts in Japan, and Ian wonders whether the band would be interested in re-forming to tour there. David at first acts outraged at the suggestion, but later asks Nigel to join the band on stage, and Spinal Tap is reunited. The traditional male bond is reestablished, and Jeanine, the feminine "intruder," is no longer seen on the stage. The film's narrative ends with a return to former "glory," as the energized band plays to wildly cheering crowds in Tokyo. Jeanine and Ian give each other cold glances, enduring an uneasy truce.

This is both a comic and an ironic ending. However much it seems "tacked on" or "throw-away," it softens the hard edge—the bleakness—of irony by ending with the comedy of social integration.[3] *This Is Spinal Tap* encourages allegiance with the band members, and especially with Nigel, David, and Derek. Thus, when the band reunites and their fortunes take a wildly fortuitous turn, the audience may be relieved. However, the ending cannot be taken at face value, for this social integration also signifies moral defeat. It ironically suggests that the band has learned nothing from its trials, that its newfound fortunes are undeserved and temporary, and that an audience can be found for just about any music, as long as it's for sale. Moreover, the ending furthers the film's critique of gender discourse in rock culture; this return to the status quo also reconfirms Spinal Tap's hypermasculine posturing.

The ending also raises problematic issues for the film's cultural critique, suggesting ideological contradictions in its thematic project. Portraying Jeanine as a stereotyped "bitch" encourages us to take pleasure in her final exclusion and the re-formation of the original male group, and to justify such pleasure by appealing to her personal shortcomings—her controlling nature, lack of humor, inability to manage the band, and so on. The critique of gender relations in *This Is Spinal Tap* would have been far stronger had Jeanine been made a more likeable, well-rounded character, with negative *and* positive qualities like those of Nigel, David, and Derek. Had she been portrayed more sympathetically, *This Is Spinal Tap* would more clearly highlight the cultural practices leading to her exclusion.

Among the handful of pseudodocumentaries and documentary parodies, *This is Spinal Tap* is most similar to *Zelig* and *Bob Roberts*. While *This is Spinal Tap* may in fact have deceived some spectators, its status as parody and satire depends on the spectator's recognition of its numerous comic markers. The audience must recognize the film as a "false" documentary fully to appreciate its art. The same is true for *Zelig* and *Bob Roberts*, during which the viewer recognizes that despite textual markers indexing the films as "documentary," Woody Allen and Tim Robbins play fictional characters in fiction films.

Films which satirize the documentary, such as *Mondo Cane* (1963) and Chris Marker's *Letter from Siberia* (1957), target the "serious" or "classical" documentary by pointing to silly, incongruous, or shocking subjects, while ironically wearing the mantle of serious investigation. In contrast to these films, the purpose of *This Is Spinal Tap* is not primarily to mock or investigate the sober informational function of the conventional documentary, but, like *Zelig* and *Bob Roberts*, to mimic the documentary for other ends. Thus *Bob Roberts* explores the relationships between popular culture and the American electoral process, and *Zelig* examines the possibility of finding personal identity in a world where illusion and reality seem confused, and where the self is defined from the outside.

The effect of *This Is Spinal Tap*, then, is not so much to explore the nature of documentary, as to focus outward, on to another kind of representation—what we might call the social representation of the self. *Bob Roberts*, *Zelig*, and *This Is Spinal Tap* all explore social representation—the representation of the self as political figure (*Bob Roberts*) or masculine ideal (*This Is Spinal Tap*), or the social construction of personal identity generally (*Zelig*). As Hutcheon notes, satire is a means "of bringing the 'world' into art" (104); both satire and parody are useful to contest and/or examine social codes or practices. In this way *This Is Spinal Tap* uses satire to examine and critique heavy metal generally, and, in particular, its promotion of a "hypermasculine" mythology, an ethos which reduces sexuality to animal instincts, devalues feminine qualities, and excludes women.

Notes

Thanks to Barry Keith Grant and Jeanette Sloniowski for their insightful comments on an earlier version of this essay.

1 An actual heavy metal band would more likely incorporate death than birth imagery into its stage show. This is one respect in which Spinal Tap misses the mark in its imitation of heavy metal.
2 One significant development in heavy metal has been androgynous bands such as Poison and Motley Crüe, and the adoption by male performers of make-up, costumes, and elaborate hairstyles that have traditionally been associated with female display. While some commentators see such bands as progressive in their deliberate confusion of traditional gender boundaries (Walser 131–33), I prefer a less sanguine explanation for their popularity. "Glam" metal, with its stage flamboyance, is calculated to appeal to young women, with whom it finds its largest audience. (Male heavy metal fans are often disdainful of the subgenre.) Through the performers, who are "made-up" in traditionally feminine ways, females gain identificatory entry into a "masculine" world of aggressive power, without threatening traditional feminine identity. This Is Spinal Tap was released just as such bands were gaining popularity. Although during concert performances the band occasionally wears stage make-up, the film deals little with the phenomenon of androgyny.
3 I use the terms "irony" and "comedy" here much as Northrop Frye uses them in The Anatomy of Criticism: Four Essays (Princeton: Princeton University Press, 1957). Although romance, tragedy, comedy, and irony are usually discussed in reference to the narrative structure of fiction, they are applicable to This Is Spinal Tap for two reasons. First, I have argued that This Is Spinal Tap is fiction. Second, even were this not the case, Hayden White, in his Metahistory: The Historical Imagination in Nineteenth-Century Europe (Baltimore: Johns Hopkins University Press, 1973), has made a convincing argument that nonfiction texts, and specifically narrative histories, make use of the kind of narrative structures Frye describes. Various scholars have extended White's claims beyond written histories to nonfiction films (e.g., Nichols 60, 143, 244: Plantinga). Frye notes that narrative forms are often mixed, as This is Spinal Tap blends comic and ironic narrative structure to become an ironic comedy. It features the social integration characteristic of comedy, but one which signifies the moral disintegration of irony.

References

Frith, Simon, and Angela McRobbie. "Rock and Sexuality." Screen Education 29 (winter 78/79): 3–19; reprinted in On Record: Rock, Pop, and the Written Word, ed. Simon Frith and Andrew Goodwin, 371–89. New York: Pantheon Books, 1990.

Harmetz, Aljean. "Reiner Has Last Laugh with His Rock Spoof." New York Times, April 25, 1984, sec. C, p. 20).

Hutcheon, Linda. A Theory of Parody. New York: Methuen, 1985.

Jenkins, Henry III. "The Amazing Push-Me/Pull-You Text: Cognitive Processing and Narrational Play in the Comic Film." Wide Angle 8, nos. 3/4 (1986): 35–44.

Kaplan, E. Ann. *Rocking around the Clock: Music Television, Postmodernism, and Consumer Culture.* New York: Methuen; 1987.

Lewis, Lisa A. *Gender Politics and* MTV: *Voicing the Difference.* Philadelphia: Temple University Press, 1990.

Munro, D. H. "Humor," In *The Encyclopedia of Philosophy*, ed. Paul Edwards, 3: 90–93. New York: Macmillan, 1967.

Nichols, Bill. *Representing Reality: Issues and Concepts in Documentary.* Bloomington: Indiana University Press, 1991.

Plantinga, Carl. *Rhetoric and Representation in Nonfiction Film.* Cambridge: Cambridge University Press, 1997.

Walser, Robert. *Running with the Devil: Power, Gender, and Madness in Heavy Metal Music.* Hanover: Wesleyan University Press, 1993.

Weinstein, Deena. *Heavy Metal: A Cultural Sociology.* New York: Lexington Books, 1991.

Manufacturing Authenticity 13

Imagining the music industry in Anglo-American cinema, 1956–62

KEIR KEIGHTLEY

Profiling the record industry in 1958, a major US family magazine with over 5 million readers suggested that rock 'n' roll was a manufactured product, part of the mass media's manipulation of its audience:

> Mitch Miller, director of popular artists for Columbia Records, contends that "the kids don't want recognized stars doing their music. They don't want real professionals. They want faceless people doing it in order to retain the feeling that it's their own." . . . But the music is not, of course, "their own." It is manufactured for them by fairly cynical businessmen who find the naive tastes of their young audience easy to manipulate . . . The kids are mostly unaware of the manipulation practiced by the music makers, although sociologist David Riesman found that "some are aware that their group standards are set by outside forces. But their loss of innocence has made them cynical, not rebellious."
>
> (Schickel 1958, 28)

Most popular music scholars read passages like this through the lens of the infamous "generation gap" viewing it as nothing more than hostile adults dismissing classic rock 'n' roll by ignorantly claiming, "it's so bad, it *has* to have been forced on the kids—why else would anyone listen to this junk?" Few would look beyond the ostensible object of the passage's analysis (rock 'n' roll music) to see the significance of the critique of the music industry, or to wonder whether teen readers at the time might have internalized such attacks on industrial structures and practices without giving up on the music itself.

In this chapter, I contend that the cinematic circulation of critiques of cultural industries like the record business before the mid-1960s birth of rock culture[1] needs to be seen as an important contributor to the development of that culture and its investment in authenticity. Rock authenticity wasn't simply adopted wholesale from the marginalized blues and country strands of rock's complex ancestry; it was equally encouraged by certain sectors of the mainstream, even, at times, by the culture industries themselves. As we shall see, the passage above is far from unique in the dominant popular culture of the USA in the 1950s. This suggests that rock's contestatory concern with authenticity must be understood to have mainstream as well as marginal roots. While authenticity was central to other musical cultures such as folk or jazz in the mid-1950s, the vast majority of rock 'n' roll fans at the time were not explicitly concerned with authenticity in the ways that rock fans would begin to be a decade later.[2] The rise of a strong culture of authenticity in popular music from the mid-1960s onward has consistently been attributed either to the influence of non-mainstream musical traditions such as folk, blues, and country, or to forms of radical social critique that have "trickled down" from theorists such as those of the Frankfurt School. The role of popular, mainstream mass media in disseminating the values that shaped rock ideology has tended to be understated or overlooked. This chapter examines the way the narratives of early rock 'n' roll films articulated critical discourse on mass culture and mass society that was already in wide circulation at rock 'n' roll's birth, and thus eventually contributed to the foundation of rock culture in the mid-1960s.

Echoing critics of the "revue" musicals of Hollywood's early sound era (see Barrios 1995, Rubin 1993), diverse commentators have claimed that the plots of early rock 'n' roll films are negligible or even irrelevant. Jeff Smith (1998, 261 n.8) refers to the "slight narrative" of such films, which is "to some extent a pretext for a series of musical numbers" (157), while Rick Altman (1989, 121) critiques the "flimsy plot" of films where narrative has become "just an excuse for music" rather than a key component, as he argues was the case in the classical Hollywood musical. Ehrenstein and Reed are perhaps most dismissive of the plots of early rock 'n' roll films, suggesting that "The sole purpose of movies like *Rock around the Clock* and *Go Johnny Go!* was only to squeeze in as much music as possible into their . . . running time" and referring to their "dopey plot[s]" as merely "dramatic filler" between the songs (1982, 17). John Mundy claims there is "barely a pretext of a plot" in many of these films, and suggests that "If the integrated narrative of the classical Hollywood musical implied ideological coherence, then the broken-backed, fractured narrative of films such as *The Girl Can't Help It* (1957) articulates the ideological, social and cultural tensions which surround rock 'n' roll and the historical moment of its emergence" (1999, 110). While Mundy's last point about the tensions surrounding the emergence of rock 'n' roll is valid, I contend there is actually a very consistent ideological position articulated in selected rock 'n' roll films between 1956 and 1962. If we look closely at the films mentioned above, along with *Jailhouse Rock* (1957), *Expresso Bongo* (1959) and *Wild Guitar* (1962), we will discover that they are united by much more than the crude exploitation and spectacularization of a teenage musical fad. The stories told by these films matter a great deal, insofar as they consistently proffer a cutting critique of the culture industries—a critique that subsequently becomes foundational for rock culture. These films portray the music industry in such critical terms that they effectively "manufacture authenticity" for audiences; by consistently representing the antitheses of authenticity (alienation, fraud, manipulation, phoniness, corruption, etc.) as evils to be avoided, these films contributed to the ideological foundation of rock culture in the mid-1960s.

The roots of rock 'n' roll cinema, part one

In 1955, a drama about inner-city juvenile delinquency entitled *Blackboard Jungle* used a failed 1954 recording by Bill Haley and the Comets in its opening credits. This attempt to enhance the authenticity of the teenage world portrayed in the film was the first use of a rock 'n' roll song in a major Hollywood film. It led to the song, "Rock around the Clock," being re-released and eventually reaching number one on the *Billboard* charts (thereby beginning the "rock" era according to some, though not all, historians).[3] Just as the ascension of "Rock around the Clock" to the top of the charts signalled the new importance of an exclusively adolescent audience to the record industry, the coeval rise of what Thomas Doherty (1988) calls "teenpics" (movies created solely for teenage viewers) was due to Hollywood's realization that teenagers were becoming the dominant segment of its audience. Though juvenile delinquent films pioneered the teenpic, the rock 'n' roll cycle of teenpics begins in 1956 with *Rock around the Clock*, made as a direct result of the success of the re-released "Rock around the Clock" and *Blackboard Jungle*. In discussing the paternity of rock 'n' roll films of the 1950s, historians usually point to the teenpic, with some Hollywood musical ancestry thrown in.

Interestingly, however, *Blackboard Jungle* is neither musical nor teenpic. It is a "serious" drama, coming out of a long tradition of Hollywood-produced films dealing with contemporary social problems. *Blackboard Jungle*'s director, Richard Brooks, had previously directed *Deadline USA* (1952), a film that presented a strong critique of corrupt and monopolistic practices in the mass media. As we shall see, this kind of "social consciousness film" contributed to the construction of many rock 'n' roll narratives. Also known as "message movies", these films explicitly engaged with social issues and frequently evinced liberal or even left-leaning political stances. They form a large and important cycle within mainstream cinema, part of what Roffman and Purdy (1981) label "the Hollywood social problem film," which begins in the early 1930s and runs into the 1960s, concurrent with the rock 'n' roll cycle. These populist-inspired films critique corruption, conspiracy, and manipulation, in areas such as politics (*The Phantom President* (1932), *The Dark Horse* (1932), *Mr Smith Goes to Washington* (1939), *The Great McGinty* (1940)); boxing (*Body and Soul* (1947), *The Set-Up* (1949), *The Harder They Fall* (1956), *Requiem for a Heavyweight* (1962)); and the mass media (*Meet John Doe* (1941), *Citizen Kane* (1941), *The Hucksters* (1947), *Ace in the Hole* (1951)).

The 1950s especially saw a remarkable increase in the latter type of social problem film, which articulated growing anxieties about mass society and media, as Douglas Brode notes: "Madison Avenue's massive power over the TV and radio networks—and thus, indirectly, over the mentality of the American people—was one of the most significant sources of movie material during the decade" (Brode 1976, 223). The year 1957 alone saw three important, Hollywood-produced, social consciousness films warning of the dangers of individuals appropriating the mass media for their own, authoritarian aims: *The Great Man*, *Sweet Smell of Success*, and *A Face in the Crowd*. The last was seen at the time as drawing upon the career of Elvis Presley for its narrative, as the film shows the rise to stardom of an uneducated singer from the US South, Lonesome Rhodes (played by Andy Griffith). At first, Lonesome, a self-described "country boy", is a champion of the "little people" using his broadcasts to criticize racism, poverty, and the pretensions to power of Establishment figures. However, Lonesome's populism eventually disintegrates into no more than a mask for his own growing alignment with the power elite. Success corrupts him and he sells his media influence to right-wing politicians who share his final view of the masses as "dummies." Social consciousness films such as these mobilized period discourses about the dangers of a mass media seen to have the power to brainwash the populace, turning the US into a nation of passive and easily manipulated dupes.

Rock 'n' roll emerged at this conjuncture, and was quickly articulated, at least by adults, with pre-existing anxieties over the alleged moral, political, and aesthetic declines seen to have been precipitated by the enormous post-war expansion of advertising and the rapid rise of television. A 1957 *Playboy* article, entitled "Down with Rock 'n' Roll" links its attack on Elvis Presley to a broader critique of advertising, television, and political image manipulation:[4]

> America has found something that has stopped it from thinking. And most of them seem to be delighted. The highest officials in the government don't make a move without an advertising agency's supervision. People seated in the highest chairs of the nation have their faces made up and their speaking voices approved for each public appearance. And the question is not "What is he going to say?" but "How is he going to look and how is he going to sound?" . . . And it's all because of |Elvis| who . . . is the biggest thing in show business.
>
> (Jessel 1957, 20)

While Senator Estes Kefauver's televised hearings into racketeering and organized crime had begun to expose massive corruption in US cities in the early 1950s, the almost simultaneous payola and quiz show scandals of the later 1950s reinforced a growing popular feeling that the cultural industries were equally guilty of manipulation, deception, and fraud.[5] For instance, a letter to the editor of a 1956 scandal magazine, featuring a cover story on a popular TV quiz show entitled "Do They Fix the $64,000 Question?", claimed, "If I believed everything I read in *Inside Story*, I'd go round feeling everything is crooked, fixed or phony" (February 1956, p. 34). Stalking the inauthentic, the false, and the phony in US culture was quickly becoming a national pastime. J.D. Salinger's 1951 best-seller *The Catcher in the Rye* deploys "phony" 37 times throughout the novel as a term of derision and dismissal, the antithesis of everything its protagonist, Holden Caulfield, stands for.[6] Holden also calls his brother a "prostitute" because he has left New York to work in Hollywood. Here we can see the prominence of discourses of authenticity, opposed to commercialization, alienation and fraud, circulating widely as rock 'n' roll emerges in the mid-1950s.

The growing links between media fraud, manipulation, and rock 'n' roll can be glimpsed in a 1956 *Variety* piece which claimed that rock 'n' roll had a "Svengali grip"[7] on teenagers, implying that its fans were victims of brainwashing. A massive 1957 non-fiction bestseller, *The Hidden Persuaders*, argued that blissfully unaware US citizens were being duped by advertising and mass media in general. The author, Vance Packard, went on to testify at Senator George Smathers's hearings on anti-trust legislation aimed at the broadcast industry.[8] Packard claimed that song-licensing body BMI was foisting rock 'n' roll on "passive" teenagers, and that gatekeepers such as DJs were manipulating playlists to keep "cheap music" on the air (quoted in Denisoff and Romanowski 1991, 102). It is into this context of growing anxiety about the manipulative and corrupt(ing) tendencies of mass media that a series of films dealing with rock 'n' roll and the music industry are released. What will later become rock's specific concern with authenticity may be glimpsed in the ugly encounters of innocent protagonists with the machinations of record business practices and personnel.

Rock around the Clock (1956)

The first rock 'n' roll film[9] sets a pattern for rock 'n' roll films in at least two important ways. First, it is what Denisoff and Romanowski (1990: 68) call a "filmed jukebox," a series of performances by stars such as Bill Haley and the Platters which they liken to a concert film

(68). Less obviously, its narrative concern with contractual relations, business negotiations, and various forms of deception, begins the cycle of rock 'n' roll films concerned with manipulation in the music industry. The plot hinges on two negotiations: first, when an out-of-work swing band manager, Steve Hollis, discovers Bill Haley and the Comets playing in a remote rural area, he's so impressed he decides to take the band under his wing and make them stars. Hollis attempts to convince their manager, Lisa Johns (who doubles as a dancer with the band) to accept an exploitative 60/40 percent deal, assuming that the female "hick" won't know she's being taken. Lisa replies that she reads *Variety* and that a manager's usual cut is only 10 per cent. Hollis then uses romance, attempting to seduce her into agreeing to the higher rate. However, she turns the tables on him again, making him fall for her, and reducing his percentage. The second contractual negotiation involves a powerful female booking agent, Corinne Talbott, who is in love with the new male manager, and who wants her romantic rival, Lisa, out of the picture. Corinne attempts to do this by insisting that Lisa, who still dances for the band, sign a contract with a clause precluding her from marrying for three years. If she doesn't sign, Bill Haley and the Comets will be "blackballed" and never work again. Thus, from the outset the music industry is imagined to be a jungle of contractual traps fraught with deception and corruption.[10]

The Girl Can't Help It (1957)

The Girl Can't Help It offers extensive footage of performances in "live" settings (nightclubs, television studios, rehearsal halls) of rock 'n' rollers who have no dialogue, along with dialogue and musical performances by actors Edmond O'Brien and Jayne Mansfield which are integrated into (and which propel) the narrative. The contrast between the deliberate mediocrity of the rock 'n' roll parodies performed by the latter pair (e.g., "Rock around the Rockpile") and the "real thing" of Little Richard, Fats Domino, Gene Vincent, Eddie Cochran, *et al.*, serves to underline the authenticity of the genuine rock 'n' rollers. The film's narrative is motivated by gangster "Fats" Marty Murdoch's (O'Brien) desire to turn his fiancée, Jerri Jordan (Mansfield), into a star. Murdoch cynically believes that if "talentless" rock 'n' rollers like Eddie Cochran can be successful, then *anyone*—with the right promotion—can become a singing star. He hires a showbiz professional, down-on-his-luck agent Tom Miller (Tom Ewell), to "manufacture" both celebrity and a hit for Jeri. Miller refuses at first, protesting that it wasn't him who made the stars he worked with in the past: "Not me—the public makes stars . . . it takes talent." Fats is impressed: "Integrity—even when you can't afford it. I like that," to which Miller replies, "That's what makes it integrity," suggesting that authenticity will be an important subtext of the film. Because he's broke, however, Miller eventually takes the job. While Miller manipulates gossip columnists to "build up" a public illusion that Jeri is already a "somebody" (thereby laying the groundwork for her record release), gangster Murdoch uses his control of the jukebox industry to create a hit for her. As Doherty describes it, "Through guile and intimidation (in a cynical acknowledgement of mob influence in the record business, former slot machine king Murdoch corners the jukebox market), the talentless Mansfield gets a manufactured hit record, complete with banner headlines in *Billboard* confirming the million-dollar sales" (Doherty 1988, 95). A *Variety* reviewer noted that the film gives the impression that the music industry "is controlled from top to bottom by warring mobsters" while *Time* magazine articulated the film's view of "no-talent"[11] success with the rise of Elvis:

"the underlying theory behind the enterprise seems to be that if Elvis could do it, so could anybody . . . little ado about nothing" (quoted in Denisoff and Romanowski 1991, 52). The reference to Shakespeare here underlines a convergence of elitist critical discourse on class and taste with widespread cynicism about the manipulative powers of the contemporary cultural industries.

Jailhouse Rock (1957)

Elvis Presley's third film presents him in the most unsympathetic role he would ever play. Elvis's character, Vince Everett, is unjustly jailed for manslaughter; in jail he witnesses the corruption of prison life, and is beaten by the warden. His cell-mate, former country and western singing star Hunk Houghton, teaches Vince/Elvis to sing and play guitar, and features Vince in a variety show, which is broadcast nationwide from within the prison. Vince is the hit of the broadcast, but he doesn't know it, because the warden and Hunk have conspired to keep hundreds of fan letters from Vince. Hunk then quickly signs Vince to a 50/50 "partnership" contract. Vince wonders why Hunk is being so generous, so "willing to split," and Hunk replies that it is out of a paternalistic concern for Vince: "I'm levelling with you, boy. Alone, you'd be like a lamb in a pack of wolves." Upon his release, the warden gives Vince the withheld fan mail, and Vince realizes Hunk has conned him. Vince then meets a female music industry professional, self-described "exploitation man" Peggy Van Alden. Together they form their own record label, after a larger label rejects Vince but then steals his style and his "sound," Vince and the new independent label become a huge success. Throughout the post-prison section of the film, Elvis's character is portrayed as obsessed with money, using lawyers to break contracts, and eventually becoming a figure not unlike the monstrously manipulative Lonesome Rhodes of A Face in the Crowd (1957). Vince becomes a television, then a film, star. Subsequently, the record company which had ripped off his style earlier offers to buy Vince and Peggy's now-successful record label, which includes Vince's recording contract. The following speech, telling junior partner Peggy (who loves Vince and the record label) that he has decided to sell out, indicates that Vince's corruption is complete: "We've got an offer for the label . . . it's just too good to turn down . . . to sell out, to Geneva Records . . . $750,000, a capital gain. $225,000 in cold cash for you after taxes . . . I'm afraid you've got no choice kid— I own [60 percent]." Here it is the rock 'n' roll star himself who has become the cynical and corrupted controller.[12]

Go Johnny Go! (1958)

Disk jockey Alan Freed's last film begins with a manipulative publicity stunt. Drawing on the myth of the celebrity-manufacturing Svengali-manager, the stunt is quickly revealed to be a fraud. At a rock 'n' roll stage show, Freed announces to the audience: "As of now, I'm looking for a boy with a beat. A youngster who will go straight to the top with a one-record smash. When I find him, I'm going to call him 'Johnny Melody' and start him spinning to the top." When unknown Jimmy Clanton approaches Freed backstage after the show, he is given the brush-off and told, "That's just a publicity stunt dreamed up by my press agent, and he's getting fired tomorrow." Freed then actively discourages Clanton from getting involved in the music business, telling him that staying in school is more important. Of course Clanton eventually does become "Johnny Melody" after a series of struggles, many of which are organized around financial matters in the music industry. The film is insistent about the importance of economics, referring to studio overtime, rehearsal costs with union musicians, and high taxation rates. It is also noteworthy that Jimmy Clanton's struggle to "make it big" is in fact a struggle to be accepted by gatekeeper Freed, after which Clanton's success is, presumably, clearly assured. Go Johnny Go! effectively reveals Freed—not the audience—as the true source of rock 'n' roll popularity and celebrity, whether through a misguided (and misleading) publicity stunt or through his power as a well-known radio disk jockey to make or break a hit record.

Expresso Bongo (1959)

These themes were not exclusive to US cinema at the time, however. The 1959 UK film Expresso Bongo was released in the USA and Canada in 1960, and also features a corrupt, cynical, Svengali-like manager, Johnny Jackson (Laurence Harvey). Upon discovering a talented but naive singer, Bongo Herbert (played by British pop star Cliff Richard), Johnny signs him to the by-then-established signifier of rock 'n' roll exploitation, the 50/50 contract, and attempts to manipulate Bongo to the top. Johnny gives Bongo advice about not acting "superior" to the "grimy yobs"; the moment the mass audience doesn't think you're one of them, Johnny tells Bongo, you're finished. The elitist view of the teenage public as constituting a debased taste to be manipulated is also articulated in the film by the president of Garrick Records, who complains that "Public taste has degenerated so far I'm finding great difficulty getting down to it. How low can you sink?" The singer and the diegetic audience are shown to be con- tinuously manipulated by the record business, as embodied by Johnny. An equivalence is thereby set up between performer and fans that ultimately encourages identification and a sense of intimacy: both are in effect "victims" of the music industry, and the struggle of the star against the system may encourage or resonate with listeners' own moments of resistance. The rock 'n' roll musician's attempt to avoid "over-commercialization" parallels the individual's attempt to maintain a sense of integrity, of authenticity, in the face of a mass society and a massive consumer culture. Thus, escaping commercialization becomes a goal of both artist and fan that in turn links them closer together. The film ends with Bongo breaking away from his sleazy manager and going on to likely stardom in New York City, where perhaps he may equally escape the corruption of the British class system. That someone as naive as Bongo might evade manipulation and reach unmanufactured (i.e., authentic) stardom is a sign of hope for an audience interested in investing emotionally and otherwise in rock 'n' roll stars.

Wild Guitar (1962)

This emphasis on the fabrication of fame, and on contractual enslavement, money, and manipulation, saturates Wild Guitar. Reportedly made for a cost of US$12,000, Ray Dennis Steckler's cult film contains the fullest exposition of the discourses I have been describing. The poster for the film explicitly refers to social consciousness traditions, exposé exploitation marketing practices, and the pitfalls of the music business in its tag line, "Record Racket Exposed!"[13] Yet another naive country boy, this time named Bud Eagle (Arch Hall Jr.), rides his motorcycle into Hollywood, gets a lucky break and appears on a live television talent show. Before he has even met the notorious manager who will later sign him, Mike MacCauley ("William Watters" a.k.a. Arch Hall Sr.) is seen lying to booking agents that he represents Bud and making deals on his behalf. MacCauley subsequently demands slave-like obedience from Bud as he exploits him, ironically proclaiming, "I can't afford to take less than a hundred percent . . . cooperation." It is later revealed that MacCauley's clients never see a penny of their earnings. But before Bud discovers this, he is upset at MacCauley's repeated manipulation of both press and public alike. Pleasantly surprised to read a music trade paper article claiming four record companies are interested in signing him, Bud asks MacCauley about it. MacCauley responds by saying, "I put that in—*publicity*. There's something I want you to get straight. You don't believe what you read, only what I tell you." Here the mind-control generally seen to victimize the mass audience is applied explicitly to the star himself, once more aligning star and fan against media system.

Subsequently, a meeting between MacCauley and the paid, teenaged presidents of fake fan clubs he's set up to boost record sales reveals the depth of the Svengali's manipulation. The brazenness of MacCauley's disdain for the rock 'n' roll audience pushes the following dialogue beyond satire, effectively highlighting authenticity via its total evacuation: "These are the presidents of your fan clubs—every major high school in Los Angeles is represented here . . . we've got a little business to transact." Turning to the six assembled adolescents, MacCauley continues to outline his exploitation campaign: "As I was saying, this kid's got appeal—I think we can go the whole route—swooners and everything."[14] A greedy teen interjects: "Speaking of money, Mike . . ." MacCauley responds: "The usual rates will apply— I've never cheated any of you, have I?" The teens giggle knowingly, suggesting that fraud is MacCauley's *modus operandi*. A cynical teen asks: "How about a fad? What kind of a fad do you want us to start?" MacCauley lights up: "Oh, this one is a natural—eagle feathers. Bud *Eagle*—you get it? You wear them behind your ear, you stick them in your hair, put 'em around your wrist . . ." When another expresses concern about the rarity of real eagle feathers— "Where're you going to get eagle feathers, Mike?"—MacCauley replies dismissively, "Oh, turkeys, chickens, magpies—what difference does it make?"

As any form of authenticity seems to be irrelevant, a disgusted Bud leaves the room and begins packing to leave, unbeknownst to MacCauley, whose spiel is intensifying: "I want you to get those county schools into the line up—I want action! We've got to work fast. This kid's first record's got to be a million-seller. That'll get the attention nationally that I want." When a club president asks, "Without payola?" MacCauley retorts, "Payola, buzzola, or just call it ola—that's *my* business!" At the precise moment the film explicitly ties the inauthentic (phony fan clubs, phony eagle feathers, and phony radio play, i.e., payola) to a corrupt industry professional, Bud re-enters the room and asks the question that rock culture will answer in a few years with a resounding "no": "Does everything have to be so phony?" MacCauley's reply, however, is matter-of-fact about Bud's reification and about the commercial nature of popular music: "Bud, you're in a serious business, a big business . . . Now let's analyse this business. We've got a product to sell—you. Now to sell our product, we advertise, we publicize, we promote every angle to increase sales. Now, in the course of this business, we use fan clubs, we supply them with pictures, with information . . . Fan clubs are very important in this business." Bud protests that popularity ought to depend on the tastes of individuals: "But you can't make people, force people to like me. You just can't take a group of people and say, 'You like Bud Eagle and you go buy his records'." MacCauley rebuts this with his version of David Riesman's sociology of other-direction: "That's *exactly* what you do—life is a big game of follow-the-leader . . . That's the way of the world, kid, get with it."[15] But Bud disagrees: "I don't think you're right Mr McCauley, and I don't think I have to be a part of it." MacCauley then explicitly links the music industry to wider critiques of the corruptions of mass media and mass society (albeit disingenuously): "I admire you for that. If more people thought like you we wouldn't have so many crooked politicians and payola and brainwashing."

Nonetheless, MacCauley compels Bud to stay, not by contractual coercion this time, but by appealing to Bud's innate sense of fair play, reminding Bud of all the money MacCauley has invested in his career. Bud agrees to remain until the debt is paid. However, he finally leaves when he learns from a former protégé of MacCauley's that MacCauley is a swindler with a "fast pencil" and cooked books, who will get Bud to sign away his royalties. Eventually Bud captures MacCauley on tape uttering threats of blackmail and violence, trying to coerce Bud into returning to the fold. Turning the tables on MacCauley, Bud uses the incriminating tape to force him to sign a presumably authentic "new deal" with "no payola, and none of those phony fan clubs." Despite protests from Bud's brother, Bud continues an affiliation with MacCauley precisely because he is an industry insider who knows the system, tacitly acknowledging the commercial contexts of popular music making, even as Bud has struggled for greater authenticity throughout the film.

The roots of rock 'n' roll cinema, part two

So, what accounts for the consistency of these critical cinematic representations of the music industry? Numerous observers view films like these as examples of a kind of "trickle down" of Marxist criticism into rock culture (for example, Coyle and Dolan 1999, 26). Andy Medhurst implies this in his discussion of a UK film made a year before *Expresso Bongo*. In *The Golden Disc* (1958), Terry Dene's stardom is, according to Medhurst,

> sponsored by a group of older and conspicuously middle-class friends who open the coffee bar, a record shop and a record label in rapid succession . . . the fact that so much of the film is blatantly concerned with the economics of pop points to a broader cultural assumption—that pop . . . needed only shrewd manipulative management to turn it into profit made from dupes on the street. *The Golden Disc*, then, has almost Frankfurt School undertones, which will later become overtones with the filming of the satirical stage musical *Expresso Bongo* (1959). There the witless economic determinism of *The Golden Disc* blossoms into a fully-fledged conspiracy theory of rampant cynicism.
>
> (Medhurst 1995, 62–63)

Though he doesn't refer to the US tradition of imagining music industry manipulation for cinema audiences, Medhurst goes on to argue that the British articulation of the capitalist exploitation narrative extends all the way to the Sex Pistols' *The Great Rock 'n' Roll Swindle* (1979). While his account of yet another fifties rock 'n' roll film critical of the music industry is extremely useful, I wish to take issue with the suggestion that the radical critique of the culture industry by the Frankfurt School is the most likely source of the worldviews expressed in these films. As I have suggested above, it is clear that a more mainstream genealogy of this "broader cultural assumption" is possible. A number of potential sources circulated widely from at least the 1930s onward; along with those already discussed—populist social consciousness films (like those of Frank Capra) and popular press writing (Packard, Boorstin, critiques of brainwashing and of Elvis Presley's success)—we must also include Hollywood discourses on celebrity, backstage musicals, the post-war *film noir*, and the legend of Faust.

All of the rock 'n' roll films discussed here are equally narratives about the manufacture of celebrity, featuring the transformation of a "nobody" into a "somebody." Innumerable movies and fan magazine stories about the rise and fall of stars have been part of Hollywood's output since at least the 1930s, and these have frequently revelled in the disparaging display of publicity machinery (e.g., *Bombshell* (1933), in which the star's nemesis is her PR agent!). This self-reflexivity contributed to the rise of what Joshua Gamson (1994, 48) calls "artificial authenticity": "As early as 1931, the *Nation* wrote that fame 'is largely manufactured and that those best known are those who have seen to it that they should be' . . . This skepticism about the connections between celebrity and authenticity updated earlier anxieties about the trustworthiness of public selves" (38). He adds that "By the 1950s, how the publicity system works to manufacture celebrity and to fabricate sincerity were already central topics: stories covered press agents, deals, and the arts of appearances" (49). This led to a tension that Gamson identifies between manufactured versus merited celebrity, wherein the audience is, at once, aware that forms of fraud are common *and* willing to search for worthy, true, *authentic* stars. Likewise, the rock 'n' roll films under examination are stories of the manufacture of stardom in which merit and authenticity are demonstrated, in part, through the final repudiation of the mechanisms of that manufacture.

Some of the most celebrated Hollywood narratives about the making of stars have also been musicals (e.g., A *Star is Born*). While it may seem obvious that the musical influenced rock 'n' roll films in terms of, for instance, direct address in musical performance, other aspects, such as the classical Hollywood musical's self-reflexivity (Feuer 1993), were arguably of even greater importance. Rick Altman is insistent that the Hollywood backstage musical (or what he calls the "show musical") is a form of exposé that often unveils "the evil under-side of the stage" (1989, 205) as well as working to oppose "the show as business transaction to the show as entertainment" (341). Altman notes that many backstage musicals "mix . . . music and the underworld in shady night-club back rooms" (205). He goes to argue that it is "the show musical that takes most literally the need to reconcile entertainment with work and business, for the show musical alone regularly confronts directly the question of entertainment's monetary value" (342), even though musicals in general labour "to erase the shameful spectre of [their] mediated status as well as . . . commercial function" (357). The revelatory aspects of the backstage musical mean that, almost from its inception, it has been linked with questions of truth and authenticity. We can also see prototypes of the manipulation/fraud theme of the rock 'n' roll cycle in the plots of film musicals well known (for instance, *Singin' in the Rain*'s (1952) vocal-ghosting), and not so well known (*Radio City Revels* (1938): a washed-up songwriter regains celebrity by stealing the ideas of an amateur who hums original, hit melodies while asleep;[16] or *Rhythm on the River* (1940): Bing Crosby is a truly talented songwriter who ghostwrites for a famous but talentless "star" songwriter). In these films, the fraudulent songwriter gets his comeuppance and the authentic talent is finally recognized and rewarded, just as the rock 'n' roll films recuperate their protagonists.

Well known for their deceitful, desperate, and cynical characters, many *films noirs* equally concern a society alienated by commerce, driven by contracts, and filled with conspiracy and corruption, according to Brian Neve (1992). *Film noir* influenced the moral as well as visual style of post-war Hollywood cinema, and no doubt contributed to popular cynicism about business in general and contracts in particular.[17] Neve also points out that "the emphasis in *film noir* on contractual relationships, governed by money" strongly echoes the story of Faust (164). Faust is almost always portrayed as a "long-haired boy" and "intellectual nonconformist" (Berman 1982, 38). At a crossroads, Faust makes a deal with the devil, Mephistopheles; in return for his everlasting soul, Faust receives, in various versions of the story, knowledge, money, power, fame. In some Faust legends, he obtains the ability to create illusions in the minds of others, suggesting the brainwashing anxieties of 1950s criticisms of mass media idols. Berman sees Goethe's *Faust* (1790–1832) as a quintessential story of modernity, in part because it connects capitalism and enlightenment in the form of Faust's desperate desire for development—intellectual, emotional, economic—at any cost. It seems easy to draw parallels with the scenarios of the films under discussion, with the manager (Mephistopheles) offering a contract to the "long-haired boy" (Faust); the very idea that what is at stake is an everlasting soul can be read, like the "soul" of soul music, as integrity, genuine feeling, authenticity. However, there are signal differences: Faust summons Mephistopheles, actively seeking him out, since without his assistance he cannot achieve his goals; Faust is ultimately destroyed by his ambition, with the devil collecting his due. In the films under discussion, however, the active figure is the Svengali-manager, who seeks out the young performer. In the end, the performer rejects the methods of the Mephistophelian manager, eventually achieving fame *with* soul, integrity, authenticity. These films turn out to be anti-Faust narratives, in which the protagonists resemble Goethe's Gretchen more than his Faust: innocents with pure hearts who struggle against a corrupt environment (even though they may, on occasion, be corrupted temporarily, as in *Jailhouse Rock*).

Conclusion

The refusal of the Faustian bargain becomes foundational for rock discourse. As represented within the diegesis, it turns out that the young talent never really needed the various forms of manipulation and deception to be successful; they were thrust upon the performer because of prejudices which presume that popularity is unrelated to mere talent, that mass culture is a top-down process, and that success is a product manufactured by the music industry rather than by the desires of the audience. It is these presumptions that rock culture challenges. In the encounter of authentically talented individuals with an inherently corrupting industrial system, these films negotiate the tension between popularity as function of mass industry and popularity as expression of the values and aspirations of real people. Rock culture emerges in the belief that mass popularity does not require mass manipulation, that success can be merited by truly talented performers, and that some million-selling stars can be authentic. As we have seen, the protagonist of these films starts out a naive, young person, whose antagonist is an older, industry insider embodying the Machiavellian machinery of the music industry. This showdown between callow, genuine talent and callous, ruthless greed is crucial, and not merely because it suggests a Manichean struggle between good and evil on the terrain of the popular. More importantly, it effectively displaces the implication of the performer in the commercial, music-for-profit system onto the persona of the manager, whose age clearly distinguishes him or her not only from the teen audience, but, significantly, from the performer himself (who, as we have seen, is often aligned with the fans).[18] Thus corruption and inauthenticity are not necessary features of mass success, but of industry personnel and practices. This bifurcation assists rock culture in the development of its particular (and even peculiar) process of disseminating anti-mass or subversive values via dominant mass media, or what I have elsewhere referred to as rock's status as "subdominant" culture.[19]

We may not be able, retrospectively, to ascertain whether teen audiences *circa* 1956–62 internalized these critiques, but neither can we ignore the fact that, approximately five to ten years later, a mass musical culture emerged that was organized precisely around these discourses. Even though a fully articulated conception of authenticity was not prominent in the adolescent popular music culture of the 1950s, a sort of "proto-rock authenticity" nonetheless functions as a structuring absence within these films. Despite their status as teen exploitation movies jumping on the latest musical fad of the time, these stories effectively showcase authenticity, by virtue of the onslaught of inauthentic elements (fraud, corruption, manipulation, exploitation) that are then demonized and repudiated. Here we see the privileging of a kind of anti-commercial and straightforward (direct, unmediated) relationship between performer and audience. Yet it is less a conventional struggle of art versus commerce than, as in Gamson's account of celebrity, a conflict between authentic popularity (in other words, merited commercial success) and inauthentic popularity (manipulated commercial success). And here we have a key to an often overlooked aspect of rock culture: authentic commercial success may be superior to its devious cousin, but it is commercial success nonetheless. Led by successful performers like the Beatles and Bob Dylan, rock was born inside the mainstream of popular music in the 1960s, making rock, from its inception, always already part of the music industry, a commercial product, an element of dominant mass media. But the fervid disavowal of this reality becomes central to rock ideology, and this is why, in part, its mainstream, mass media ancestry has been occluded in accounts of rock history. These early rock 'n' roll films can be said to "manufacture authenticity" for mainstream audiences because, in the process of foregrounding a young performer's resistance to the corrupt and manipulative tendencies of the music industry and thereby privileging *un*manufactured popularity (genuine talent = genuine success), authenticity is transformed into a core value in the consumption of mainstream, manufactured cultural commodities like records and stars.

I wish to close by touching on a film that at once continues this cycle of early rock 'n' roll films (in its unflinching portrayal of the music industry's manufacturing mechanisms), *and* sounds the cinematic first note of what will ultimately become the most "authentic" kind of rock movie, the documentary. The National Film Board of Canada's documentary about Paul Anka, *Lonely Boy* (1961), is stunning in its frank revelation of its subject's ambitiousness, industry insiderism, image building, and plastic surgery. An example of a cinematic movement away from manipulated illusion and toward greater "truth" in non-fiction filmmaking, the *cinema verité* approach of *Lonely Boy* means that authenticity is an explicit structuring presence. We see this in the film's many self-reflexive moments, which reveal (and even revel in) the presence of the filmmakers and the process of the film's manufacture. At the same time, it is evident that the film would not have been possible without Paul Anka's total and daring cooperation (making it, as well, the far-superior precursor to Madonna's *Truth or Dare* (1991)). Following *Lonely Boy*, documentaries like *Don't Look Back* (1967), *Monterey Pop* (1969), *Woodstock*

(1970), *Gimme Shelter* (1970), and many others emerged as emblematic of rock on film, in large part because the constructed and artificial nature of fictional films had come to be seen as inimical to rock's authenticity project; non-fiction purported to offer truth, direct, unmediated reality, and a sense of *unmanufacture* that resonated with the core values of rock culture.[20] The irony of *Lonely Boy* is that a film that seems to set out to debunk Anka and to reveal his falseness, phoniness, inauthenticity, ultimately does just the opposite. The more we hear Anka talk about his career, and watch him at work, the more we are compelled to see him as human being rather than manufactured product. The unveiling of the machinery of Anka's celebrity—and of the filmmaking process itself—enhances our proximity to him (and to some kind of "truth"); to the extent that he appears "human" he is not "manufactured." In the course of the film, it becomes clear that it is Anka, not his manager, who is in control of his music and his career. Thus *Lonely Boy* also manufactures authenticity out of the exposé materials of the rock 'n' roll film, but in a new mode that will soon become dominant with the rise of "rockumentary" realism.

Notes

I would like to thank Charles Acland, Daniela Sneppova, and Will Straw for their helpful comments on this chapter.

1 See Keightley 2001 for an argument about the need to distinguish sharply between rock 'n' roll (*ca.* 1955–58) and rock (*ca.* 1965–66 onward), a distinction flowing from rock's self-conscious adaptation and dissemination of the critique of mass society.

2 See Coyle and Dolan's (1999, 25–26) discussion of the absence of a concern with authenticity in early rock 'n' roll. We must remember here that while authenticity has been a key concern for Western societies for centuries, and one crucial to less mainstream musical cultures before rock, rock's specificity lies in the ways it foregrounds questions of authenticity in a new context, commercial popular music. For the longer history of authenticity in pre-rock US culture, see Orvell (1989).

3 For example Peterson (1990); for the anti-1955 position, see note 1 above.

4 One strand of this growing popular critique would culminate in Daniel Boorstin's 1961 best-seller, *The Image.* Subtitled "A Guide to Pseudo-Events in America," Boorstin is particularly critical of the growing culture of the celebrity, whom he describes as "a human pseudo-event" (45ff.). Like "phony," "pseudo" became a keyword signalling post-war culture's expanding search for authenticity. Dismissing mass media stardom as "a new category of human emptiness" (49), Boorstin is clearly speaking to period anxieties about mass media manipulation and deception, as congealed in the form of the false idols of teen music. For Boorstin, the post-war predominance of the artificial, illusory, and pseudo has actually contributed to a desire for their opposites, to a resurgence of the real; he concludes that the growing popular interest in news of truly spontaneous, *unmanufactured* events such as crime is actually a hopeful sign of the American people's unvanquished hunger for "uncorrupted authenticity" (254).

5 Kefauver later headed a 1955 Senate Judiciary Subcommittee investigation into juvenile delinquency and the "possible deleterious effect upon . . . children of certain of the media of mass communication" (quoted in Doherty 1988, 117). The report of the Subcommittee

contributed to the growing belief that mass media audiences could be unduly influenced by the output of the cultural industries. See also (Gilbert 1986, 143ff. (esp. the reference to brainwashing and Rock All Night (1957) on p. 155)).

6 The statistic is cited in "'The Catcher' On the Web." Entertainment Weekly, 16 November, 2001: 176.

7 "Alltime B'klyn 204G B.O. High on Rock 'n' Roll," Variety, 11 April, 1956, p. 60. "Svengali" is a term inextricably tied to discussions of pop idols, to this day. Referring to a behind-the-scenes manager or handler of a performer, its negative connotations developed in the novel Trilby (1894) by George du Maurier. "Svengali" is the name given to the orchestra conductor who trains the tone-deaf, poor and innocent young woman, Trilby. Trilby becomes an international singing star, but can only sing while looking at Svengali, who appears to have magical powers over her. When Svengali dies, she comes out of the spell, can no longer sing, and has no memory of being a star. Thus Variety's reference to a "Svengali grip" on teens suggests that, like Trilby, the adolescent audience is unaware of its manipulation by a puppet-master now called "rock 'n' roll."

8 It is interesting that Packard, whose expertise did not extend to the record industry or even to popular music, was seen as an important witness; obviously, rock 'n' roll was already by 1957 implicated (in the minds of many) in a broader media conspiracy. See Horowitz (1994, esp. 150ff.) on the role of liberal and left-leaning writers like Packard in helping to "shape the transition from the 1950s to the 1960s," which in part involved questioning "the extent of the nation's commitments to justice, equality, and authenticity" (150).

9 It is likely not the first film with "rock 'n' roll" in its title, however; that honour probably belongs to the 1955 film Rock 'n' Roll Revue, whose title is honest about its structure—a plotless series of musical performances strung together one after the other—if less so about its musical content. It was originally entitled Rhythm and Blues Revue, and contains performances by jazz artists such as Duke Ellington, Lionel Hampton, Nat King Cole, and Dinah Washington, along with the Clovers, Big Joe Turner, and Ruth Brown. Its revue structure is the result of the footage originating as short, single-song film clips called "Snaders" that were subsequently compiled into a feature-length film. See Smith (1998, 382) and Crenshaw (1994, 182).

10 Steve and Lisa marry before signing the contract, thereby outwitting Corinne, providing the requisite happy ending to the romantic component of the film's narrative, and ensuring Bill Haley and the Comets' commercial success.

11 The phrase is from a 1959 New York Times piece on teen idols and modern recording-studio technology entitled "How No-Talent Singers Get 'Talent'" (Wilson 1959).

12 Elvis's character is rehabilitated in the end. He loses his voice after being punched by Hunk during a disagreement about the record deal. As a result, most industry insiders write him off. Only Hunk and Peggy stick by him while he convalesces. He recovers and realizes the error of his ways.

13 This poster is reproduced in Bettrock (1986, 96); see Schaefer (1999) for a discussion of exploitation films and their marketing.

14 This is likely a reference to the widespread rumour that George Evans, Frank Sinatra's press agent during his early teen idol days (the 1940s), had paid bobbysoxers to scream, faint, and riot in order to build up Sinatra's romantic image in the press as "Swoonatra".

15 Interestingly, That's the Way of the World is the title of a 1974 film about a gangster-run record label and various forms of "Racism, graft, and corruption in the music business" (Crenshaw

1994, 226). For Riesman's idea of "other-direction" and an influential critique of the alienations of mass society, see Riesman *et al.* (1953).

16 This is an example of a sub-set of backstage musicals known as "radio musicals" in which a parade of radio stars are pictured performing at a radio station. One of the very first, *The Big Broadcast* (1932), is explicitly organized around economic issues: a group of radio stars rally around a failing station to help it get out of financial difficulties. Films like these are clearly the precursors of the "jukebox musical" of the post-war years. For a useful discussion of discourses of "art versus commerce" in Hollywood films about jazz, see Gabbard (1996).

17 See especially Neve's discussion of *Night and the City*, p. 165. Although I believe populist versions of media industry critique are the key influences on these rock 'n' roll films, it is also important to note that many *films noirs* (and many Hollywood films in general) were written by screenwriters who had been members of the Popular Front, familiar with and sympathetic to forms of Marxist political economy. On populism, see Webster (1988).

18 Discussing rock films of the late sixties and seventies, Barry Grant (1986, 203ff.) makes a similar point. However, he sees this tradition beginning much later than I do, with Sonny and Cher's *Good Times* (1967), in which the evil manager Mordicus is taken to represent the evils of the entire record industry.

19 I use this term to highlight the way rock music has historically worn subcultural clothes and espoused countercultural values at the same time as it has been a massively successful component of mainstream, dominant culture. See Keightley (2001, esp. 140–141).

20 Even some of the very best *fictional* rock films pay homage to the documentary, as seen in so-called "mockumentaries" like *This Is Spinal Tap* (1984) and *Hedwig and the Angry Inch* (2001). See also Arthur (1993) on authenticity in the documentary.

References

Altman, Rick (1989) *The American Film Musical.* Bloomington: Indiana University Press

Arthur, P. (1993) "Jargons of Authenticity (Three American Moments)" in Renoir, M. (ed.) *Theorizing Documentary.* London: Routledge, pp. 108–134

Barrios, Richard (1995) *A Song in the Dark: The Birth of the Musical Film.* NewYork: Oxford University Press

Berman, Marshall (1982) *All That is Solid Melts into Air: The Experience of Modernity.* New York: Penguin

Bettrock, A. (1986) *The I Was a Teenage Juvenile Delinquent Rock 'n' Roll Horror Beach Party Movie Book.* New York: St Martin's Press

Boorstin, Daniel (1971 [first published in 1961]) *The Image: A Guide to Pseudo-Events in America.* New York: Atheneum

Brode, Douglas (1976) *The Films of the Fifties.* Secaucus, NJ: Citadel Press

Coyle, Michael and Dolan, Jon (1999) "Modeling Authenticity, Authenticating Commercial Models" in Dettmar, Kevin and Richey, William (eds) *Reading Rock and Roll: Authenticity, Appropriation, Aesthetics.* New York: Columbia University Press, 17–36

Crenshaw, Marshall (1994) *Hollywood Rock: A Guide to Rock 'n' Roll in the Movies.* New York: HarperPerennial

Denisoff, R. Serge and Romanowski, William (1990) "Katzman's *Rock around the Clock*: A Pseudo-Event?" in *Journal of Popular Culture* 24.1: 65–78

Denisoff, R. Serge and Romanowski, William (1991) *Risky Business: Rock in Film*. New Brunswick, NJ: Transaction

Doherty, Thomas (1988) *Teenagers & Teenpics: The Juvenilization of American Movies in the 1950s*. Boston: Unwin Hyman

Ehrenstein, David and Reed, Bill (1982) *Rock on Film*. New York: Delilah Books

Feuer, Jane (1993) *The Hollywood Musical*, 2nd edition. Bloomington: Indiana University Press

Gabbard, Krin (1996) *Jammin' at the Margins: Jazz and the American Cinema*. Chicago: University of Chicago Press

Gamson, Joshua (1994) *Claims to Fame: Celebrity in Contemporary America*. Berkeley: University of California Press

Gilbert, James (1986) *A Cycle of Outrage: America's Reaction to the Juvenile Delinquent in the 1950s*. NewYork: Oxford University Press

Grant, Barry K. (1986) "The Classical Hollywood Musical and the 'Problem' of Rock 'n Roll" in *The Journal of Popular Film and Television* 13/4: 195–205

Horowitz, David (1994) *Vance Packard and American Social Criticism*. Chapel Hill: University of North Carolina Press

Jessel, George (1957) "Down with Rock and Roll" in *Playboy* January: 20

Keightley, Keir (2001) "Reconsidering Rock" in Frith, Simon, Straw, Will and Street, John (eds) *The Cambridge Companion to Pop and Rock*. Cambridge: Cambridge University Press, 109–142

Medhurst, Andy. 1995. "It Sort of Happened Here: The Strange, Brief Life of the British Pop Film" in Romney, Jonathan and Wootton, Adrian (eds) *Celluloid Jukebox: Popular Music and the Movies Since the 50s*. London: BFI, 60–71

Mundy, John (1999) *Popular Music on Screen: From Hollywood Musical to Music Video*. Manchester: Manchester University Press

Neve, Brian (1992) *Film and Politics in America: A Social Tradition*. London: Routledge

Orvell, Miles (1989) *The Real Thing: Imitation and Authenticity in American Culture, 1880–1940*. Chapel Hill: University of North Carolina Press

Packard, Vance (1957) *The Hidden Persuaders*. New York: David McKay

Peterson, R. (1990) "Why 1955? Explaining the Advent of Rock Music" in *Popular Music* 9:1, pp. 97–116

Riesman, David, Glazer, Nathan and Denney, Reuel (1953 [first published in 1950]) *The Lonely Crowd: A Study of the Changing American Character*. Garden City: Doubleday

Roffman, Peter and Purdy, Jim (1981) *The Hollywood Social Problem Film: Madness, Despair, and Politics from the Depression to the Fifties*. Bloomington: Indiana University Press

Rubin, Martin (1993) *Showstoppers: Busby Berkeley and the Tradition of Spectacle*. New York: Columbia University Press

Schaefer, E. (1999) *Bold! Daring! Shocking! True! A History of Exploitation Films, 1919–1959*. Durham, NC: Duke University Press

Schickel, Richard (1958) "The Big Revolution in Records" in *Look* 15 (April): 26–35

Smith, Jeff (1998) *The Sounds of Commerce: Marketing Popular Film Music*. New York: Columbia University Press

Webster, Duncan (1988) *Looka Yonder! The Imaginary America of Populist Culture*. London: Comedia/Routledge

Wilson, John S. (1959) "How No-Talent Singers 'Get' Talent" in *New York Times Magazine* 21 June: 16, 52

A Madonna "Wanna-Be" Story on Film

LISA LEWIS

In the spring of 1985, Madonna's debut Hollywood film *Desperately Seeking Susan* was released. Madonna co-starred with actor Rosanna Arquette in a narrative line that *Rolling Stone* likened to the Carole Lombard and Claudette Colbert "caper comedies" of the thirties:

> Arquette's bored housewife, Roberta, follows the trail of Madonna's gutterball schemer, Susan, into a slapdash murder mystery that scrambles suburbanites and hipsters into something between farce and dreamy fable.

> (Schruers 1985, p. 30)

But a description of the film might also read like this:

> Rosanna Arquette plays the part of a Madonna "wanna-be." Unappreciated and unnoticed in her dreary and exploited life as a young middle-class wife, she turns her vague desire for recognition and adventure into a fantasy identification with a textual persona. Arquette's character, Roberta, follows the trail of Madonna, the woman of the text. Roberta is a voyeur who observes from afar and participates vicariously in the narrative of Madonna that she, in part, creates. She buys Madonna fashions, and dressing in them, becomes Madonna. Or rather, she becomes the image of what Madonna represents to her. As a result, she is suddenly noticed by strangers, and acquires a complex personality based on Madonna's reputation, a prior public knowledge of who she is and what she represents. In living out her fantasy, she moves in directions she was previously too inhibited to pursue. She performs on stage and is recognized for the first rime as an individual with her own style and talents by the very people who were indifferent before. She gains the confidence to change her life, to change the conditions that hampered her ability to know herself, and to act on her desires.

The decision to hire Madonna for the role of Susan was in part a decision to make the Susan character into Madonna. What appears to have been unintentional was the way in which Madonna's selection for the role of Susan made Arquette's character, Roberta, into a Madonna "wanna-be." The film's storyline about a young woman who impersonates another woman, whom she has come to adore as a textual persona, was written a number of years before Madonna's rise to fame, yet it wonderfully encapsulates the "wanna-be" impulse. Those who worked on the film were quick to point out that *Desperately Seeking Susan* is not "Madonna's film." Madonna played a character role in an ensemble cast, a role in a screenplay that circulated Hollywood for five years before being sold as a package to Orion Pictures, teaming Director Susan Seidelman with Rosanna Arquette as the starring actor. The film's publicist, Reid Rosefelt, has distinguished *Desperately Seeking Susan* from a "vehicle film," such as Prince's *Purple Rain*, in which the script and starring role are designed around a particular performer: "This was a part that Madonna could look at and say, 'I could play that!' And she could find things in her personality that could fit that, but that's not her. Susan's nor Madonna" (Bego 1985, p. 116). Yet Seidelman has said that she cast Madonna over some two hundred actors who tested for the part because she believed her style and image provided elements suited to Susan's character:

> There was something about Madonna. I think it's just kind of her . . . She's got a sort of a bad girl/good girl quality that I think is real interesting. She's a little tough, but not too tough. A little "street" but also, I think, real appealing. Earthy in a way that I thought was essential to the character . . . I thought Madonna had a sort of authentic quality that would be really good to try to capture on film.
>
> (Bego 1985, pp. 102–103)

In any event, the character of Susan clearly became blended with Madonna's star persona. A repertoire of intertextual references to Madonna blurred the lines between her film character and her already popularized image. Most obvious was the adoption of Madonna's style to create Susan's character. Fans of Madonna recognized the black bra straps, sunglasses, exposed midriff, crucifix and star jewelry, headbands fashioned from stockings, layered clothing, and stringy hair that had become Madonna signature marks in the several videos she had produced prior to the film. Reportedly, the film's costume designer, Santo Loquasto, originally conceived of Susan as having more of a "West Side old clothes and thrift-shop" look, but after Madonna's selection for the role, he decided to create an adaptation of her style and worked with her to recreate Susan's look (Bego 1985, p. 113). Costume pieces that serve as plot functions, such as Susan's pyramid-eye jacket and the rhinestone boots for which she trades the jacket, were combined with Madonna's own clothing (Bego, 1985). This touch makes Roberta's assumption of Susan's look in the film all the more susceptible to the reading that she represents a Madonna style imitator. A Madonna song also was used in one scene. Although apparently not written for the movie,[1] "Into the Groove" explicitly states the film's thematic content with its lyric, "Live out your fantasy here with me." The location chosen for the song's debut in the film was New York's Danceteria, a club Madonna fans know as the place that led to her first record contract. Footage from *Desperately Seeking Susan* was reorganized in the music video produced for "Into the Groove" and distributed by MTV, which had the intent and effect of attracting Madonna fans to the movie. But most striking of all are the character traits exhibited by Arquette's character, Roberta, the de facto "wanna-be." Roberta is oppressed by her gender condition and this motivates her to create an identification with Susan, whose unconventional life becomes an attraction. Roberta is media literate and (like a fan) actively uses her contact with media texts to formulate a response, indeed, to effect a positive change in her life.

In the film, Roberta is first shown in a beauty parlor, where she is one among many suburban housewives getting their hair done. Shots of identically disposed women, with the manufactured uniformity of their looks, call attention to the similarity of their social condition and locate gender as a central theme. The song blaring over the scene, Carole King's "It's in His Kiss," associates the beauty "work" underway with the women's insecurities over their husbands' love (e.g., lyrics such as "Does he love me I want to know? How can I tell?") and identifies monogamous heterosexuality as their chief social doctrine. Roberta is accompanied by her sister-in-law Leslie, who has brought her to the shop for a new hairstyle. "This is your birthday, I want to give you something different," Leslie says to Roberta. The hairdresser chimes in, "Her husband will love it." The gesture of her sister-in-law's birthday present, a "new look" that Roberta does not want, but that her husband will love, demonstrates her effacement, and the general disregard for who she is as a person and for her potential as an individual. Later, we see Roberta's birthday celebrated by a party full of her husband's friends, at which she is obliged. to play hostess. Her social position is summarized visually in a low-level photographic shot that severs her head from her body, leaving only her arms to serve hors d'oeuvres. Background lyrics of another King song float in as if in admonition, "You don't have to prove to me that you're beautiful." Roberta is portrayed as an appendage of her husband, a woman trapped within a female role and having very little sense of worth. Immersed in her middle-class values and female role, Roberta lives in fear of change and risk. When her hairdresser holds up a page from a hair fashion magazine and chortles, "The look is you," Roberta's reply is, "But I only want a trim." But as the film unfolds, Roberta's textual identifications, particularly with Susan, will change her into an active risk-taker.

Roberta's infatuation with the on-going correspondence between Susan and her boyfriend, Jim, in the personal ads of the newspaper appears initially to revolve around the intensity of Jim's romantic desire for his love, Susan. He beckons to her in dire tones through personals with the heading "Desperately Seeking Susan." But soon it becomes clear that it is Susan and what she represents, in short, everything that Roberta is not, but desires to be, that is the basis of her attraction. Susan is an adventurous spirit. She has style and purpose and is wildly desired, all of which makes her exhilarating to Roberta. Susan is introduced in the film self-confidently snapping Polaroid pictures of herself, a device that Seidelman used in her first film, *Smithereens*, but one that also neatly coincides with the figure of Madonna, who authored her own public image. Rather than fashioning herself after a photograph of a model, as Roberta does to achieve her new and "different" look, Susan has command of the photographic apparatus and her representation. She takes pictures of men (the man asleep in her hotel bed (not her boyfriend, Jim) and the bellboy who delivers a room-service meal), an activity that develops her as a character who reverses traditional gender roles and who assumes a dominant posture alongside men. Whereas Roberta is shown giving and serving in her scenes, Susan takes and is served. When she leaves the man in the hotel room, she takes his cash and the Egyptian earrings he has also stolen, thereby laying the foundation for his murder and her endangerment, the film's primary jeopardy.

In her first scene, Susan is dressed in the pyramid-eye jacket ("like on a dollar bill") that Roberta will later purchase and wear, beginning her assumption of Susan's life. She exudes an idiosyncratic, personal style that is far distant from the commercial fashions through which Roberta's world seeks difference and change. Susan (like Madonna) *is* different, partly because she has her *own* style. The comparison the film makes between Roberta's fulfillment of gender expectations and Susan's breach of the same establishes gender oppression as a context for

Roberta's identification with the textual persona of Susan. And Roberta's desire for attention, recognition, and excitement, qualities of life that she sees embodied in Susan, are basic components of the "wanna-be" impulse. Roberta's use of textual identification as a means to discover her own identity replay's the girl-fan response to Madonna.

Although the film begins by showing Roberta's fantasy identification with Susan as a vague and passive longing for change, this stance expands as the film develops to give textual identification the power to motivate Roberta's actions, to launch her style-imitation behavior. She is inspired by a number of textual encounters to start making changes in her life. In the kitchen after her party, seated next to the remains of her birthday cake, Roberta watches the movie *Rebecca*. The clip shows a scene from late in the movie. Maximilian de Winter (Sir Laurence Olivier) is unburdening his guilty conscience to his wife (Joan Fontaine), "Gone forever, that funny young lost look I loved. It won't ever come back. I killed that when I told you about 'Rebecca.'" The description, "funny young lost look," fits Roberta's expression perfectly, and the film's narrative line, which speaks of a change undergone and a husband at fault, creates an alignment between the film and Roberta's story. The scene in the kitchen takes place early in the film, immediately before Roberta makes her first initiatory move, before she goes to Battery Park to watch Jim meet Susan. It is the act of watching *Rebecca* that provokes her to act on her fantasy attraction to Susan.

Another textual interaction immediately precedes Roberta's first move to contact Susan personally—in order to return the key Susan had left in the pyramid-eye jacket. Although Roberta has already purchased and begun to wear Susan's jacket, she has not as yet become completely committed to the imitation of her persona. Roberta rushes home, after remembering to pick up Gary's dry cleaning (but not his radio), to start dinner. She runs a Julia Child videotape on her kitchen VCR and begins to mimic each step the video cook makes. Julia breaks eggs, Roberta breaks eggs; Julia grates cheese, Roberta grates cheese. By imitating Julia Child's video image, she creates without being creative, makes a gourmet meal without being a gourmet cook. The video program symbolically establishes a solution for Roberta— by imitating Susan/Madonna, she will become her and thereby produce the changes in her life that she cannot seem to make of her own volition.

After Roberta sees Susan "in the flesh" at Battery Park (although it is her image that she sees through the mediating device of a coin-operated telescope), Susan's clothes come to embody for Roberta a world of adventure and independence. As Susan walks off down the street after meeting Jim in the park, Roberta is compelled to follow her. Susan tries on a pair of sunglasses and a hat from a street vendor. Roberta, at her heels, her "lost look" in place, repeats Susan's actions. She moves as if in a trance, as if immersed in a dream. All of Roberta's textual interactions are called up to constitute her motivation at this moment: her identification with the victimized wife in *Rebecca*, her imitation of Julia Child's video cookery, even her participation in re-creating the look of others through her new hairstyle. She moves into full style imitation of Susan and begins to live Susan's life. This moment in the film is one that style imitators in the audience would see as epiphanal, the moment Roberta decides (is driven) to be a style imitator. Madonna's "wanna-be" fans were already organizing around the practice of style imitation before principal shooting on the film was completed in November 1984. They were described in Madonna's first *Rolling Stone* cover story the same month: "The Madonna clones are ratting their hair, putting on rosaries and baring their bellies from coast to coast" (Connelly 1984, p. 81). For these fans, the film's portrayal of Roberta's identification with and style imitation of Susan was surely striking in its similarity to their own identification with and imitation of Madonna.

Desperately Seeking Susan organized a clearer, more accurate picture of the "wanna-be" connection to a textual persona than any produced by critics of actual "wanna-be" fans. Roberta never fully assumes the personality of Susan. But neither does she maintain the persona of Roberta, at least not the Roberta of "Gary's wife," which the film's audience comes to recognize was never who she really was in the first place. It is as if her imitation of Susan's style enables her to develop a personality all her own. This is crucial to understanding Roberta's response, particularly if it is proposed to extract from the film any insight into the imitative practice of Madonna "wanna-bes." More than a mindless reproduction of a star's clothing and hairstyle, style imitation operates as a medium that allows the discovery of creative impulses and the initiation of transformations.

In the world of the movie, assuming the identity of Susan produces a number of changes in Roberta. She leaves suburbia and discovers urban living. She leaves Gary and falls in love with another man. She ends her isolated existence as a housewife by getting a job in which she helps onstage to perform magic tricks for an audience. Even the murder adventure that Roberta inadvertently becomes involved in provides a contrast to her previous boring and staid existence. By the film's end, her husband, Gary, and sister-in-law, Leslie, are ready to admit, "She's really got style in a way; she's good," upon seeing Roberta's perfected stage act. Roberta also gets to meet Susan, her textual inspiration, in a scene in which they join forces to capture a murderous thug. In the last moment of the film, the two are shown hand-in-hand in a photograph on the cover of their beloved newspaper, being cited by the city for their efforts. The headline reads, "What a Pair!" Roberta has become what Susan represented to her initially, a textual figure worthy of recognition and perhaps worthy of yet another woman's identification.

Throughout the film, Susan serves as a guide through Roberta's dissatisfactions and fantasies She discovers (in the not-so-hidden bedside chest of drawers) the books that are evidence of Roberta's intense involvement with textual products and her quest for relief from isolation in the home—*How to Be Your Own Best Friend*; *I'm OK, You're OK*; and *Dr Ruth's Guide to Good Sex*. But it is Roberta's diary, which Susan unabashedly reads aloud, that reveals the intricacies of her fascination with the "text" of Susan: "He's looking for Susan again. She's late returning from Mexico. This is the fifth ad he's run. Why does he want to see her so badly? Who is she?" The exposure of Roberta's secret textual fantasy causes Gary and Leslie to ruminate wildly about her disappearance. They summon up fantastic scenarios about the secret lives of women. Perhaps she is a prostitute by day and returns to be a suburban housewife only in the evenings. But how to explain Roberta's selection of a woman, Susan, as her object of desire? Unable to fathom an identification rooted in social condition, they evoke the model of sexual attraction. She must be a lesbian, they conclude. The logic reproduces the common confusion over the same-sex star–fan identifications generated by Madonna's popularity with female audiences.

This confusion entered the dialogue of the movie's prerelease promotion. Two months before the film's release, *Rolling Stone* alluded to a parallel in the relationship between actors Arquette and Madonna and that of the characters they play in the film. The story, with an accompanying photograph, appeared in "Random Notes," a section that typically contains comments on a promotional photograph, using upbeat, gossipy prose while providing information on release dates or pertinent career moves of media stars. The headline reads, "Two Lucky Stars Take a Shine to Each Other." In its use of the phrase "lucky stars" the headline makes reference to Madonna's hit video/song "Lucky Star." The phrase, however, uses the plural form of "star," thereby collapsing the two women together in "Madonna-ness." The headline suggests that the two actors have grown to like each other, to become something of a team, even friends, through the process of making *Desperately Seeking Susan*. The story's text emphasizes their closeness:

> In their co-starring movie, *Desperately Seeking Susan* (due in March), Rosanna Arquette takes on aspects of Madonna's personality—but who's borrowing whose style here? Well, both say they recognized similarities in each other right away. "'We're like sisters— we've got lots of miseries in common, and boyfriend problems," says Madonna of her friend. "I love her," reciprocates Rosanna, "She's my long-lost sister." Now that they've found each other, the two intend to share social lives as much as possible.
>
> (Ginsberg 1985, p. 6)

In the account, Madonna is quoted as calling Arquette her "sister." Arquette also refers to Madonna as a "sister," but with the additional inference of a "lover" ("I love her"). The author, Merle Ginsberg, uses the more neutral word "friend" to describe Arquette's relationship with Madonna, but at the text's end employs flowery descriptions more suited to lovers. Phrases in the last sentence, "now that they've found each other" and "share social lives as much as possible," are written in veiled language that could describe lovers.

The accompanying photograph is more ambiguous and provocative than the text in describing their relationship. Both women are dressed alike as Susan/Roberta–Madonna/ Rosanna in pyramid-eye jackets. The jacket is more coded by Madonna's wearing of it than by its presence in the film, which had yet to be released. Both wear tights tied around their hair, the Madonna signature style that she brought to Susan's costuming. Arquette's leather pants, however, have no direct reference to the film's costume design. They are a sign of Arquette's own statement, and she wears them with the jacket in the mode of the female fans at Madonna's concerts, combining an item of star imitation with an item of personal clothing. The leather pants also contribute to the subtly sexual pose Arquette holds as she looks directly into the camera. The only visible key lighting is the sheen on her leather-clad hip. Although she is shown standing in profile, it is evident that her legs are parted. Madonna's pose is far more demonstrative, more dominant in its body language. Her right arm encircles Arquette's neck, and her left hand is placed so as to strengthen the hold. Her arm circles as if to choke—or is it to embrace? Arquette's right hand is placed over Madonna's elbow as if to pull her arm away—or is it to reciprocate the caress? Therein lies the core of the dilemma posed by the photograph: Is it hatred? Sexual love? Or is it friendship? Is the relationship reciprocal, or does Madonna dominate? The portrait must have intrigued fan viewers, planting a question in their minds: Did Arquette become a Madonna "wanna-be" during the making of *Desperately Seeking Susan*?

Macy's "Madonna Look-Alike Contest"

The shopping mall became one key site around which the Madonna and |Cyndi| Lauper fan communities coalesced. "Madonna is everywhere," one biographer wrote. "There is even a mall in California that people have nicknamed 'the Madonna mall' because so many girls who shop there try to look just like her" (Matthews 1985, p. 8). Music video displays began popping up in "Juniorwear" departments at shopping malls across the country, the connection between MTV and girl culture having been recognized. While Lauper and Madonna videos were not the only ones shown in the displays, it was their clothing styles that the marketplace scrambled to emulate. Responding to the popularity of the two musicians, the fashion industry manufactured ready-to-wear fashion lines inspired by the stars' styles. *Seventeen* magazine ("Funky Frills," 1985) billing itself as "Young America's Favorite Magazine," disseminated word of Lauper-inspired fashion accessories: black rubber bracelets, twelve for $4; multicolored rhinestone bracelets, $9 each; black leather wristband with rhinestone cluster, $26; and gun-metal and rhinestone bracelets, $30 each. The Macy's Department Store in New York City created a whole department called "Madonnaland," devoted to cropped sweaters ($30), cropped pants ($21), and a variety of jewelry accessories such as crucifix earrings and outsized "pearl" necklaces ($4–$59) that resembled those worn by Madonna. The department became the location for the mobilization of Madonna fans in the summer of 1985, when Macy's sponsored a "Madonna Look-Alike Contest" to coincide with the star's New York concert date.

To encourage attendance, the store ran a full-page ad in the *Village Voice*, with text designed to capitalize on fan familiarity with Madonna's *Material Girl* video and the movie *Desperately Seeking Susan* (both released in 1985), in which she performed the song, "Into the Groove":

> JRS!
> DESPERATELY SEEKING MADONNA LOOK-ALIKES
> Join our Madonna Day contest, Thurs., June 6 in
> Madonnaland on 4, Macy's Herald Square. If you're a
> brassy material girl, get into the groove and prove it.
> (*Village Voice*, 1985)

Contestants presented themselves before judges (one of whom was Andy Warhol), who were seated beside a bank of video monitors that continuously played Madonna videos. A giant reproduction of Madonna's *Time* magazine cover (May 1985) presided over the event. The parade before the judges summoned up that ideological apogee of female competition, the beauty contest, but gave it a new context by involving girls who were united by membership in the same fan community. As a group, the contestants demonstrated a wide range of interpretations of Madonna's look. The differences were partly a product of Madonna's own cultivation of many looks, but they were also clearly a product of creative recombination. The fans balanced imitation of the star with the projection of self. On this instance, style imitation was, more accurately, style appropriation. Assuming the appearance of Madonna meant, in actuality, the dynamic taking-over of her style for their own personal and collective uses.

In sponsoring the contest, Macy's was clearly motivated by the desire to sell its "Madonnaland" clothes and accessories. The "Look-Alike" contest provided a direct incentive to peruse the department and purchase ensembles: But the fans' active participation in the store-sponsored contest also represented the fan community's selection of the store for its fan event. Style imitators involved stores as point of reference in an assertion of shopping and fashion as an authentic arena of female-adolescent culture.

The sexual division of labor and the regimen of female domesticity has long positioned women as the primary consumers in American society (Gardiner, 1979; Weinbaum and Bridges, 1979; Harris and Young, 1981). But stores came to be defined as female social space, as female cultural arenas, in the late nineteenth century. Leach (1984) has linked the rise of consumption culture before the turn of the century to a transformative effect on women's experience of gender. Centralized sites of consumption, in the form of department stores, offered middle-class women a socially acceptable way to escape the confines of the house and provided a richly imaginative culture in which to explore social possibilities. Leach's historical research provides details of how the department store also became an important center of women's political life. Newly cultivated advertising methods and modes of store display prompted suffragists of the period to adopt colorful, graphic forms of political expression. Stores were selected as sites from which suffrage activities were publicized and coordinated:

> Stores everywhere volunteered their windows and their interiors for suffrage advertising. In June 1916 Chicago's Carson, Pirie Scott [a department store] installed a wax figure of a suffragist in one of its windows, a herald of the coming convention of the Woman's Party in that city. At about the same time, Wanamaker's set a precedent by permitting all female employees to march in suffrage parades during working hours. In 1912 suffragists chose Macy's in New York as the headquarters for suffragette supplies, including marching gowns, bonnets, and hatpins.
>
> (Leach 1984, pp. 338–339)

Culture critics have been reluctant to consider arenas of consumption as sites of cultural production. Characteristically, they express an aversion to all forms of commercial culture, coding the marketplace as the antithesis of authentic cultural expression and as essentially a mechanism of capitalist economic reproduction. Such assumptions create obstacles to the analytical treatment of consumer girl culture, operating to reduce girl participation in consumption to a kind of "false consciousness,"[2] of use only to the dominant order as a means to prepare girls for reproductive social roles. Carter (1984, p. 186) developed McRobbie's (1980) critique of male bias in theoretical work on youth subculture[3] by focusing on the way certain culture critics have blended commercialism and gender, deprecating both consumption and women simultaneously: "The analyses themselves are founded on a number of unspoken oppositions: conformity and resistance, harmony and rupture, passivity and activity, consumption and appropriation, femininity and masculinity."

In contemporary life, the shopping mall has come under the reign of teen and preteen girls. Consumer culture helps define and support female-adolescent leisure and culture practices. The mall is a popular female substitute for the streets of male adolescents. Its corridors offer active and semi-anonymous areas for adolescent loitering and peer gatherings, but within a more restricted and supervised setting. Girls at the mall have the option to retreat into stores, which provide the added attraction of shopping, an activity girls like to do together. Visiting the mall and shopping are not merely behaviors about the act of consumption, they are ways for girls to involve themselves in their own brand of adolescent culture, peer bonding, and the construction of style.

Both Madonna and Lauper adeptly created styles and video texts that acknowledged and celebrated adolescent girls' involvement in appearance and consumer girl culture. Madonna manipulated the "glamour" look and the codes of high fashion into appropriations and recombinations that tap into girls' fascination with fashion models and the ability of celebrities to direct trends. Lauper wore thrift store and boutique outfits that recirculated fashions from the past, calling attention to the circularity of consumption, pointing out ways to construct personal style on a budget, and suggesting how to exercise control over the terms of prevailing fashion. The styles of the two stars articulated the tensions between conforming to and resisting codes of gender-specific appearance, between following marketplace dictates and innovating fashion trends.

The overwhelming response to Macy's "Madonna Look-Alike Contest" by Madonna's fans was featured on both MTV and "ABC World News Tonight," where the "wanna-bes" reveled in their new-found fame. On camera, they gushed that they too "wanted to be famous" and "to be looked at" like their idol, Madonna. And for one magical moment, in front of ABC and MTV viewers, it came to pass.

[. . .]

Notes

1 The following excerpt from Madonna's interview with Harry Dean Stanton (1985, p. 66) for *Interview* discusses how "Into the Groove" found its way into the film: "The director, Susan Seidelman, said to me she was shooting a sequence where we needed a song that had a really good dance beat. She asked if we could just bring in the tape of the song that Steven Bray and I wrote. I said okay, and I brought in this tape we had been working on. Actually I wanted to test it out on all the extras who were dancing to it, to see if it was a good song. I had no intention of using it in the movie. So I brought it in and we played it, and we had to do take after take and pretty soon everyone was starting to like the song and they were saying, 'What's this song, and where's it coming from?' I said, 'it's just a song,' and as the film got nearer to the end and they were doing the final cuts, Susan called me up and said, 'Look . . .' Originally, I think they were going to use all songs that were already recorded in the soundtrack. I didn't go into this film thinking I'm going to get a hit song out of this, or an MTV video. No way! I think everybody wanted to turn the other cheek to that song and not bring it in because nobody wanted to make it that kind of a movie. So it was getting closer and closer and Susan Seidelman said to me, 'We're trying to find another song for that scene and we just think yours really works—it's a great song, the producers loved it, Orion loved it, everybody loved it.' I said, 'Okay, fine.' They synched the song to that sequence in the movie and showed it to me. I thought it was great and it didn't interfere with my character or what I was doing acting-wise, and we ended up using the original 8-track demo Steven and I had made. We never went into the recording studio and made a record out of it."

2 For a detailed discussion of Karl Marx and Frederick Engels' concept of ideology, and for comments on the context in which the term "false consciousness" has been used, see Raymond Williams (1977).

3 Erica Carter (1984) cites the work of Richard Hoggart (1957), Phil Cohen (1972), Stuart Hall and Tony Jefferson (1976), Dick Hebdige (1979), and Paul Willis (1977) as examples.

References

Bego, M. (1985) *Madonna!* New York: Pinnacle Books

Carter, E. (1984) "Alice in the Consumer Wonderland" in McRobbie, A. and Nava, M. (eds) *Gender and Generation*. London: Macmillan, 185–214

Connelly, C. (1984) "Madonna Goes All the Way" in *Rolling Stone* 22 November: 14–20, 81

Gardiner, J. (1979) "Women's Domestic Labour" in Eisenstein, Z. (ed.) *Capitalist Patriarchy and the Case for Socialist Feminism*. New York: Monthly Review Press, 173–189

Ginsberg, M. (1985) "Two Lucky Stars Take a Shine to Each Other" in *Rolling Stone* 17 January: 6

Harris, O. and Young, K. (1981) "Engendered Structures: Some Problems in the Analysis of Reproduction" in Kahn, J. and Llobera, J. (eds) *The Anthropology of Pre-capitalist Societies*. London: Humanities Press, 109–147

Leach, W. (1984) "Transformations in the Culture of Consumption: Women and Department Stores 1890–1926" in *Journal of American History* 71(2): 319–342

Matthews, G. (1985) *Madonna*. New York: Wanderer Books/Simon and Schuster

McRobbie, A. (1980) "Settling Accounts with Subcultures: A Feminist Critique" in *Screen Education* 34: 37–49

Schruers, F. (1985) "Lucky Stars" in *Rolling Stone* 9 May: 27–32

Stanton, H. (1985) "Madonna" in *Interview* December: 58–68

Weinbaum, B. and Bridges, A. (1979) "The Other Side of the Paycheck: Monopoly Capital and the Structure of Consumption" in Eisenstein, Z. (ed.) *Capitalist Patriarchy and the Case for the Socialist Feminism*. New York: Monthly Review Press, 190–205

Williams, R. (1977) *Marxism and Literature*. Oxford: Oxford University Press

Further Reading

Adorno, T. and Eisler, H. (1994) *Composing for the Films*. London: Athlone Press

Altman, R. (ed.) (1980) *Cinema/Sound. Special Issue of Yale French Studies* 60/1

Arnold, A. (1992/3) "Aspects of Production and Consumption in the Popular Hindi Film Song Industry" in *Asian Music* XXIV: 122–136

Atkins, I. (1983) *Source Music in Motion Pictures*. Rutherford: Fairleigh Dickinson University Press

Batchelor, J. (1984) "From 'Aida' to 'Zauberflote': The Opera Film" in *Screen* 25/3: 26–38

Bazelon, I. (1975) *Knowing the Score: Notes on Film Music*. New York: Van Nostrand Reinhold Company

Berg, C. (1978) "Cinema Sings the Blues" in *Cinema Journal* 17/2: 1–12

Betrock, A. (1986) *The I Was a Teenage Juvenile Delinquent Rock'n'Roll Horror Beach Party Movie Book: A Complete Guide to the Teen Exploitation Film 1954–1969/* London: Plexus

Brophy, P. (1991) "The Animation of Sound" in Cholodenko, A. (ed.) *The Illusion of Life: Essays on Animation*. Sydney: Power Publications

Brophy, P. (1997–8) "The Secret History of Film Music." A Series in *The Wire* 158–174 and also available at http://media-arts.rmit.edu.ac/Phil_Brophy/soundtrackList.html

Brophy, P. (ed.) (1999) *The World of Sound in Film*. North Ryde: AFTRS

Brophy, P. (ed.) (2000) *Cinema and the Sound of Music*. North Ryde: AFTRS

Brophy, P. (ed.) (2001) *Experiencing the Soundtrack*. North Ryde: AFTRS

Brown, R. (1994) *Overtones and Undertones: Reading Film Music*. Berkeley: University of California Press

Bruce, D. (1985) *Bernard Herrmann: Film Music and Film Narrative*. Michigan: Ann Arbor

Buhler, J., Flinn, C. and Neumeyer, D. (eds) (2000) *Music and Cinema*. Hanover: Wesleyan University Press

Carlson, T. (1998) "The Comeback Corpse in Hollywood: *Mystery Train, True Romance* and the Politics of Elvis in the '90s" in *Popular Music and Society* 22/2: 1–10

Chion, M. (trans. Gorbman, C.) (1994) *Audio-Vision: Sound on Screen*. New York: Columbia University Press

Cook, N. (1998) *Analysing Musical Multimedia*. Oxford: Clarendon Press

Creekmur, C. (1988) "The Space of Recording: The Production of Popular Music as Spectacle" in *Wide Angle*. 10/2: 32–34

Crenshaw, M. (1994) *Hollywood Rock: A Guide to Rock'n'Roll in the Movies*. London: Plexus

Curry, R. (1990) "Madonna from Marilyn to Marlene—Pastiche and/or Parody?" in *Journal of Film and Television* 42/2: 15–30

Custen, G. (1992) *Bio/Pics: How Hollywood Constructed Public History*. New Brunswick: Rutgers University Press

Darby, W. and DuBois, J. (1990) *American Film Music: Major Composers, Techniques and Trends 1915–1990*. Jefferson: McFarland

Dellar, F. (1981) NME *Guide to Rock Cinema*. Middlesex: Hamlyn

Denisoff, R. and Plasketes, G. (1990) "Synergy in 1980s Film and Music: Formula for Success or Industry Mythology?" in *Film History* 4/3: 257–276

Denisoff, R. and Romanowski, W. (1991) *Risky Business: Rock in Film*. New Brunswick: Transaction Publishers

Donnelly, K (1998a) "The classical film score forever?: *Batman*, *Batman Returns* and post-classical film music" in Neale, S. and Smith, M. (eds) (1998) *Contemporary Hollywood Cinema*. London: Routledge

Donnelly, K. (1998b) "Sir Cliff Richard and British Pop Musicals" in *Journal of Popular Film and Television* 25/4: 146–154

Donnelly, K. (2001a) *Pop Music in British Cinema: A Chronicle*. London: BFI Publishing

Donnelly, K. (ed.) (2001b) *Film Music: Critical Approaches*. Edinburgh: Edinburgh University Press

Doty, A. (1988) "(Re) New (ed.) Conservatism in Film Marketing" in *Wide Angle* 10/2: 70–79

Dwyer, R. (2000) *All You Want Is Money, All You Need Is Love: Sex and Romance in Modern India*. London: Cassell

Egorova, T. (1997) *Soviet Film Music: An Historical Survey*. Amsterdam: Harwood Academic Publishers

Eisenstein, S. (trans. and ed. Leyda, J.) (1970) *The Film Sense*. London: Faber and Faber Ltd

Eisenstein, S. (trans. Marshall, H.) (1987) *Nonindifferent Nature*. Cambridge: Cambridge University Press

Eldine, S. (1962) "Arab Documentary Film Production and the Use of Music in Arab Films." UNESCO Report

Evans, M. (1975) *Soundtrack: The Music of the Movies*. New York: Hopkinson and Blake

Fawkes, R. (2000) *Opera on Film*. London: Gerald Duckworth and Co.

Fehr, R. and Vogel, F. (1993) *Lullabies of Hollywood: Movie Music and the Movie Musical 1915–1992*. London: McFarland and Co. Inc.

Flinn, C. (1990) "The Most Romantic Art of All: Music in the Classical Hollywood Cinema" in *Cinema Journal* 29/4: 35–50

Flinn, C. (1992) *Strains of Utopia: Gender, Nostalgia and Hollywood Film Music*. Princeton: Princeton University Press

Frith, S. (1984) "Mood Music: An Inquiry into Narrative Film Music" in *Screen* 25/3: 78–87

Frith, S. *et al.* (eds) (1993) *Sound and Vision: The Music Video Reader*. London: Routledge

Gabbard, K. (ed.) (1995a) *Jazz among the Discourses*. Durham, NC: Duke University Press

Gabbard, K. (ed.) (1995b) *Representing Jazz*. Durham, NC: Duke University Press

Gabbard, K. (1996) *Jammin' at the Margins: Jazz and the American Cinema*. Chicago: Chicago University Press

Gay, P. and Negus, K. (1994) "The Changing Site of Sound: Music Retailing and the Composition of Consumers" in *Media, Culture and Society* 16: 395–413

Gorbman, C. (1987) *Unheard Melodies: Narrative Film Music*. London: BFI

Hagen, E. (1971) *Scoring for the Films*. Los Angeles: Alfred Publishing Co.

Hanson, C. (1988) "The Hollywood Musical Biopic and the Regressive Performer" in *Wide Angle* 10/2: 15–23

Healey, J. (1995) "All This Is for Us: The Songs in *Thelma and Louise*" in *Journal of Popular Culture* 29/3: 103–119

Hope, A. (1966) "Blues in the Stalls" in *Jazz Monthly* September: 2–4

Huntley, J. (1972) *British Film Music*. London: Arno Press

Kalinak, K. (1992) *Settling the Score: Music and the Classical Hollywood Film*. Madison: University of Wisconsin Press

Kassabian, A. (20001) *Hearing Film: Tracking Identifications in Contemporary Hollywood Film Music*. London: Routledge

Knobloch, S. (1999) "(Pass through) The Mirror Moment and *Don't Look Back*: Music and Gender in the Rockmentary" in Waldman, D. and Walker, J. (eds) (1999) *Feminism and Documentary*. Minneapolis: University of Minnesota Press

Lack, R. (1997) *Twenty Four Frames under: A Buried History of Film Music*. London: Quartet Books

Lapedis, H. (1999) "Popping the Question: the Function and Effect of Popular music in Cinema" in *Popular Music* 18/3: 367–379

Larson, R. (1985) *Musique Fantastique: A Survey of Film Music in the Fantasy Cinema*. London: Scarecrow Press.

Lichter, P. (1975) *Elvis in Hollywood*. New York: Simon and Schuster

Limbacher, J. (ed.) (1984) *Film Music: From Violins to Video*. Metuchen: Scarecrow Press

London, K. (1970) *Film Music: A Summary of the Characteristic Features of Its History, Aesthetics and Possible Developments*. London: Faber and Faber

Luckett, M. (1994) "Fantasia: Cultural Constructions of Disney's 'Masterpiece'" in Smoodin, E. (ed.) *Disney Discourse: Producing the Magic Kingdom*. London: Routledge

MacDonald, L. (1998) *The Invisible Art of Film Music: A Comprehensive History*. New York: Ardsley House Publishers

McLafferty, G. (1989) *Elvis Presley in Hollywood: Celluloid Sell-Out*. London: Robert Hale

McLean, A. (1993) "'It's Only That I Do What I Love and Love What I Do': Film Noir and the Musical Woman" in *Cinema Journal* 33/1: 3–16

Malkmus, L. and Armes, R. (1991) *Arab and African Film Making*. London: Zed Books

Manuel, P. (1993) *Cassette Culture: Popular Music and Technology in North India*. Chicago: Chicago University Press

Manvell, R. and Huntley, J. (1975) *The Technique of Film Music*. London: Focal Press

Marks, M. (1997) *Music and the Silent Film: Contexts and Case Studies 1895–1924*. Oxford: Oxford University Press

Marmorstein, G. (1997) *Hollywood Rhapsody: Movie Music and Its Makers 1900 to 1975*. New York: Schirmer Books

Marshall, B. and Stilwell, R. (eds) (2000) *Musicals: Hollywood and Beyond*. Exeter: Intellect Books

Meeker, D. (1981) *Jazz in the Movies*. London: Talisman Books

Mundy, J. (1999) *Popular Music on Screen: From Hollywood Musical to Music Video*. Manchester: Manchester University Press

Nandy, A. (ed.) (1998) *The Secret Politics of Our Desires: Innocence, Culpability and Indian Popular Cinema*. London: Zed Books

Neaverson, B. (1997) *The Beatles Movies*. London: Cassell

Prendergast, R. (1992) *Film Music: A Neglected Art*. New York: W. W. Norton

Rai, A. (1994) "An American Raj in Filmistan: Images of Elvis in Indian Films" in *Screen* 35/1: 51–77

Romanowski, W. and Denisoff, R. (1987) "Money for Nothin' and the Charts for Free: Rock and the Movies" in *Journal of Popular Culture* 21/3: 63–78

Romney, J. and Wootton, A. (eds) (1995) *Celluloid Jukebox: Popular Music and the Movies since the Fifties*. London: BFI Publishing

Rothman, W. (1997) "Cinema Verite in America (II): Don't Look Back" in *Documentary Film Classics*. Cambridge: Cambridge University Press

Sackett, S. (1995) *Hollywood Sings: An Inside Look at Sixty Years of Academy Award-Nominated Songs*. New York: Billboard Books

Schelle, M. (1999) *The Score: Interviews with Film Composers*. Los Angeles: Silman-James Press

Scheurer, T. (1998) "The Score for 2001: A Space Odyssey" in *Journal of Popular Film and Television* 25/4: 173–182

Shafik, V. (1998) *Arab Cinema: History and Cultural Identity*. Cairo: American University in Cairo Press

Shelton, M. (1995) "Whitney is Every Woman? Cultural Politics and the Pop Star" in *Camera Obscura* 36: 135–153

Shumway, D. (1999) "Rock and Roll Soundtracks and the Production of Nostalgia" in *Cinema Journal* 38/2: 36–51

Smith, J. (1998) *The Sounds of Commerce: Marketing Popular Film Music*. New York: Columbia University Press

Straub, J.-M. (1967) "Sur *Chronique d'Anna Magdalena Bach*" in *Cahiers du cinema* 193: 56–58

Sullivan, H. (1987) "Paul, John and Broad Street" in *Popular Music* 6/3: 327–338

Tasker, Y. (1994) "Music, Video, Cinema: Singers and Movie Stars" in *Working Girls*. London: Routledge

Thomas, T. (1991) *The Film Score: The Art and Craft of Film Music*. Burband: Riverwood Press

Thomas, T. (1997) *Music for the Movies*, second edition. Los Angeles: Silman-James Press

Thoraval, Y. (2000) *The Cinemas of India*. New Delhi: Macmillan India

Tietyen, D. (1990) *The Musical World of Walt Disney*. Wisconsin: Walt Disney Company

Wocjik, P. and Knight, A. (eds) (2001) *Soundtrack Available: Essays on Film and Popular Music*. Durham, NC: Duke University Press

Wyatt, J. (1994) *High Concept: Movies and Marketing in Hollywood*. Austin: University of Texas Press

Zmijewsky, S. and Zmijewsky, B. (1983) *Elvis: The Films and Career of Elvis Presley*. New York: Citadel Press

Index